IMAGES
of America

PORTER COUNTY LAKES AND RESORTS

IMAGES
of America

PORTER COUNTY LAKES AND RESORTS

Larry G. Eggleston

ARCADIA
PUBLISHING

ISBN 978-0-7385-3277-0

Published by Arcadia Publishing
Charleston, South Carolina

Printed in the United States of America

Library of Congress Catalog Card Number: 2004103636

For all general information contact Arcadia Publishing at:
Telephone 843-853-2070
Fax 843-853-0044
E-Mail sales@arcadiapublishing.com
For customer service and orders:
Toll-Free 1-888-313-2665

Visit us on the Internet at www.arcadiapublishing.com

Contents

Acknowledgments

I would like to take this opportunity to thank the following people and organizations for their generous help and kind assistance in compiling the photographs and data needed for this book:

Bailly Homestead Historical Park, Chesterton, Indiana.
Fulton County Historical Society, Rochester, Indiana.
Indiana Dunes State Park, Chesterton, Indiana.
Indiana State Library Archives, Indianapolis.
Harold L. Rogers Lakewood Park, Valparaiso, Indiana.
Edwin S. Kuehl Jr., Valparaiso, Indiana.
Porter County Historical Society, Valparaiso, Indiana.
Porter County Public Library, Valparaiso, Indiana.
City of Valparaiso Water Department, Valparaiso, Indiana.
Valparaiso Department of Parks and Recreation, Valparaiso, Indiana.
Valparaiso University Library, Valparaiso, Indiana.
Margaret Eggleston, Wanatah, Indiana.
The Library of Congress, Washington D.C.
Eva Hopkins, Chesterton, Indiana.
Jane Walsh-Brown, Chesterton, Indiana
Westchester Public Library, Chesterton, Indiana.
Kouts Public Library, Kouts, Indiana.
The Vidette Messenger, Valparaiso, Indiana.
Kankakee Valley Historical Society, Kouts, Indiana.
Chamber of Commerce Valparaiso, Valparaiso, Indiana.
Porter County Convention Recreation & Visitors Commission, Chesterton, Indiana.
G. Bradley Publishing, Inc., St Louis, Missouri.
Dan Brauhn, Chesterton, Indiana.
Rose Lepara, Merrillville, Indiana.
The Catholic Diocese of Gary, Merrillvlle, Indiana.
John Hodson, Kouts, Indiana.

Introduction

The history of Porter County Indiana, clearly demonstrates how the challenges of opening an unsettled wilderness were met and the willingness of the people to deal with change and progress as the area grew.

This book deals with the history and growth of Porter County and the exciting history of its many beautiful lakes. The book begins with a brief discussion of Pre-Porter County history followed by an illustrated history of the many early lake resorts and the influence of the interurban electric railroad system on the county. Clearly one can see that the growth of Porter County can be attributed not only to its industrious citizens, but also to its natural beauty and desirability as a resort area with its many beautiful fresh water lakes.

The most desirable of these lakes is Flint Lake which is steeped in history and legend dating back to the early Potawatomi Indians, who first inhabited the area. The natural beauty of Flint Lake attracted many early developers who built four summer resorts on its banks. Long Lake, which is connected to Flint Lake by a quarter mile long channel; also attracted developers who erected a beautiful resort on its east bank for boating, fishing, and swimming

After the expulsion of the Potawatomi Indians in 1838 a manmade lake was established south of Valparaiso. It was later named Sager's Lake. A beautiful recreation area was established on the new lake for boating, fishing, swimming, hiking, and picnicking. Sager's Lake became a very popular attraction and drew visitors from the entire Calumet Region.

The illustrated history of the interurban electric railroad and its influence on the growth of the county is shown in this publication. The early resort areas of Porter County flourished as the interurban system gave easy access to visitors.

Along with the resort trade, the lakes served the county in several other ways. Prior to the development of refrigerators, the lakes served as a source of ice for use throughout the warm summer months. Huge icehouses were erected on several of the lakes. During the winter months ice was cut from the lakes and stored for summer use. With the use of cork insulation and sawdust the ice would last most of the summer. The demand for ice during the summer made these ice houses into thriving businesses.

The establishment of several grist, flour, and lumber mills also spurred the growth of Porter County. These mills allowed the rural community the luxury of processing their grain and lumber without the expense and burden of shipping their crops to Chicago, Michigan City, South Bend, or Lafayette for processing. These local mills made a great contribution to the economic development of Porter County. Several of these early mills are illustrated in this book.

The southern part of Porter County boarders the Kankakee River. The Kankakee River Valley was considered a sportsman's paradise and attracted visitors from around the world. Many hunt clubs were erected on the river banks. These were frequented by a great number of famous people such as John "Bronco John" Harrington Sullivan, Gen. Lew Wallace—author of Ben-Hur, Benjamin Harrison—later president of the United States, and President Theodore Roosevelt. A few of these clubs are illustrated in this publication.

Although Porter County with its many beautiful lakes has grown into a thriving populated area it has managed to retain the natural beauty which originally attracted the early settlers and visitors.

One

Porter County Beginnings

Early History

The history of Porter County and its beautiful lakes is full of exciting stories, legends, and wonder. The Legend of Flint Lake, the Sea Serpent of Flint Lake, and the Mystery of Burlington Beach are examples of these exciting stories.

The natural beauty of the Porter County lake areas has always been an attraction to people who enjoy the great outdoors or for those who just enjoy relaxing surrounded by the beautiful landscape.

The lake areas of Porter County were originally populated by the Potawatomi Indians. There were several other tribes in the area but they were not in great numbers. The other tribes were mostly in northern Porter County around the Bailly Homestead area. Those other tribes included the Oneida, Ottawa, and the Chippewa. However, the main influence in the area was the Potawatomi Indians who were led by Chief Chiqua. The main Potawatomi camp was one mile south of Valparaiso and was called Chiqua's Town. The Potawatomi established several hunting camps around the Porter County lake areas.

The first white men to arrive in the area were the French fur traders and Jesuit missionaries who arrived in the mid 1600s. Later, in 1672, two Catholic missionaries, Father Allouez and Father Dablon traveled the area from the shores of Lake Michigan to the Kankakee River. They stopped at the various Indian villages to study the people and the geographical layout of the area. In 1673, Father Marquette ventured up the Kankakee to the St. Joseph River where he found his way into Lake Michigan. He proceeded up the coast of Lake Michigan to the great fur-trading center at Green Bay.

Because of the rich fur trade in the area a French explorer named Robert Chavillier navigated and explored the entire length of the Mississippi River Basin. When he arrived at the mouth of the river, he claimed all the land drained by this great river for France. He named the area Louisiana in honor of the French King.

All of northern Indiana became a British possession in 1759. This caused a bitter rivalry between England and France over control of the lucrative fur trade.

The Louisiana Territory was given to the Spanish by the treaty of Fontainblue in 1762. This did not include the land around the head of Lake Michigan. In 1781, the Spanish decided to take possession of the excluded Lake Michigan area. They held control of the land until 1783. Under the terms of the treaty of 1783, between the United States and Great Britain, the western boundary of the United States was established at the Mississippi River. Spain was then forced to recognize the rights of the United States and withdrew their claim to the area.

Although the border of the United States was established at the Mississippi River, England continued to exercise control over the area of northern Indiana until 1796 when the area finally came fully under the control of the United States.

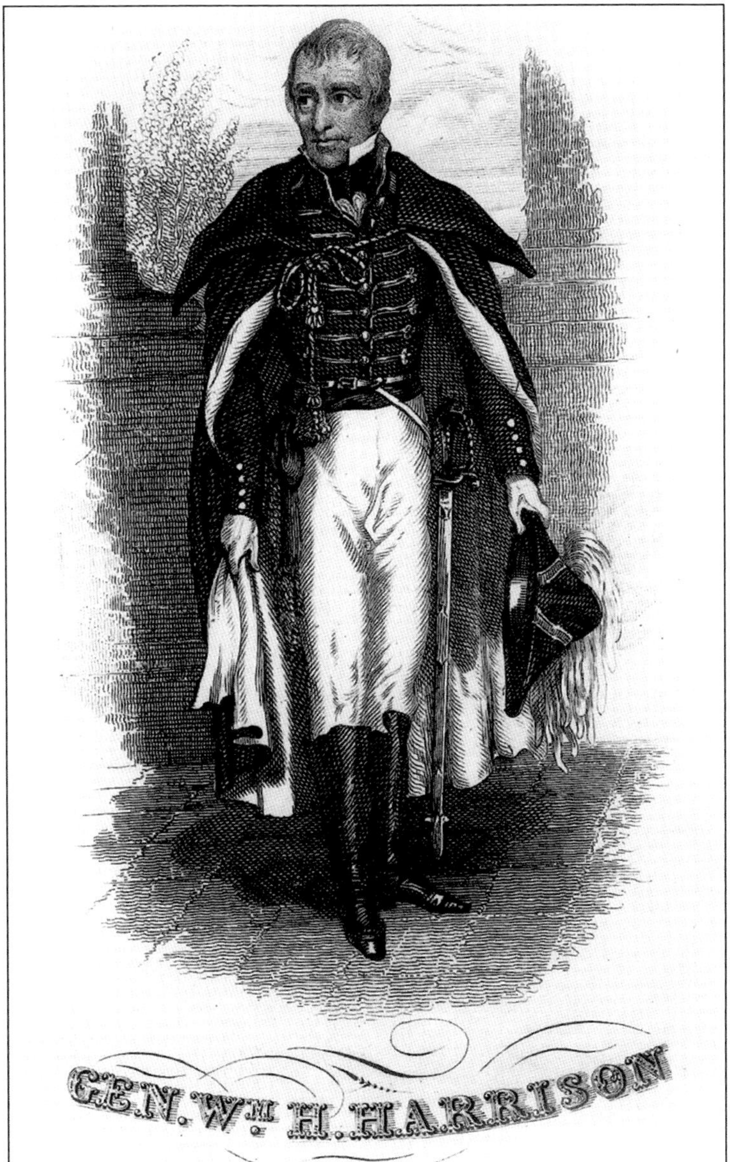

Peace agreements were soon made between the Indians and the United States, giving the United States large tracks of land, which could be opened to settlers. Such agreements were made with the Potawatomi, Luvandat, Ottawa, Chippewa, Sac, Miami, Delaware, and Shawnee tribes. The agreements provided the tribes with an initial sum of money and an annual annuity plus supplies.

An act of Congress, dated May 7, 1880, provided that the territory northwest of the Ohio River be divided into Indiana and Illinois territories.

Gen. William Henry Harrison, who later became the 9th President of the United States, was appointed Governor of the Indiana Territory. General Harrison convened a meeting of the territorial officials in Vincennes to establish the rules, regulations, and laws for the new territory.

General Harrison's military career and fame were enhanced greatly during the Indian uprising when he defeated Tecumseh and the Prophet at the battle of Tippecanoe on November 7, 1811.

The successful completion of the war of 1812 brought an end to Indian hostilities in the area.

The first permanent settlers to the Porter County area began arriving in the early 1800s. Joseph Bailly is credited with being the first white settler to establish a permanent residence in the Porter County area. He built his home in 1822 on the banks of the Little Calumet River. The trading center he established became known as the Bailly Homestead. (Photo Courtesy of the Library of Congress.)

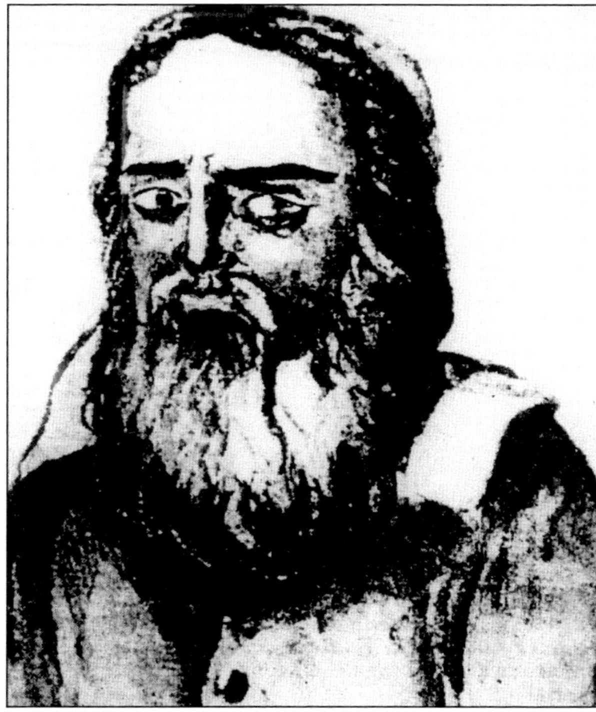

The drawing shown here is the only known image of Joseph Bailly. His daughter, Rose Victore Bailly made this drawing in 1835.

Joseph Bailly was a fur trader and an agent for the American Fur Company which was owned by Jacob Astor. He selected the site on the Little Calumet River as an ideal spot for a trading post because it was a major canoe route and where the North Sauk and Potawatomi trails converged.

Joseph Bailly was born in 1774 and died at the Bailly Homestead in Porter County in 1835, which was the year Porter County was established. Prior to building his homestead and trading post Joseph Bailly lived on Mackinac Island, Michigan where he began his fur trading career at the age of 18. He often traveled through the northern Indiana area trading supplies for furs. Joseph Bailly was well thought of by the Indians and was in no danger during the War of 1812. He was married to a French Indian woman named Marie LeFevre de La Vigne who was half Ottawa.

During the years from 1822 through 1835 while Joseph Bailly ran the trading post, the relatives of his wife Marie, maintained camps near their home. The Bailly Homestead originally consisted of six buildings; a store for trading, two warehouses, a chapel, a kitchen, and living quarters.

The first home built by Joseph Bailly was constructed on the shore of the Little Calumet River. However, after being flooded out, he rebuilt his home on higher ground. All of the buildings, which comprise the Bailly Homestead, are on the ridge overlooking the Little Calumet River and free from flood.

The Indians would arrive on the Little Calumet River with their canoes laden with furs, or by horseback on one of the two Indian trails which crossed the area. Trading was done mostly in the fur trading and storage building and sometimes at the river's edge.

In 1835, Joseph Bailly began building a new two-story home for his family. He completed the house but died prior to moving into his new home. The original house is still standing today.

The house is built of cut logs, which were cut from the surrounding forest. Wood siding was put on the outside to cover the logs. The inside walls were only painted, and plaster was placed in the cracks between the logs to make a smooth wall. Visitors to the home can see the walls of logs in areas where later applied plaster and lathe has been removed. The house was home to the Bailly family until 1917.

Both Joseph and his wife Marie died in the original chapel. He died in 1835 and she died in 1866. Prior to his death in 1835 Joseph Bailly purchased land on Lake Michigan. He laid out a town, which he named Baillytown. The plans for this town ceased with his death. The site where Baillytown would have been constructed is now occupied by Bethlehem Steel Corporation.

The Bailly Homestead was later used as a Catholic retreat, and later as rental property. In 1965 it was converted into a restaurant. The restaurant did not last very long and in 1976 the house was restored and the homestead became part of the Indiana Dunes National Lakeshore. (Drawing courtesy of Porter County Historical Society.)

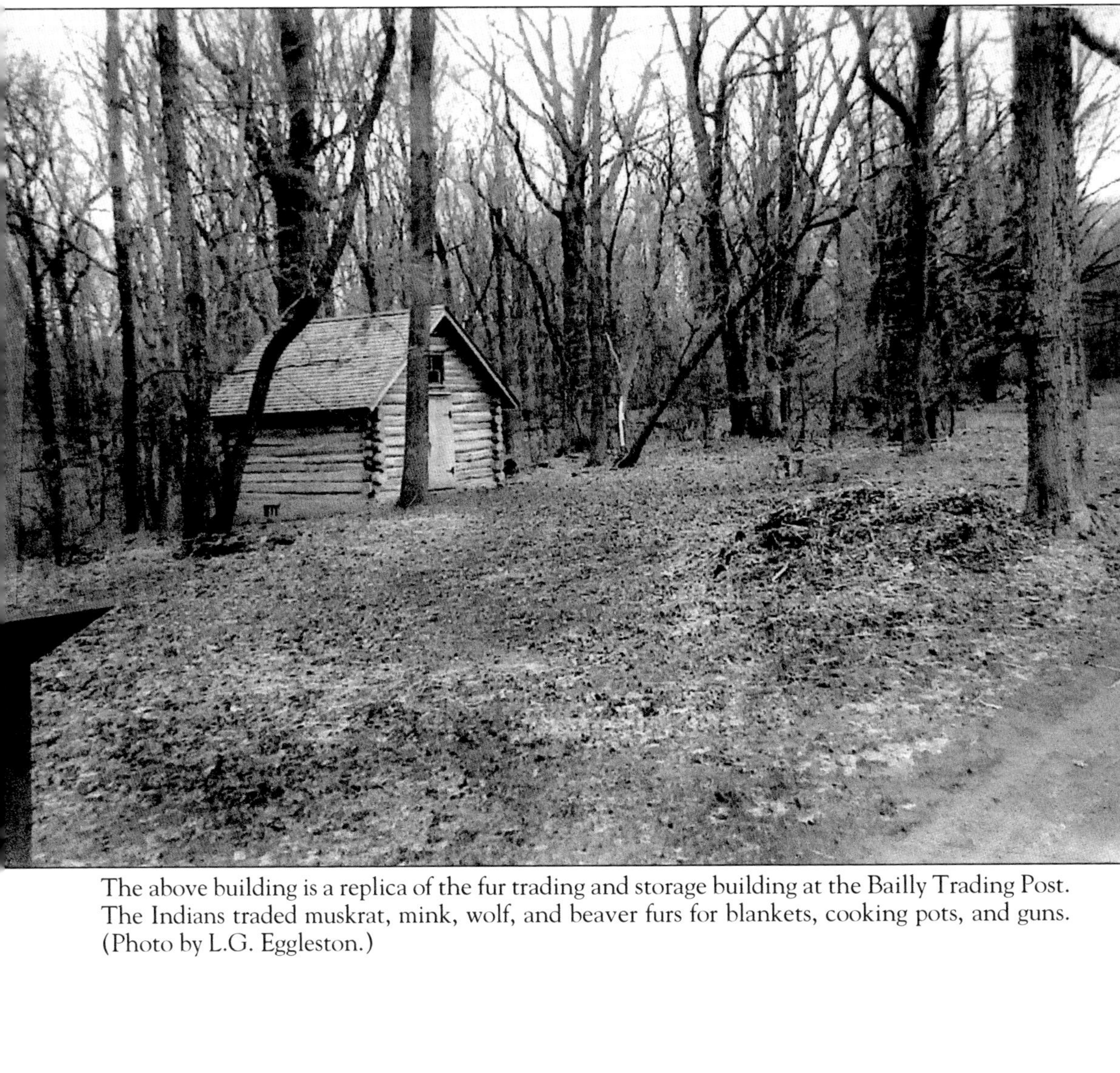

The above building is a replica of the fur trading and storage building at the Bailly Trading Post. The Indians traded muskrat, mink, wolf, and beaver furs for blankets, cooking pots, and guns. (Photo by L.G. Eggleston.)

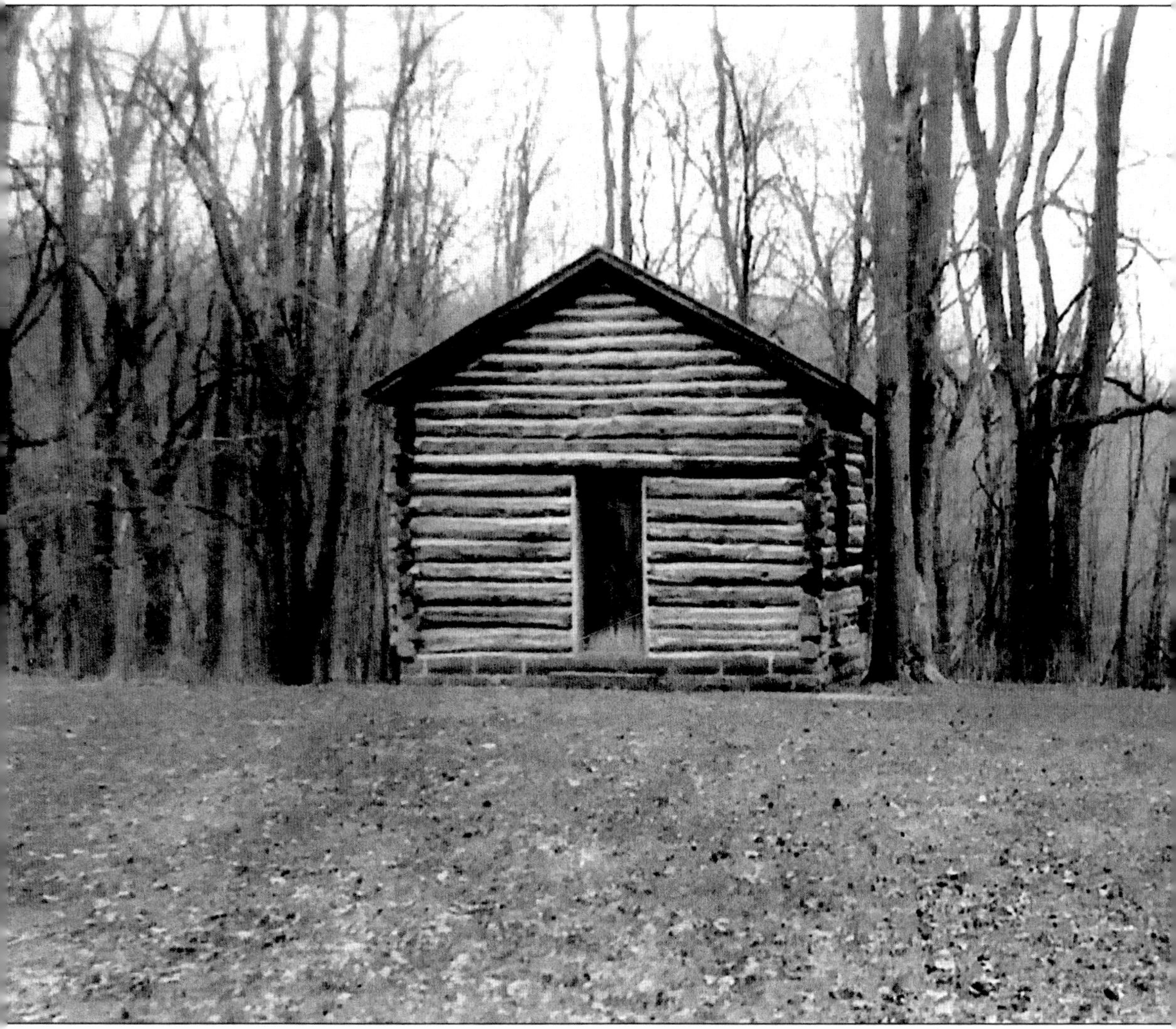

The above photograph is a replica of one of the three original buildings, which were used as living quarters, family kitchen, and chapel. This replica sits next to the main house at the Bailly Homestead. (Photo by L.G. Eggleston.)

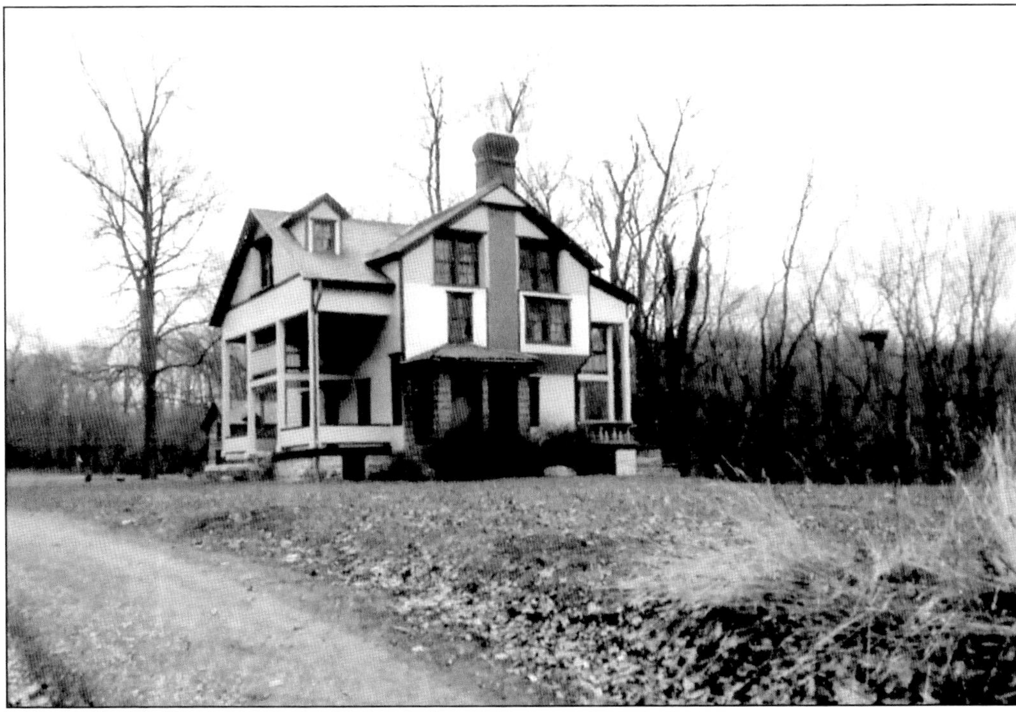

The above building is the original new home Joseph Bailly built in 1835. (Photo by L.G. Eggleston.)

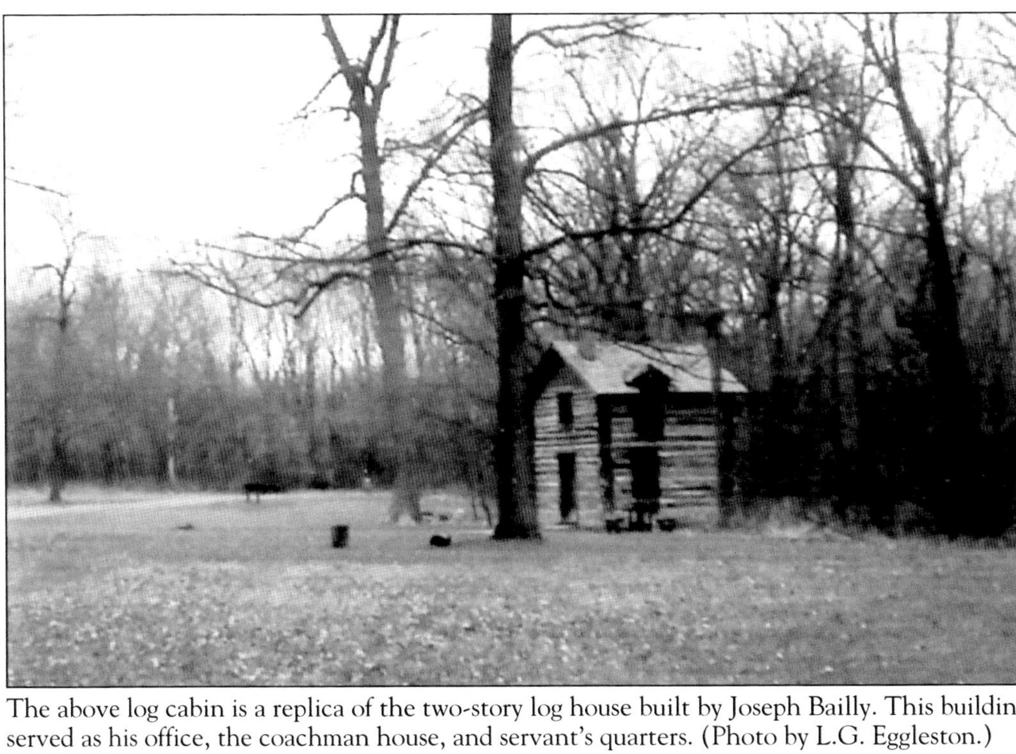

The above log cabin is a replica of the two-story log house built by Joseph Bailly. This building served as his office, the coachman house, and servant's quarters. (Photo by L.G. Eggleston.)

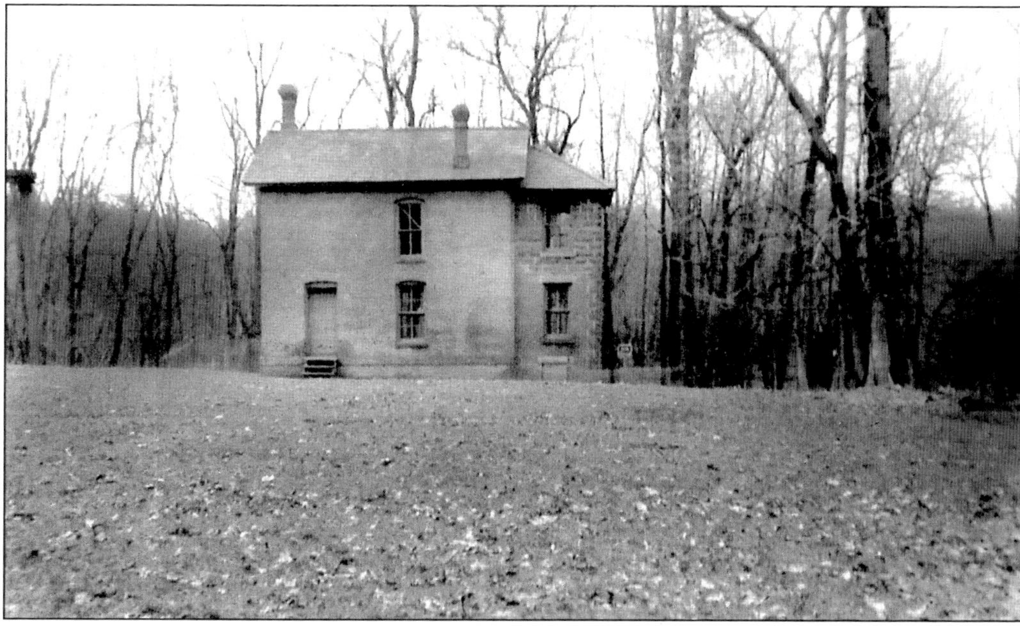

Joseph Bailly's daughter Rose had a two story brick home built in the 1870s. This house was attached to the main two-story house, which her father built in 1835. In 1904, Rose had the house moved to its present location overlooking the Little Calumet River. (Photo by L.G. Eggleston.)

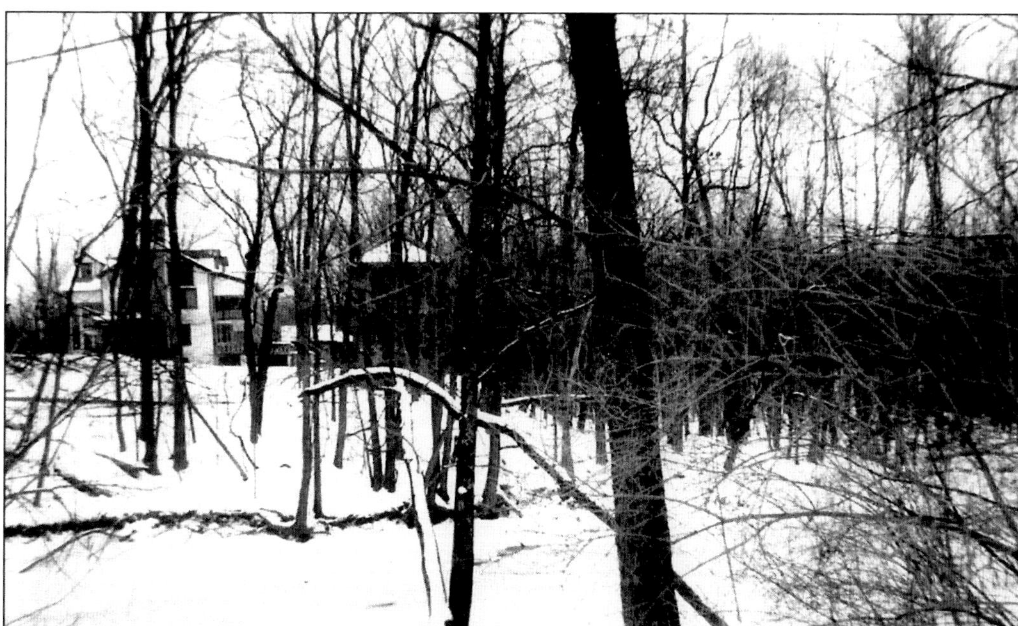

This is a view of the Little Calumet River in the winter time. The river flows in back of the Bailly Homestead. There was a platform on the river where the canoes could stop and trappers could unload their furs. (Photo by L.G. Eggleston.)

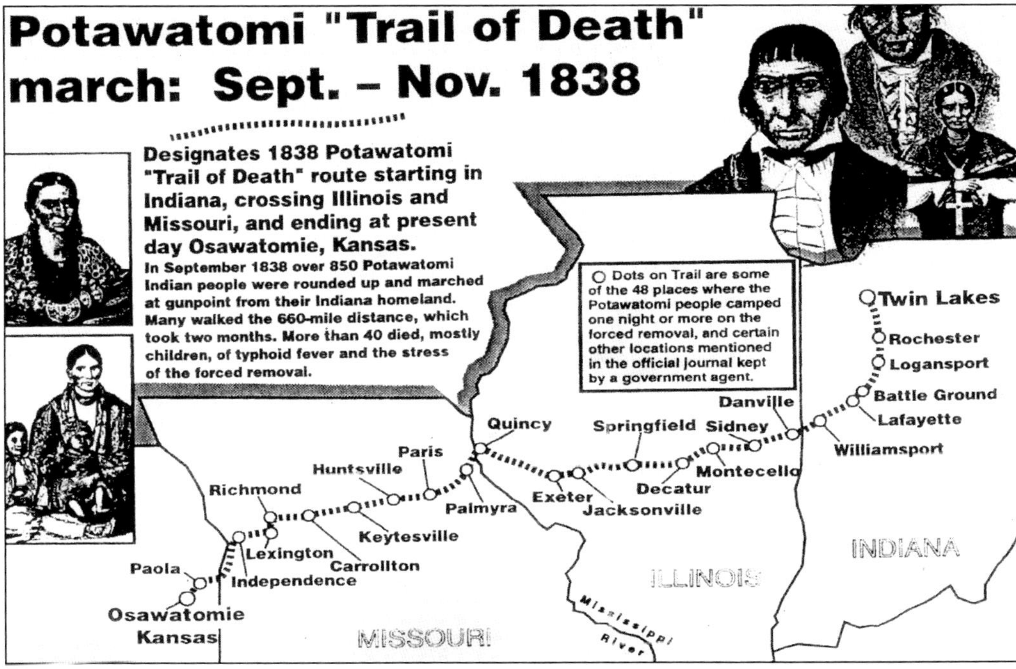

After the War of 1812 many settlers began to move into the Indiana Territory. As the population of the territory began to grow and prosper, its citizens petitioned the U.S. Government for statehood. Indiana was granted statehood in 1816.

By 1826 the U.S. had purchased all the remaining land in Indiana which was owned by the Potawatomi Indians. The entire wilderness area, which now consists of Lake and Porter Counties, was placed under the jurisdiction of LaPorte County.

The LaPorte County Commissioners met in March 1835 to divide the land west of LaPorte County into Porter County and Lake County. Porter County was established in March 1835, which was 19 years after Indiana became a state.

Upon the establishment of Porter County, several small villages began competing to become the county seat. The three main villages in contention were Flintville, Talbot, and Portersville. Flintville was located on the southeast corner of Flint Lake where the Valparaiso water works now stands. Flintville extended east over Old Highway 49, which is now Calumet. The village of Talbot was located southeast of Portersville and no longer exists. The final choice for county seat was Portersville. Portersville was selected as the county seat of Porter County on October 31, 1836. Portersville was later renamed Valparaiso.

With the purchase of the remaining Potawatomi lands by the U.S. Government in 1826, the wilderness area was now fully open for settlers. Plans began to be made for the removal of the remaining Indians and resettling them west of the Mississippi. Congress passed the Indian Removal Act in 1830. The long and anguished process of resettlement began.

In September 1838, the remaining 850 Potawatomi Indians in northern Indiana were rounded up and marched to Paola, Kansas, on the Osage River, for resettlement. The present day town in Kansas in called Osawatomi. The 660-mile march became known as the "Trail of Death." The march to Kansas started at Twin Lakes, near Plymouth, Indiana. During the march, 42 people died, mostly women and children. In addition to those who died there were 50 who escaped. Since the western border of the U.S. was the Mississippi River, the Potawatomi Indians were actually moved out of the country. The "Trail of Death" is illustrated above. The removal of the Potawatomi Indians from Porter County in 1838 coincides with the only resettlement of 1838 therefore it can be reasoned that the Porter County Indians were part of the "Trail of Death." (Image above courtesy of Fulton County Historical Society.)

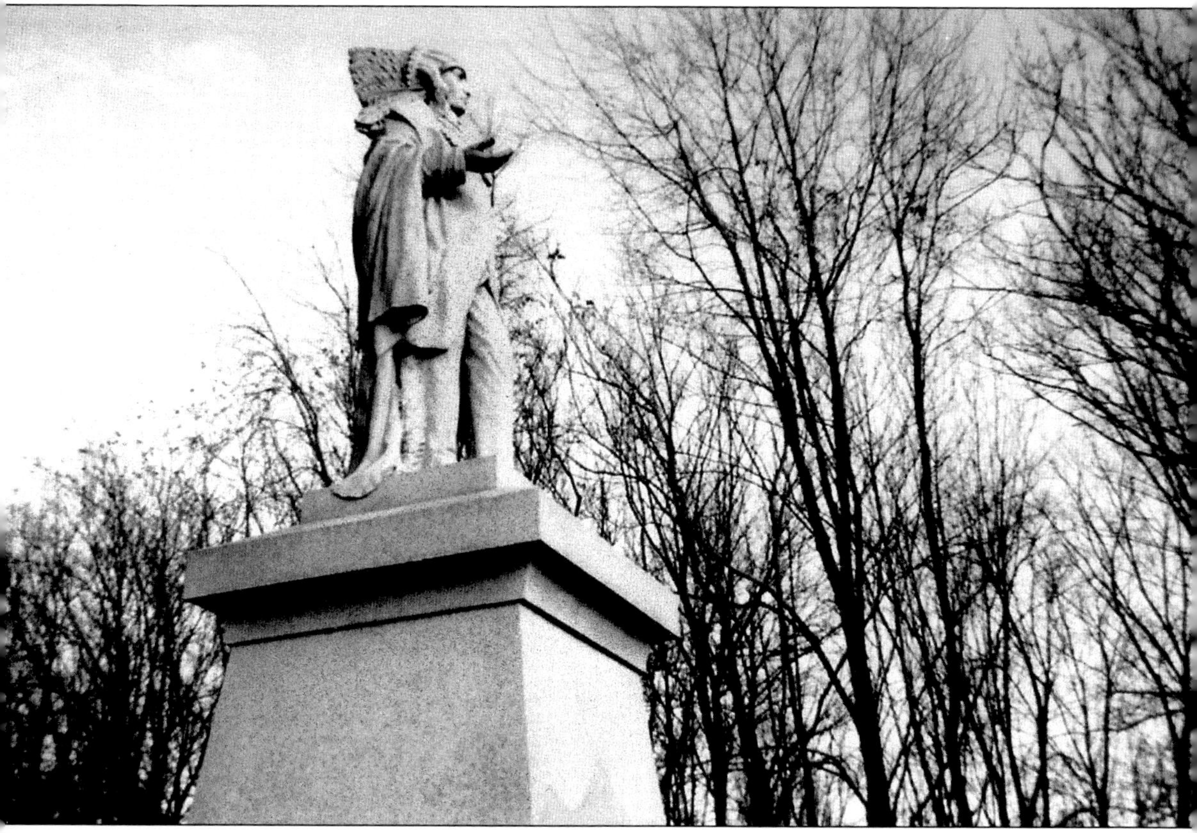

A monument to Potawatomi Chief Menominee marks the spot where the "Trail of Death" began on September 19, 1838. The monument was erected in 1909 near Twin Lakes, which is south of Plymouth, Indiana. It is located on South Peach Road, five miles west of Highway 31.

Indiana was the first state to officially designate the "Trail of Death" as a historical trail on January 28, 1994. Kansas declared the "Trail of Death" a historical trail on February 16, 1994, Illinois declared it a historical trail on November 17, 1994, and Missouri declared it a historical trail on April 15, 1996. All four state declarations were made at the request of the Indian Awareness Center which is a branch of the Fulton County, Indiana Historical Society located in Rochester, Indiana. (Photo by L.G. Eggleston.)

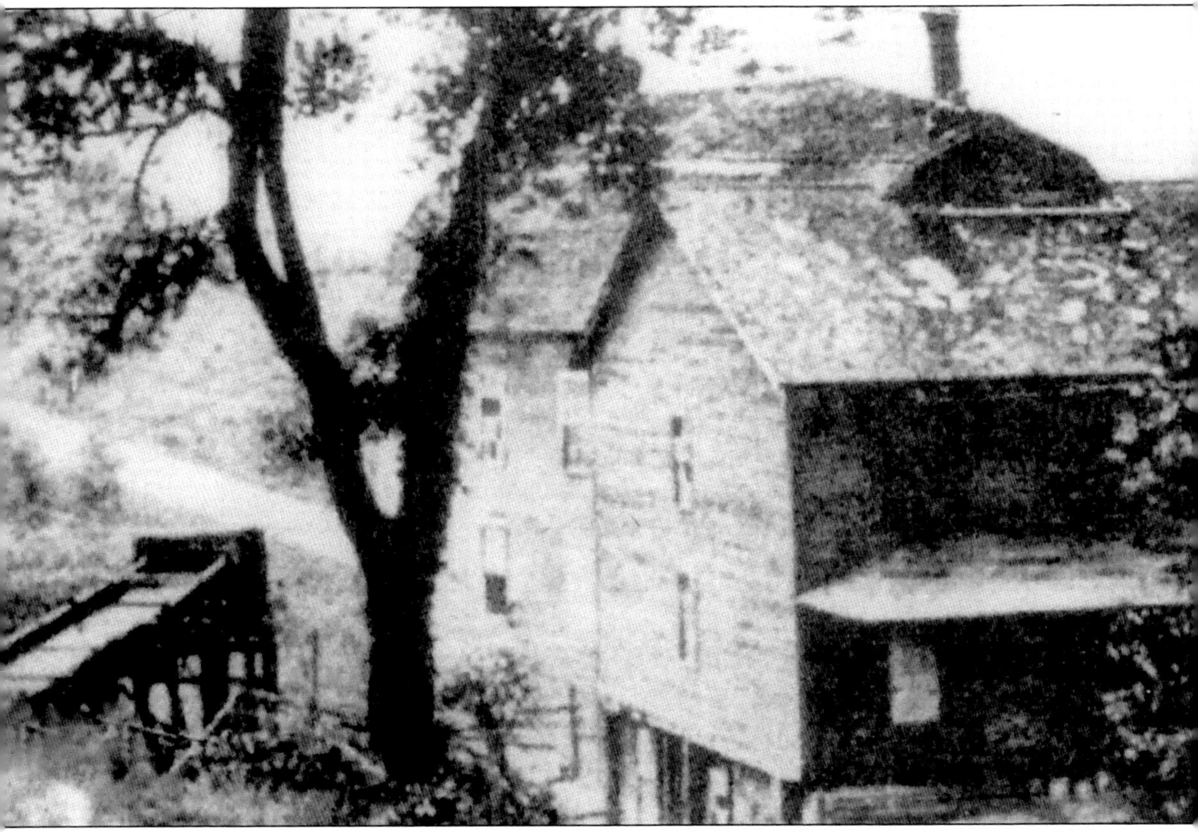

The above photograph shows the original William Cheney Mill in 1841. (Courtesy of Porter County Historical Society)

Sager's Lake and Area Mills The Potawatomi Indians made their home in a beautiful valley one-mile south of Portersville (now Valparaiso). The settlers referred to the Indian village as Chiqua's Town since Chief Chiqua was the head of the tribe. The Potawatomi Indians also maintained several hunting camps around the freshwater lakes in northern Porter County. The site for Chiqua's Town was chosen because the valley had several natural springs and being in the valley, the town would be out of the wind.

The Rand McNally map of the Indians of Indiana and several other historical documents show Chiqua's Town in the valley south of Valparaiso, which as close as one can measure, is the valley which was dammed up to form Sager's Lake.

Just prior to the 1838 relocation of the Potawatomi Indians, Chief Chiqua was stripped of his authority and cast out of Chiqua's Town by the tribal counsel. He was deposed for being drunk and causing a fire, which burned his hut down killing his wife. He and several followers set up a new camp near the area where the Strongbow Inn is today.

After the 1838 removal of the Indians it was decided to dam up the west end of the valley and let the natural springs create a millpond. In 1841, William Cheney built a gristmill on the dam. Mr. Cheney charged the local farmers a percentage of the meal he produced for them. He milled flours, cornmeal, and oatmeal. The finished products were sold to the markets in La Porte and Michigan City.

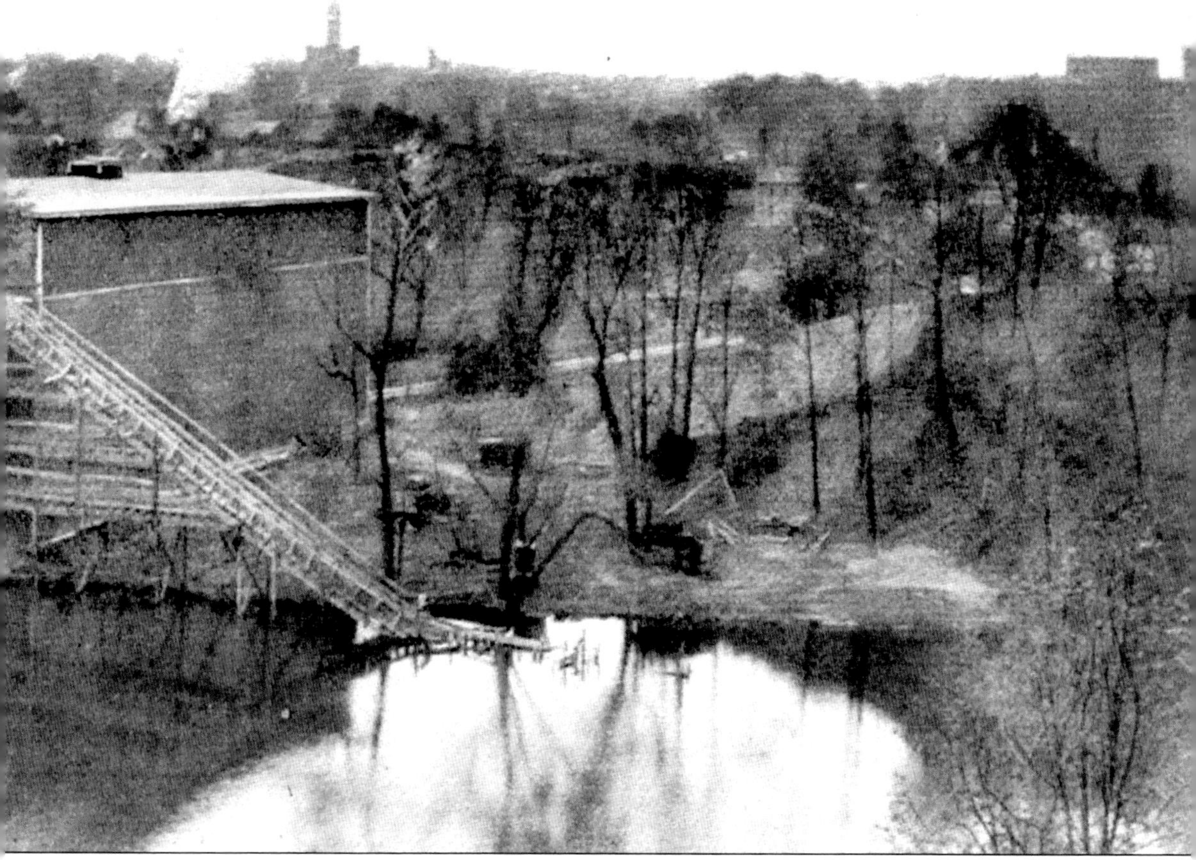

The above photograph of Sager's Mill shows the large recreational water chute, which was built on the lake. Each boat used on the water chute held up to six adults. The ride was called Chute-The-Chute and was very popular. (Photo courtesy of L.G. Eggleston.)

As the need for milling grain became greater, other mills were being built in the area. Mr. M.B. Crosby and his partner Mr. Samuel Haas built a mill inside the town limits of Valparaiso in 1855. The mill was called the Crosby and Haas Steam Flour and Sawmill. It was located north of the railroad where Highway 2 goes under the Nickleplate rails toward Highway 30.

Within a few years, just prior to 1861, the Crobsy Mill burned to the ground. Since Mr. Crosby wanted to stay in the milling business he decided to purchase the Cheney Mill which he acquired in 1861 and operated until 1864.

William Sager purchased the mill in 1864 and named the millpond Sager's Lake. Sager's Lake soon became a popular fishing, boating, and recreation area for the local residents. Mr. Sager added beaches, picnic areas, and recreation facilities to the site.

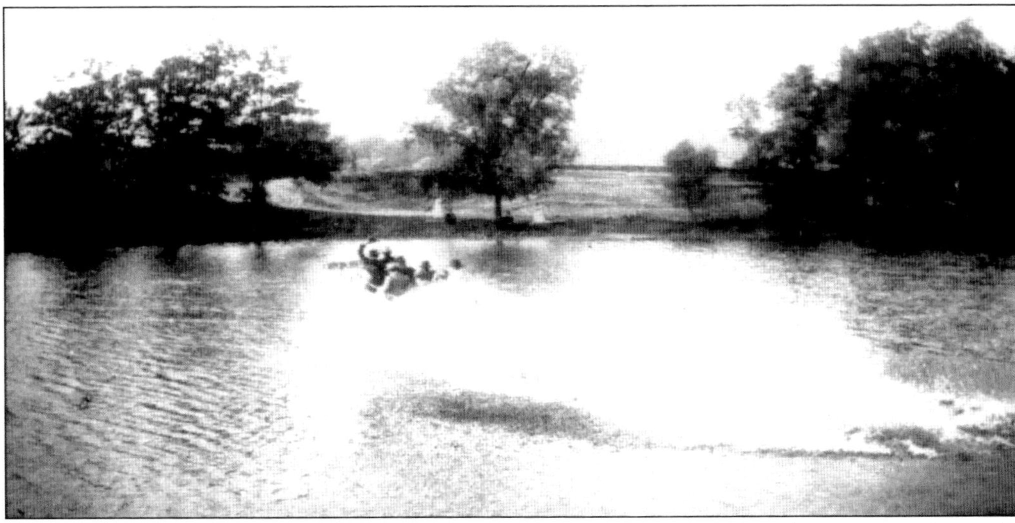

The above photograph shows the boat skimming across Sager's Lake after coming down the water chute. (Photo courtesy of G. Bradley Publishing, Inc.)

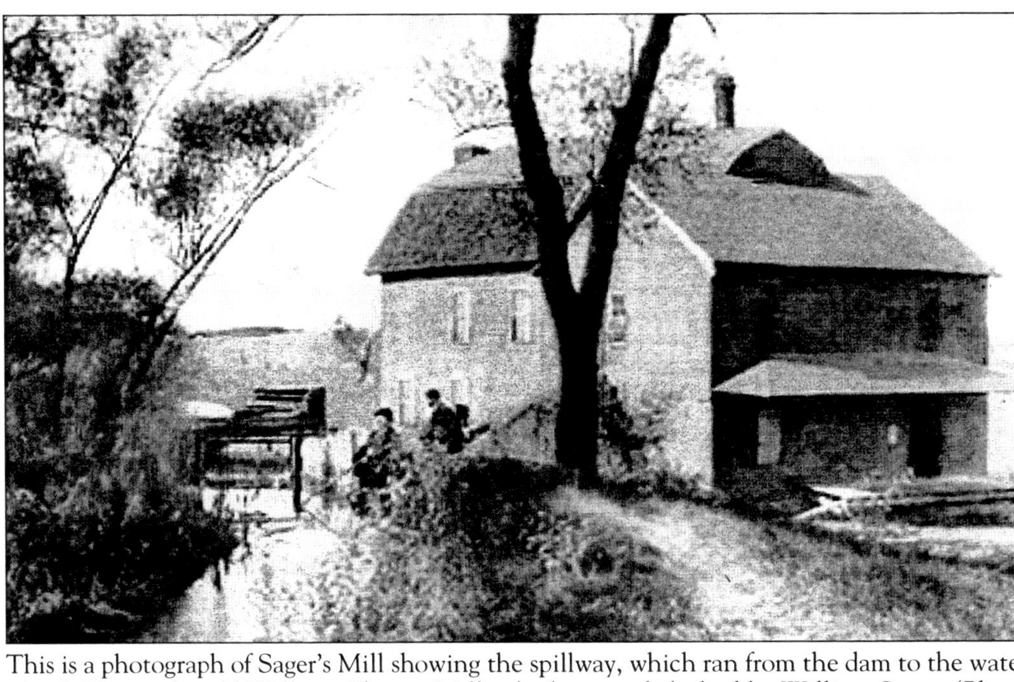

This is a photograph of Sager's Mill showing the spillway, which ran from the dam to the water wheel. This is the old William Cheney Mill, which was refurbished by William Sager. (Photo courtesy of Porter County Historical Society.)

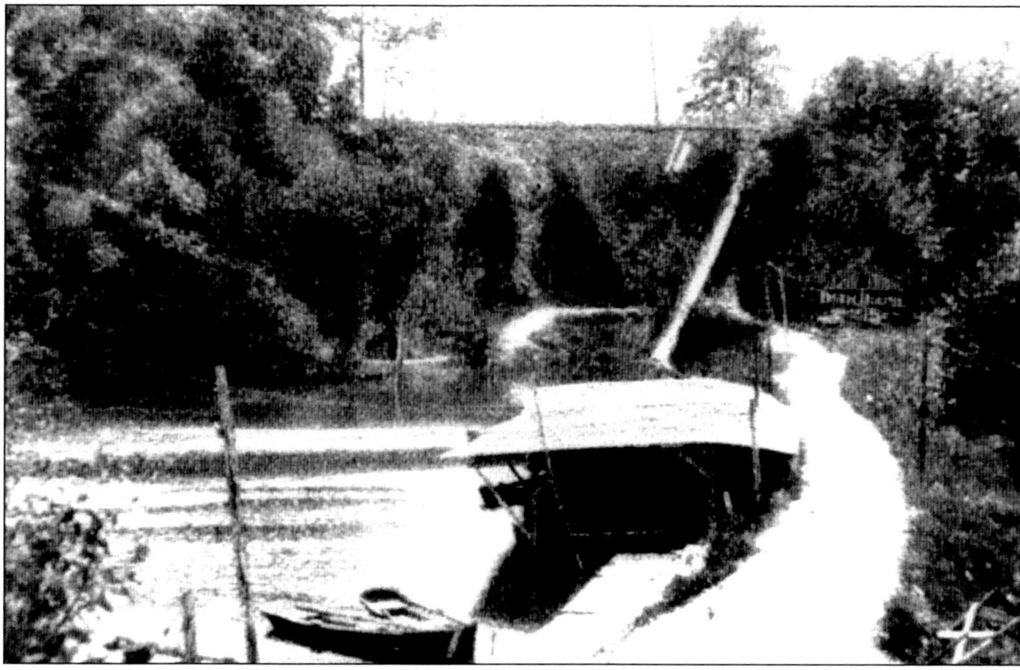

The boat rental area on Sager's Lake Dam is shown above. The Nickleplate Railroad runs across the top of the picture. (Photo courtesy of Porter County Historical Society.)

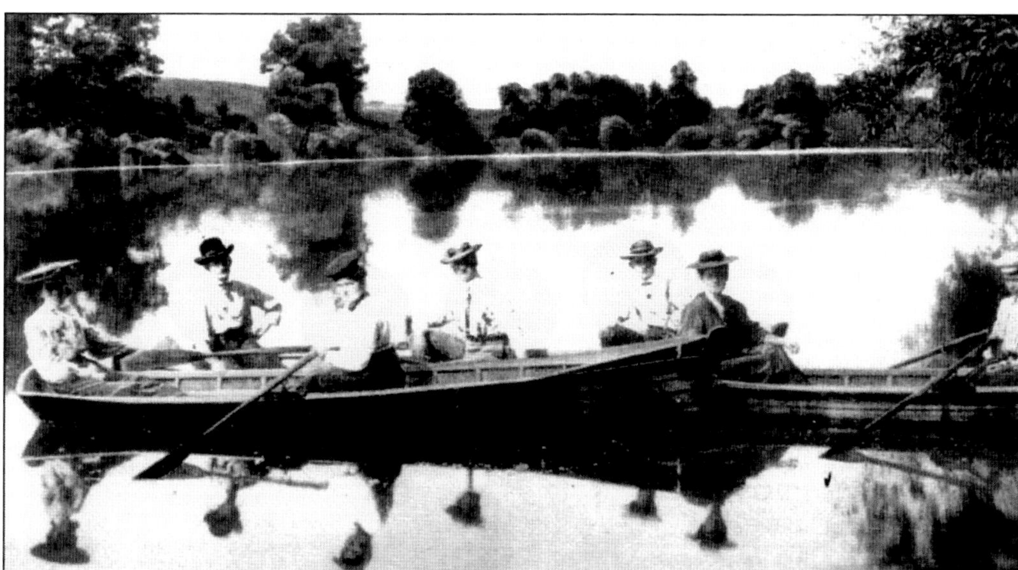

Boating on Sager's Lake in 1909 was very popular for local residents as well as tourists who stayed in the many downtown Valparaiso hotels. The above photograph shows the type of rental boats used. (Photo courtesy of L.G. Eggleston.)

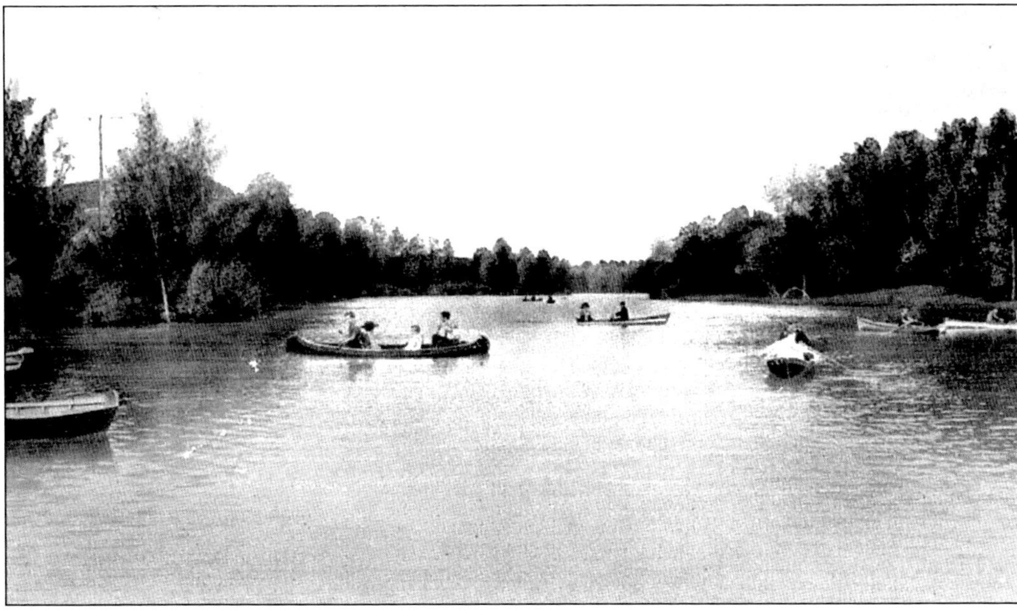

The above photograph was taken in 1910 and shows canoes and boats on Sager's Lake. (Photo courtesy of L.G. Egglcston.)

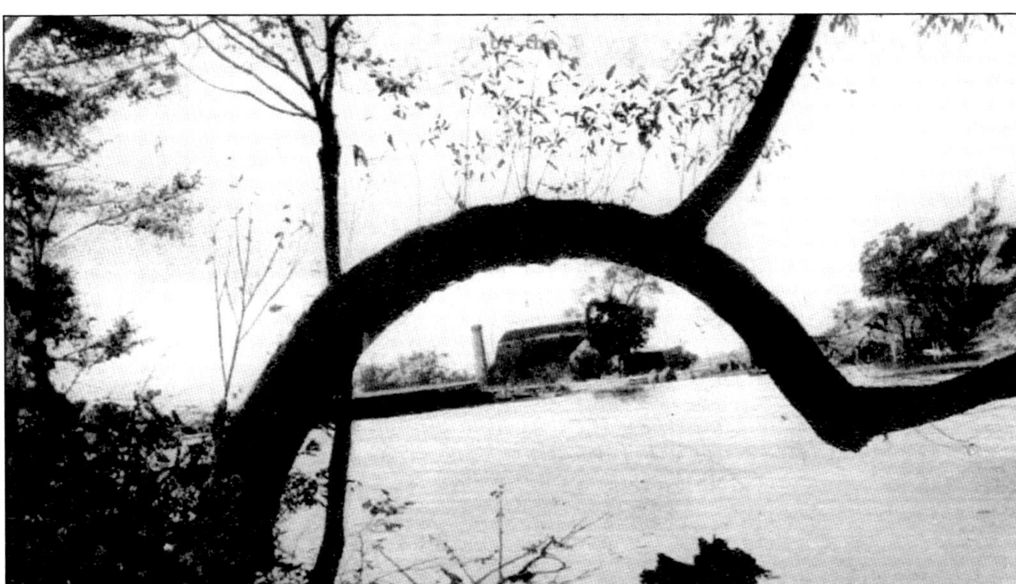

The above photograph is a view looking toward the dam and mill from the walking trail around Sager's Lake, *c.* 1908. (Photo courtesy of L.G. Eggleston)

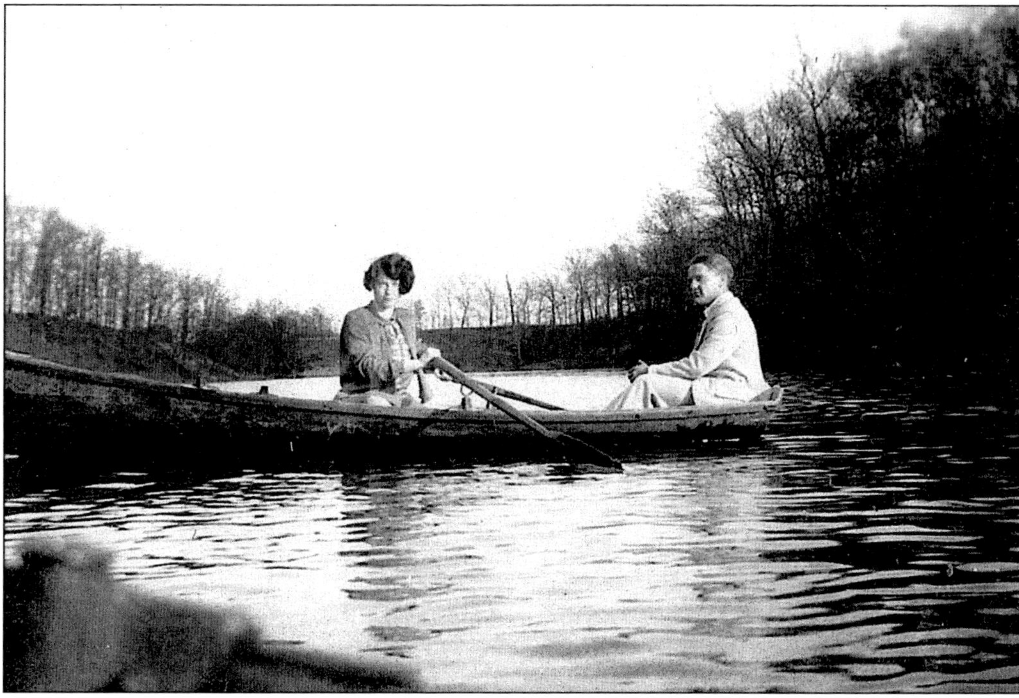

Boating was also very popular for young couples during courting. The above photograph is of Ann Murvihill and Spencer Eldridge Chester in 1927. (Photo courtesy of Margaret Eggleston.)

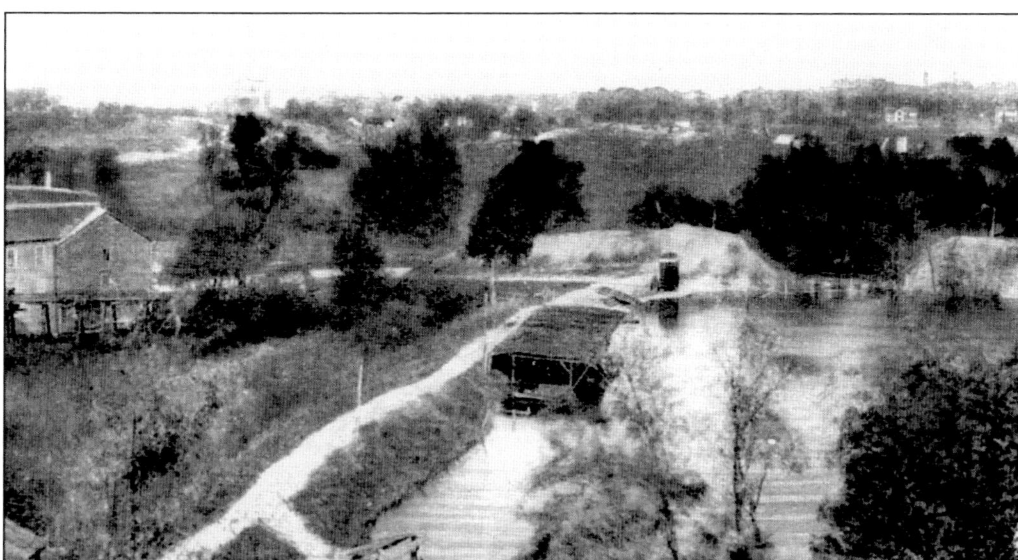

Shown here is a view from Sager's Lake with Valparaiso in the background. The spillway, from the dam to the mill, can also been seen. The walking trail seen on the dam extended completely around Sager's Lake. (Photo courtesy of L.G. Eggleston.)

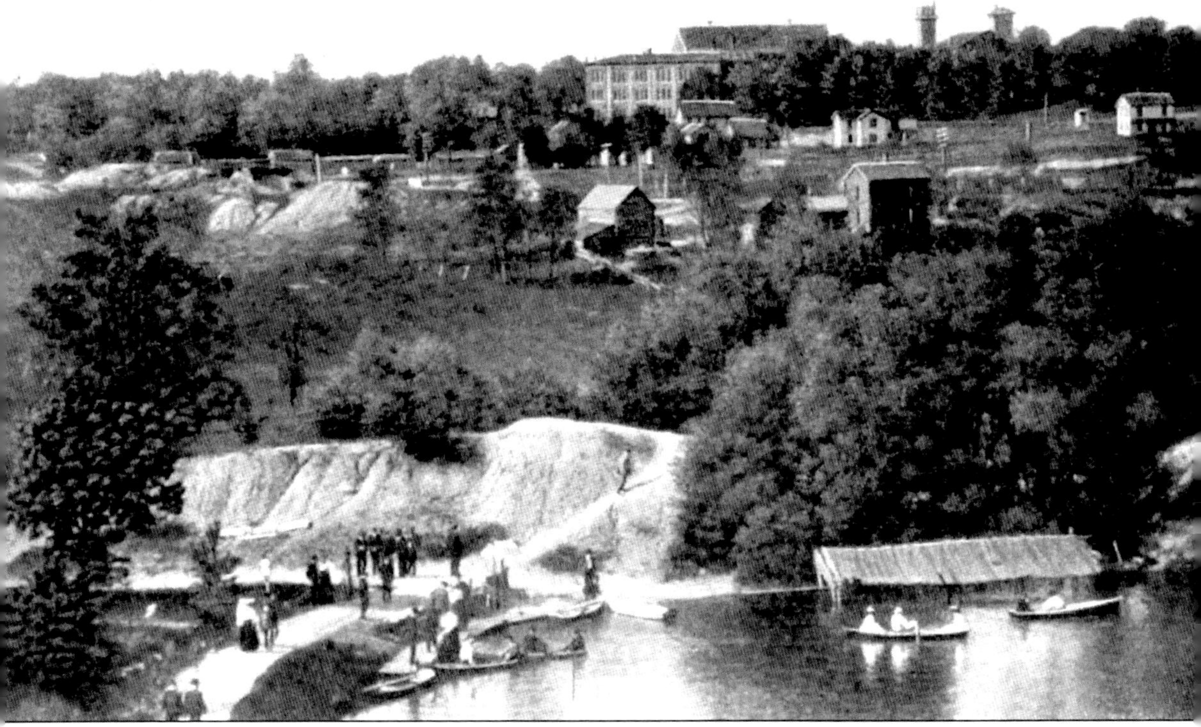

The scene above is a view from Sager's Lake in 1908 showing Valparaiso University in the background. Also seen are visitors strolling on the walking trail by the dam. (Photo courtesy of L.G. Eggleston.)

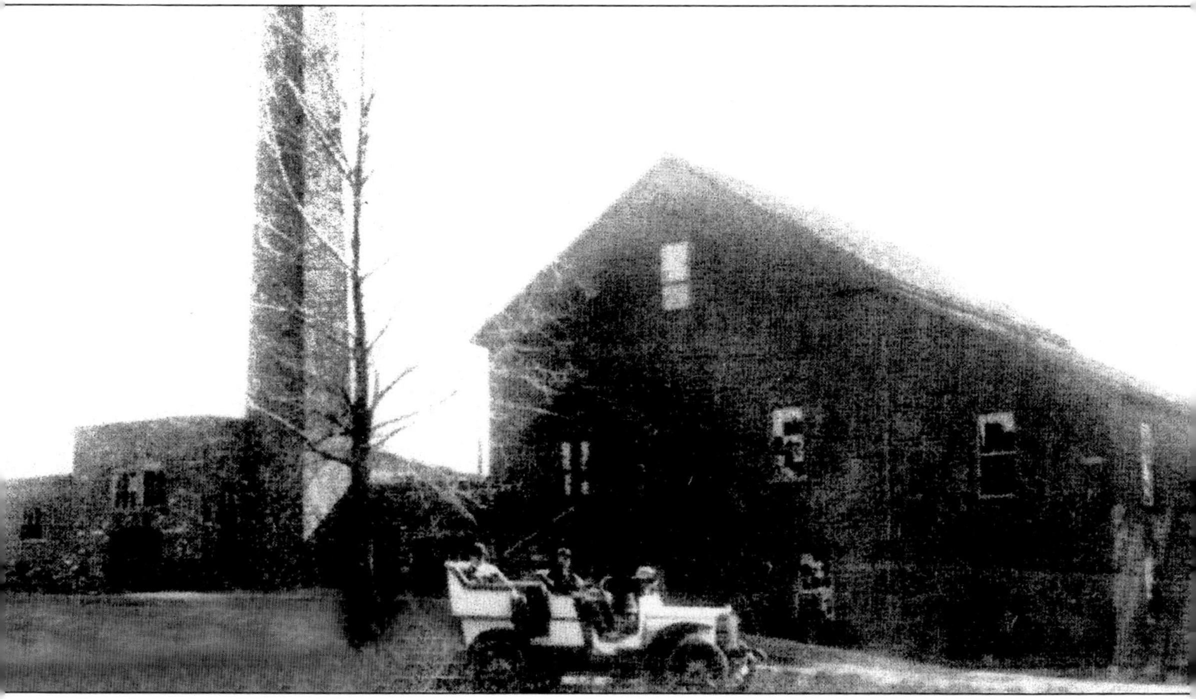

The above picture is of the old Crosby Mill in Valparaiso. (Photo courtesy of Porter County Historical Society.)

Many different types of mills were constructed as the Porter County area continued to grow. There were 13 mills built to process a variety of products. Those mills are listed below.

PAIN'S SAWMILL 1834. Built on the east side of the Joliet Bridge over Salt Creek.
KINSEY WOOL CARDING MILL. Built one-half-mile south of Valparaiso, at the base of the ridge that runs along the valley of Salt Creek. The mill used waterpower from a large wheel.
AXE CARDING MILL. Built one-half-mile above Sager's Mill on Salt Creek. Jacob Axe built the mill.
CHENEY FLOUR MILL. Built by William Cheney in 1841 on the dam, which created Sager's Lake. The mill was sold to M.B. Crosby in 1861 and then to William Sager in 1864.
ELGIN'S MILL. This mill was purchased in 1866 by William McConkey and renamed McConkey Flouring Mill.
CHENEY & FREEMAN FLOUR MILL. Built by a man named Mr. Allen Prior in 1880. The mill was sold to Captain Hixon who later sold it to Aaron Lytle. It became property of T.A. Hogan in 1861 and was sold to Richard Lytle in 1867.
PAPER MILL. This was built in the late 1860s in Valparaiso and powered by a boiler purchased from Richard Lytle's sawmill at Flintville.
HENRY'S MILL. Built in the northwest corner of Center Township.
MCQUISTON SAW MILL. Built in 1878 by John McQuinston at Flintville. The mill burned down in 1881.
UPDYKE SAW MILL. Built by J.G. Updyke near the depot of the Pennisular Railroad in Valparaiso. The Penninsular Railroad later became the Grand Trunk. The entire mill was later moved to Washington Township.
STAVE FACTORY. Built and operated near the Flint Lake steam and saw mill at Flintville and was owned by a group of businessmen from Illinois. The factory went out of business in 1867.

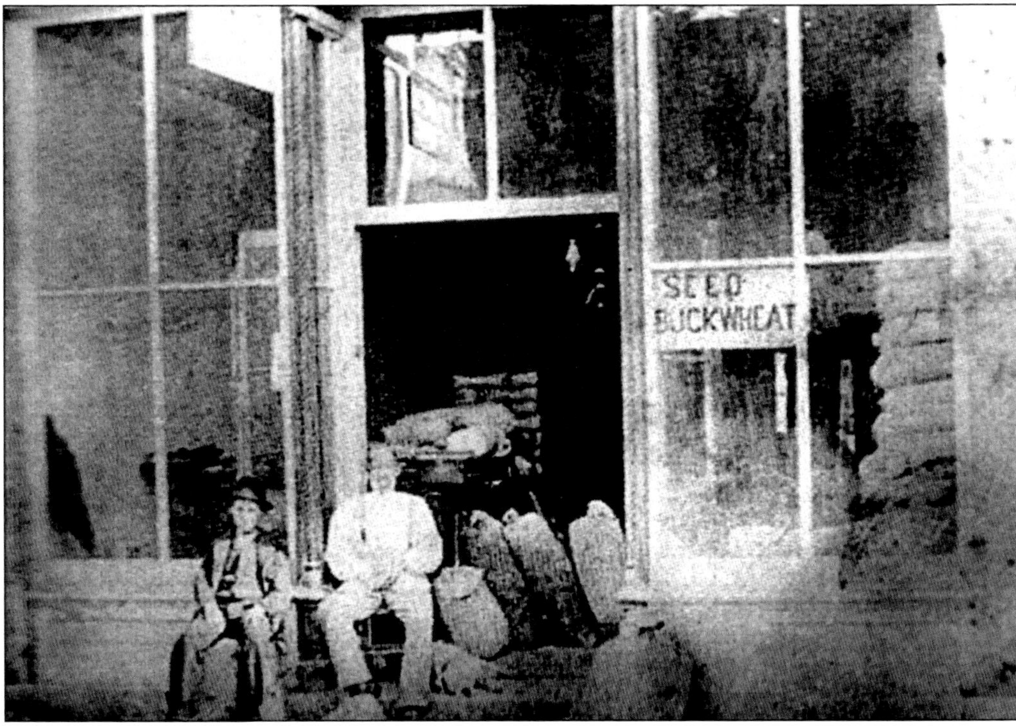

The Crosby Feed Store shown here was located on Washington Street in Valparaiso and sold products milled by the Crosby Mill. (Photo courtesy of G. Bradley Publishing, Inc.)

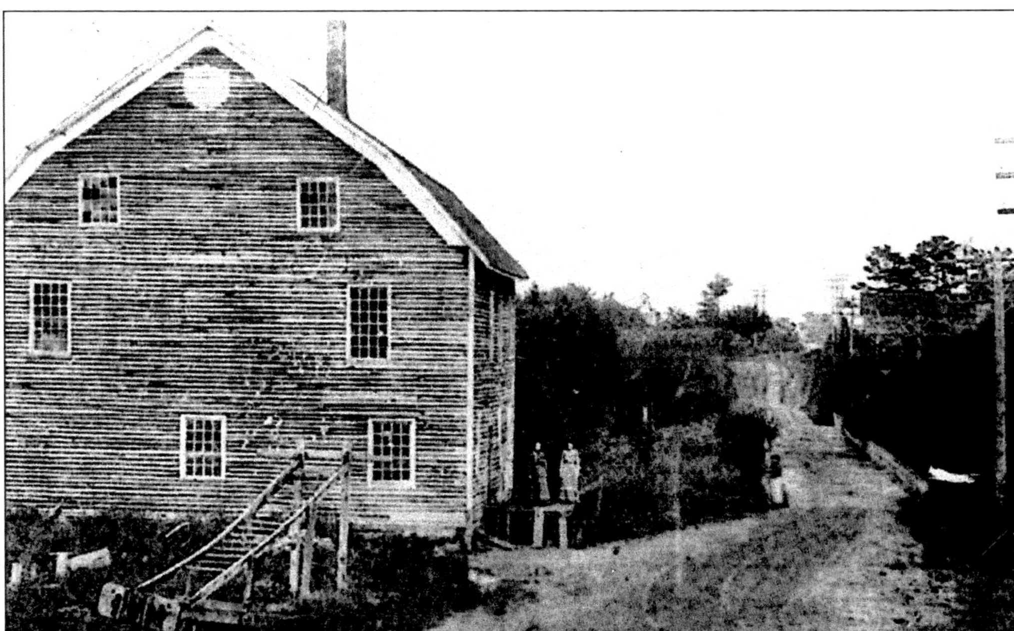

The above photograph is of Salt Creek Mill, which was built near the area now known as Salt Creek Commons. The photograph is from the late 1800s. (Photo courtesy of Porter County Historical Society.)

Two

Flint Lake Folklore

The Legend of Flint Lake

The Legend of Flint Lake The Legend of Flint Lake began in the early 1800s when a family named Van Loon came to the area and built a home in the woods on a lake, which they named Van Loon Lake. They built their home on land owned by the Potawatomi Indians. The exact date of their arrival is unknown. Estimates place them in the area in the early 1820s. Their daughter Mary Van Loon was taken by the Potawatomi Indians as a baby. Estimates show that she died in 1836 at the approximate age of 16. The fate of the Van Loon family is unknown.

The U.S. Government purchased Lake Van Loon and the surrounding area in 1826. The land was then sold to a family named Dillingham. A young man named William (Billie) Wauhob married Betsy Electra Dillingham on January 28, 1837 and acquired the land on Van Loon Lake. He renamed the lake Wauhob Lake, as it is known today.

As settlers began to arrive in the area around the lakes they noticed, while trading with the Indians, that the Potawatomi tribe had a young white girl living with them. She is described as small, plump, and beautiful. Her name was Mary Van Loon and the settlers reported that she was stolen from the Van Loon family when she was a baby.

Although the settlers knew that the Indians took Mary Van Loon, they made no effort to take her away from them. There were two main reasons for this. The first reason is that the Indians were friendly toward the settlers and they did not want to arouse any hostility. The second reason is that Chief Chiqua had plans for Mary Van Loon to marry his son and any rescue effort could be met with hostility.

Chief Chiqua allowed the settlers to teach Mary how to read and write and how to dress as a white woman. The settlers provided her with white cloth to make dresses and other articles of clothing. She was often seen wearing white dresses with garlands of white water lilies around her neck. However, most of the time her neck was adorned with a necklace of white flint arrowheads. The fact that she was usually dressed in white with white water lilies or white arrowheads around her neck, earned her the nickname of White Flint, as she was called by both the Indians and the settlers.

Since she was to become the bride of Chief Chiqua's son, the tribe treated her very well. She was given her own pony and was allowed the freedom to come and go as she pleased. She enjoyed riding the trails which encircled the lakes.

When White Flint was approximately 16 years old a young settler from Ohio came to live in the lake area. His name was James (Jimmie) Arnold. He came to live and work with his uncle. When Jimmie Arnold met White Flint they fell deeply in love. He tried several times to get White Flint to run away and marry him, but was unsuccessful. Chief Chiqua and the tribe became very angry and went as far as to shut her up for a while to keep her from seeing Jimmie. White Flint took every opportunity as it arose to slip away on her pony and ride up the trail around the lakes to meet her lover.

One day while riding the trail around the lakes she inquired about where she could find Jimmie. The settlers gladly told her that he was at Long Lake hunting white swans. By the time she reached the channel to Long Lake at the northwest corner of what is now Flint Lake, it started to rain. She dismounted and took shelter under a thick bush. Unknown to her, Jimmie Arnold was nearby and as he approached he noticed, through the mist and rain what he thought was a white swan under a bush. He quickly took aim and fired. Pleased that he had hit his mark he rushed toward the bush to retrieve his prize. His elation was short lived and quickly turned into extreme horror as he discovered that he had killed his lover, Mary Van Loon.

Shaken with grief he carried her body back to the Indian camp. The Indians seeing how shaken and grief stricken he was took pity on him and consoled him until he was able to return home to his uncle.

When he returned home he related the tragic events to his uncle. He was counseled by his uncle to report the story to the local authorities and not to flee the area in fear of prosecution. He was tried and cleared of any wrongdoing. The court found that the death of Mary Van Loon was an accident.

After a period of mourning Jimmie Arnold returned to the Potawatomi camp and remained with them the rest of his life. He went with them when they were moved west of the Mississippi.

Up to this time Flint Lake had not been named. Because of the tragic accident the settlers began to call the lake, White Flint Lake in her honor. As time passed it became known only as Flint Lake.

The settlers composed a song about White Flint to remember and honor her. The song is as follows.

Song of White Flint

It happened one evening
At the setting of the sun
She stepped under a green tree
A shower for to shun

Along came her true love
And shot all in the dark
Woe! And alas
He did not miss his mark

He stepped up to her
And found it was she
Then his limbs did tremble
And his eyes could not see

He took her in his arms
He found she was dead
A fountain of tears
All around her he shed

He went home
With his gun in his hand
Saying "Uncle, Dear Uncle"
I have shot Mary Van

I have shot that dear creature
The flower of the year
Uncle, Dear Uncle
What shall I do to get clear?

Stay in your country
Till your trial comes on
Never try to run away
For you will not be hung

One evening to his uncle
Mary's spirit did appear
Saying "Uncle, Dear Uncle"
Jimmie Arnold will be cleared

They tried and they cleared him
To finish my song
Ne'er again will he go hunting
At the setting of the sun

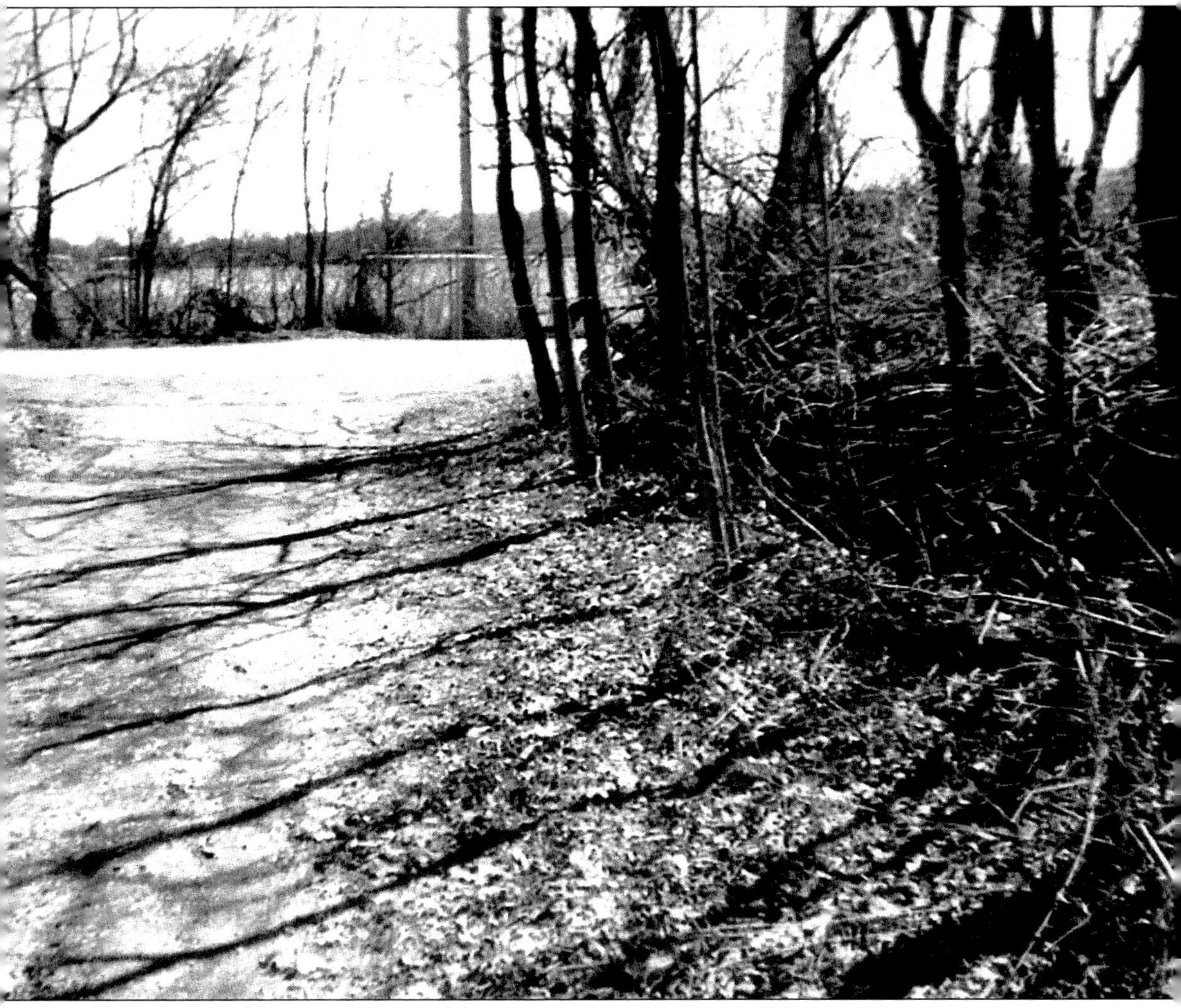

Jimmie Arnold reportedly killed his lover, Mary Van Loon "White Flint" somewhere along the area shown above which is between Flint Lake and Long Lake. The path shown in the photograph runs along the West Side of the channel between Flint Lake and Long Lake. Flint Lake is shown in the background. (Photo by L.G. Eggleston.)

Mr. George M. Merrill as reported in the *Vidette* on October 16, 1916 sang this song to Mrs. L.F. Bennett in early 1916. George M. Merrill was 83 years old at the time and had lived at Flint Lake for 80 years. He was 3 years old when his family arrived in 1836.

White Flint (Mary Van Loon) was estimated to be 16 years old when she was killed. This would place the Van Loon family in the area in the early 1820s. The date she was taken by the Potawatomi is unknown and no record can be found which shows the fate of her family. The Indians may have killed them, they may have simply died from disease or accident, or they may have left the area after the loss of their daughter.

The only actual record is that of Mr. Merrill who recalls actually seeing White Flint as the Indians visited their farm. He also related the information that Mary Van Loon "White Flint" was stolen from her family by the Potawatomi Indians. Mr. Merrill is the only person on record who remembers seeing White Flint and hearing the other settlers' remarks about how beautiful she was.

Because of this mixture of facts and hearsay the story of White Flint will remain a legend.

The Sea Serpent of Flint Lake There are many strange and exciting stories in early Porter County history. Some are based on facts or happenings while others are based on hearsay, myth, legends, or hoaxes. The story of the Sea Serpent of Flint Lake is one of these stories.

The sea serpent first appeared in the summer of 1892. The lake was just beginning to become a popular place for fishermen, hikers, picnickers, and campers. The old Indian trails around the lake gave visitors easy access.

The first description of the sea serpent was by a group of visitors to the lake who reported that they had seen a large round head with whiskers moving across the lake. Later reports as more sightings occurred included a long green round body, which looped in and out of the water.

Many people flocked to the lake to hopefully get a glimpse of the sea serpent. Some watched from shore while others rented boats and waited on the lake. On several occasions when the serpent appeared the boaters raced out to get a better view of what they were seeing. Each time they began to near the serpent it disappeared under the water.

The sightings made national headlines and many from around the country traveled to Flint Lake to get a glimpse of the unusual phenomena.

The stores in Porter County experienced large increases in sales for supplies, especially field glasses and binoculars. Many people bought shotguns, pistols, and rifles. Those who were overly curious set up watches around the lake. Speculation as to what the creature was ranged from giant turtle, huge muskrat, water moccasin, to a dog.

Finally someone seemed to solve the mystery. It seems that two seals had escaped from the Columbia Exposition grounds in Chicago and it was suggested that they swam through the underground river system till they emerged in Flint Lake. This solution fit the descriptions of a round head and the large whiskers. Everyone seemed satisfied with this explanation, and no more sightings were reported.

In the fall of 1892, a young boy named A.W. Shinabargar accompanied his parents on a visit to the Drum Farm near the lakes. There was a young boy in the Drum family who was a friend of the young Shinabargar boy. During the visit the two boys got bored and decided to explore the stable behind the house. In the rafters they found a row of old keg hoops covered with green cloth and a wooden round head with pig bristles on both sides of the mouth. The discovery by the two boys solved the mystery of the sea serpent of Flint Lake. It was a hoax.

The Mystery of Burlington Beach In the historic records of legends, myths, and mysteries, Burlington Beach is not without its unsolved mystery. The mystery revolves around the unexplained life and death of Joseph (Jimmy) DeArmond. Jimmy DeArmond was a retired circus and vaudeville performer. He was part of a circus act called "The Flying DeArmonds." He was referred to in the trade as a "knock about" (a person who goes from job to job). He was at one time thrown out of the theater but bounced back with his own act and a new group of performers who became very successful.

When he retired in 1925 he purchased a cottage at Burlington Beach on Flint Lake. Jimmy had saved $50,000, which he brought with him to his new home. He furnished his cottage with the finest house wares and linens available. Jimmy always wore the finest clothes and was well thought of in his new community. He often spoke to his friends and neighbors about his lovely wife and sons who were planning to join him at a later date. Jimmy always attended every holiday event in the Valparaiso area.

Jimmy seemed to enjoy his retirement and his new friends. He often mused about his days in vaudeville and about a young comic who was a genteel tramp with a cane and sloppy shoes. This comic always left the audience in stitches. His name was Charlie Chaplin.

On July 4, 1936 Jimmy failed to attend the 4th of July celebrations in Valparaiso. This was the first time he missed the celebrations in the ten years he lived at Burlington Beach. Everyone wondered what had happened to him. The answer soon came in a telephone call from the Allen County sheriff's office. It seems that for some reason Jimmy had left his clothes on the bank of the St. Mary's River at Hessan Castle near Ft. Wayne, and gone swimming alone in the river. His body was found by two fishermen.

The Allen County Sheriff contacted Porter County Sheriff Fry for instructions as to the disposition of the body and/or burial instructions.

Sheriff Fry went to Jimmy's cottage at Burlington Beach to find the address of his wife and sons. He found nothing to indicate that Jimmy had ever had a family. Neighbors stated that Jimmy often talked of his wife and two grown children who supposedly were somewhere in New York. The $50,000, which Jimmy had when he came to Porter County, could not be found. The Porter County recorder's office showed that the cottage at Burlington Beach was in the name of Mr. and Mrs. Joseph DeArmond.

Jimmy was buried in Potter's Field in Ft. Wayne, Indiana. Sheriff Fry locked the cottage and referred the matter to the courts for disposition.

Many unanswered questions surrounded his death. Why did Jimmy go to the St. Mary's River on the 4th of July instead of celebrating it in Valparaiso as he always had? Why did he decide to go swimming alone? Why didn't he have a return train ticket to Valparaiso? The return ticket only cost $1.67. What happened to the $50,000 he brought with him to Porter County? Did he have a family, and if so what happened to them?

The mystery of Jimmy DeArmond was reported in the *Vidette Messenger* on July 7, 1936. The true story of Jimmy DeArmond will remain one of the mysteries in Porter County history.

Three

Flint Lake Resorts

Burlington Beach Resort Flint Lake is a 98-acre lake fed by an underground spring, which is located near the southwest side of the lake. The southern edge of Flint Lake was owned by George Merrill who in 1862 built a fishing and boating resort, which he named Burlington Beach. The resort consisted of rental cabins, a boathouse, a picnic area, and a swimming beach.

The Merrill Family owned the southern edge of Flint Lake for over three decades. Charles Specht purchased the property in 1902. Mr. Specht built a beautiful resort hotel on the lake and named it "The Willows Resort." Mr. Specht rejuvenated the property and turned it into a popular summer resort.

The Burlington Beach resort was located at the end of Flint Lake Gateway Road which runs from Burlington Beach Road to the lake. The Burlington Beach resort no longer exists. The only remaining area is a small fenced-in beach which is private, and owned by the Burlington Beach Association. Flint Lake Gateway Road goes to the water's edge and allows public access to the lake.

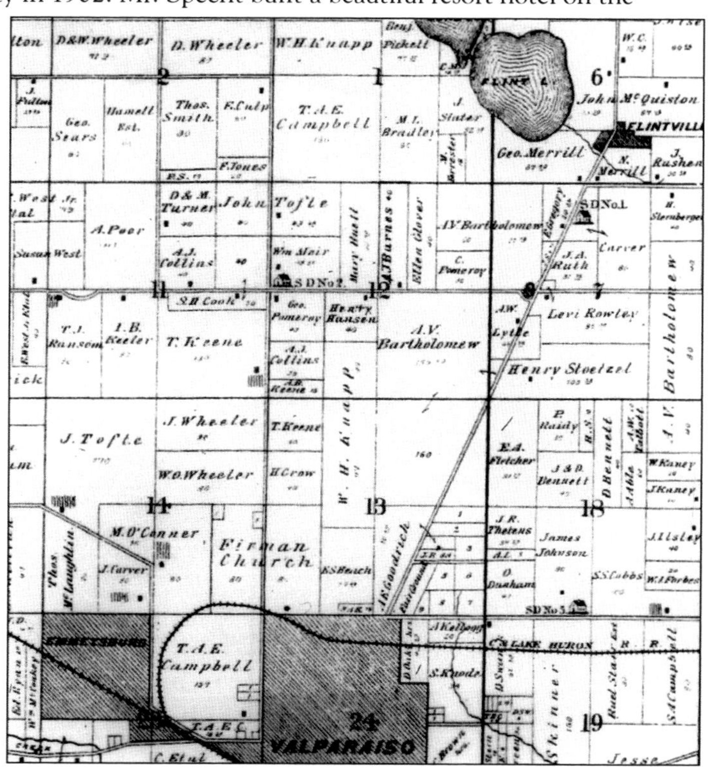

The map to the right shows ownership of lake property north of Valparaiso in the early days of Porter County. (Map courtesy of Valparaiso Public Library.)

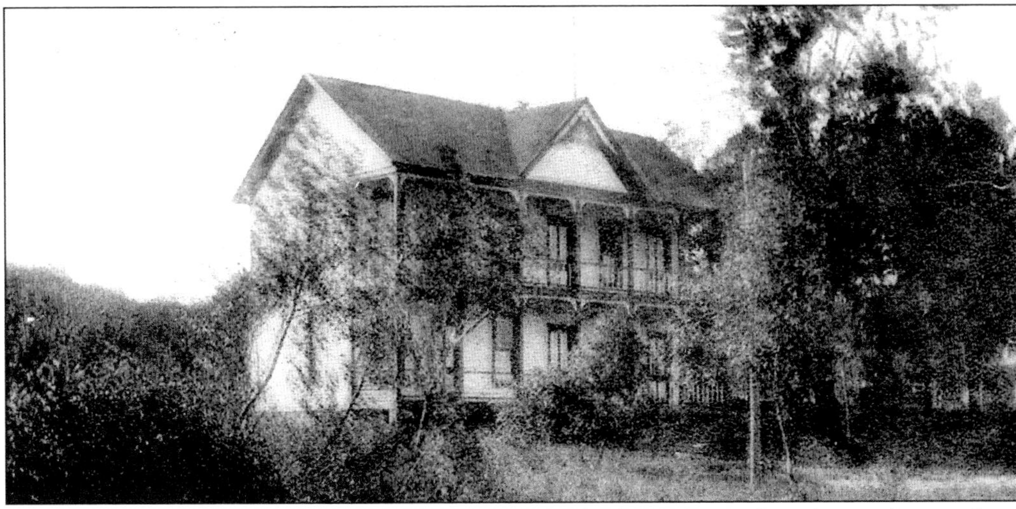

The above picture shows the Willows Resort Hotel, which was located on the southeast edge of Flint Lake at Burlington Beach. (Photo courtesy of L.G. Eggleston.)

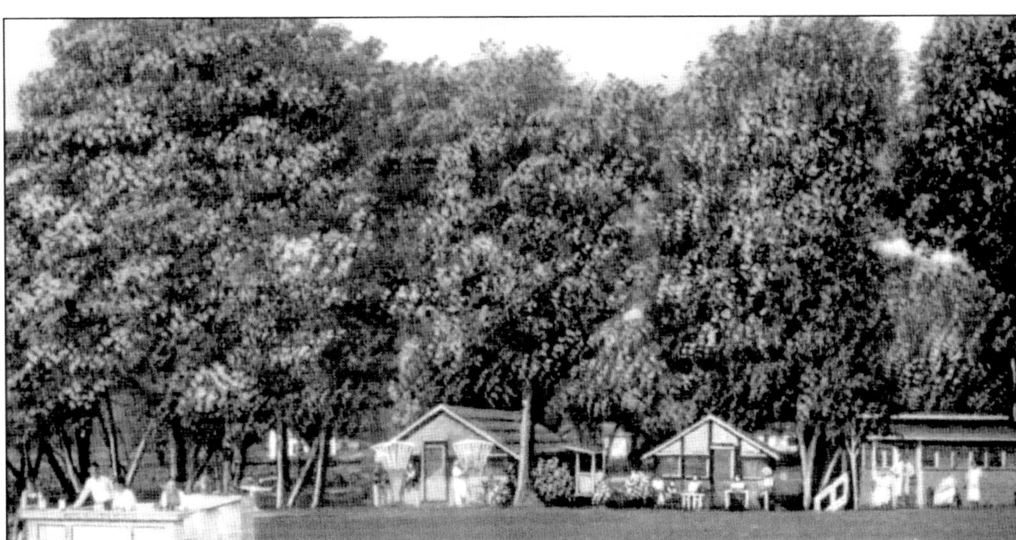

This is a picture of the rental cabins and recreation area at the Burlington Beach Resort. (Photo courtesy of L.G. Eggleston.)

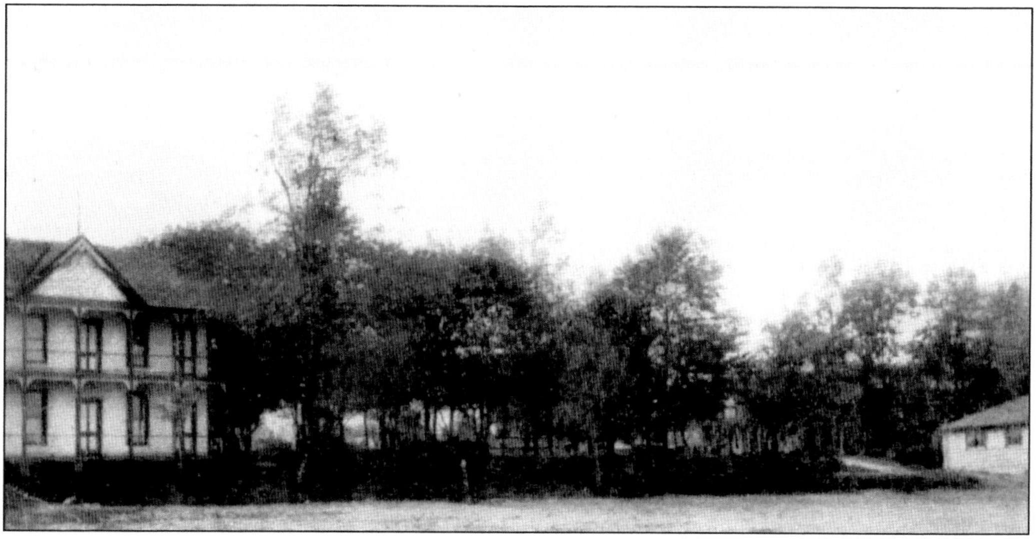

The above picture is a view of The Willows Resort from the lake showing the hotel, the main access road, (which is now Flint Lake Gateway) and the boat house. (Photo courtesy of L.G. Eggleston.)

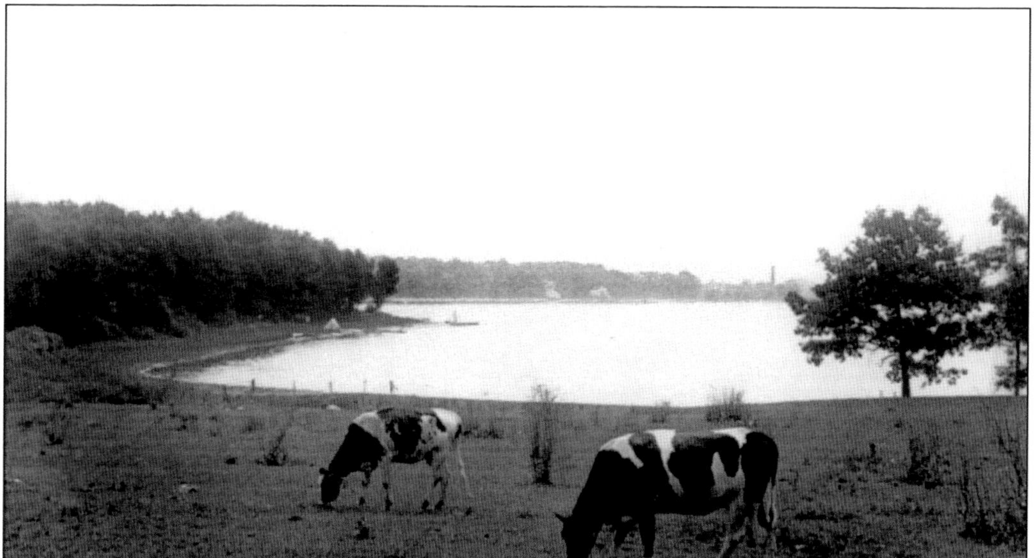

This photograph shows the grazing land on Flint Lake, west of The Willows Resort at Burlington Beach. (Photo courtesy of L.G. Eggleston.)

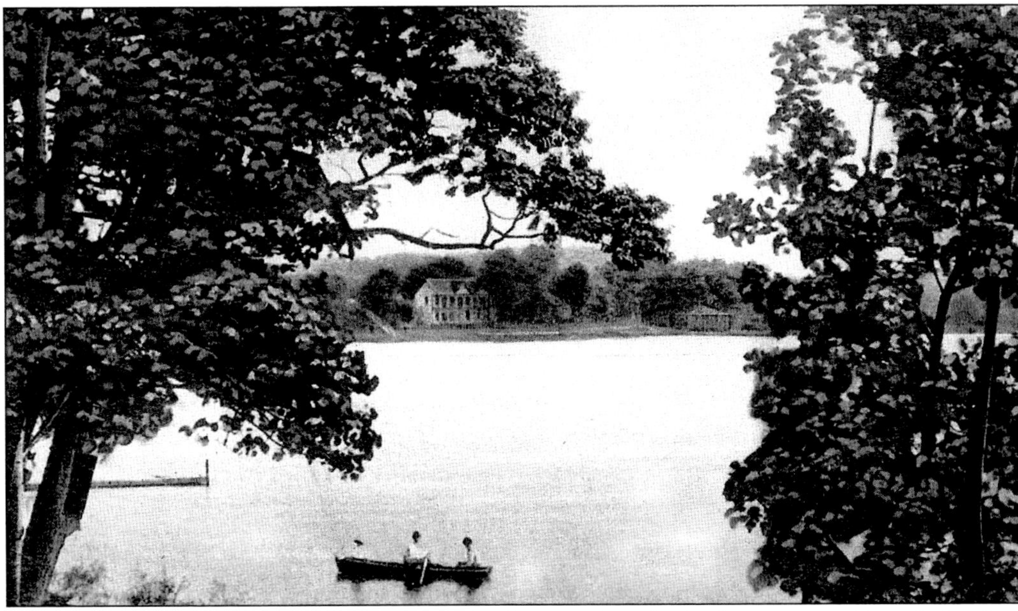

This is a view of the Willows Resort at Burlington Beach, looking across Flint Lake from Sheridan Beach. (Photo courtesy of L.G. Eggleston.)

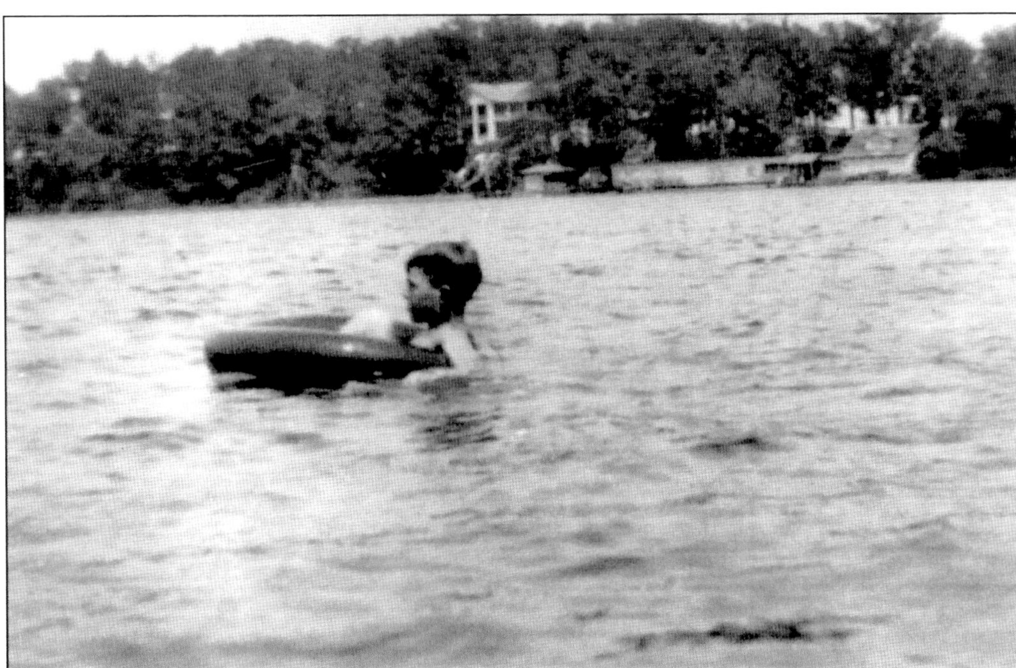

Here is a young boy tubing at Burlington Beach Resort. The view is from Burlington Beach Resort and shows Blackhawk Beach Resort on the other side of the lake. (Photo courtesy of Edwin Kuehl.)

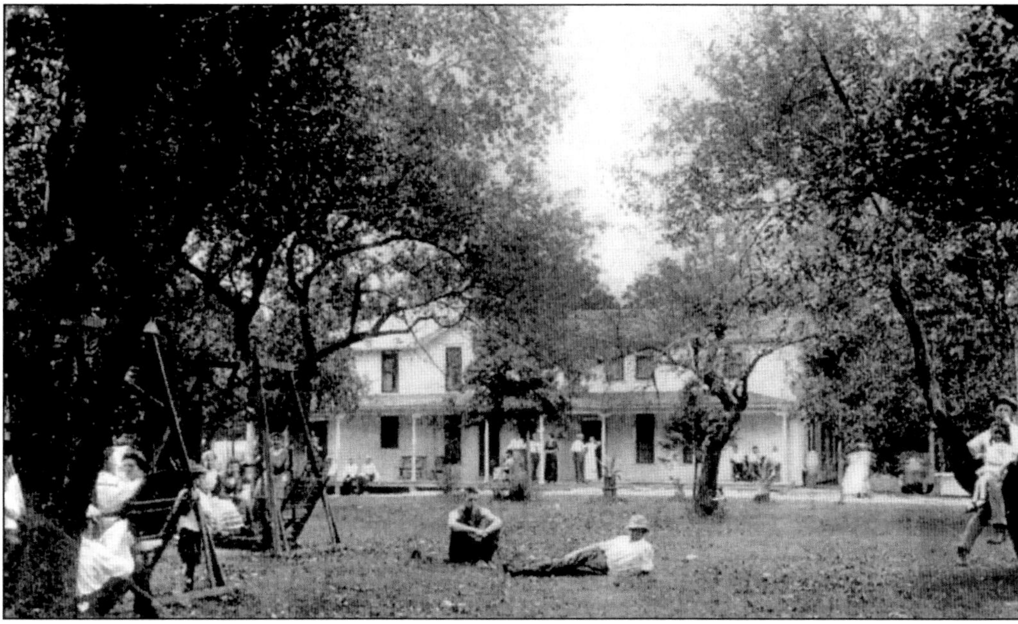

This is a view of the recreation area of the Willows Resort Hotel at Burlington Beach. Flint Lake is to the left of this picture and the rental cabins and tennis courts are to the right. (Photo courtesy of L.G. Eggleston.)

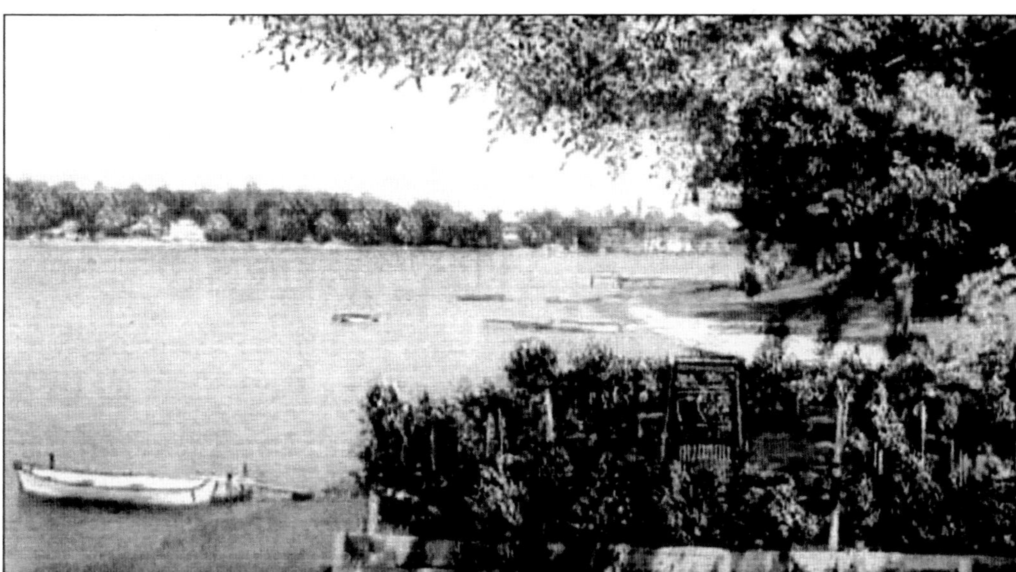

These gardens are on Flint Lake west of the Willows Resort. (Photo courtesy of L.G. Eggleston.)

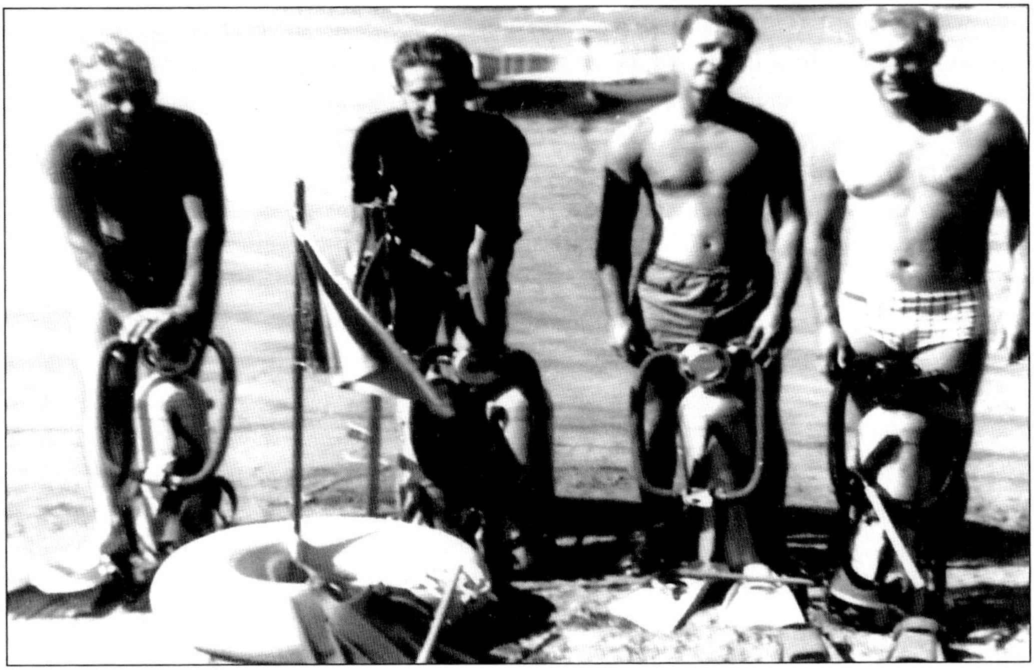

The public access to Flint Lake at Burlington Beach attracted scuba divers in the 1950s and '60s. Seen here are four members of the Midwest Aquatiers Skin Diving Club. From let to right are Fred Myers, David Boyer, David Johnston, and Edwin Kuehl. (Photo courtesy of Edwin Kuehl.)

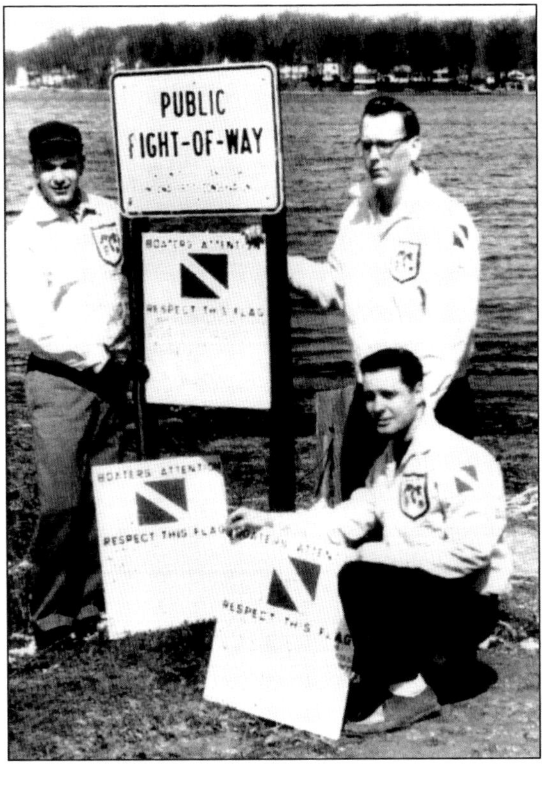

Three members of the Midwest Aquatiers Diving Club are shown here erecting safety signs for boaters to be aware of the skin diving flag used to show that divers are in the area. Left to right are Edwin Kuehl, Allen Brown, and David Johnston. The Midwest Aquatiers Diving Club also served as the Porter County Sheriffs underwater recovery team. (Photo courtesy of Edwin Kuehl.)

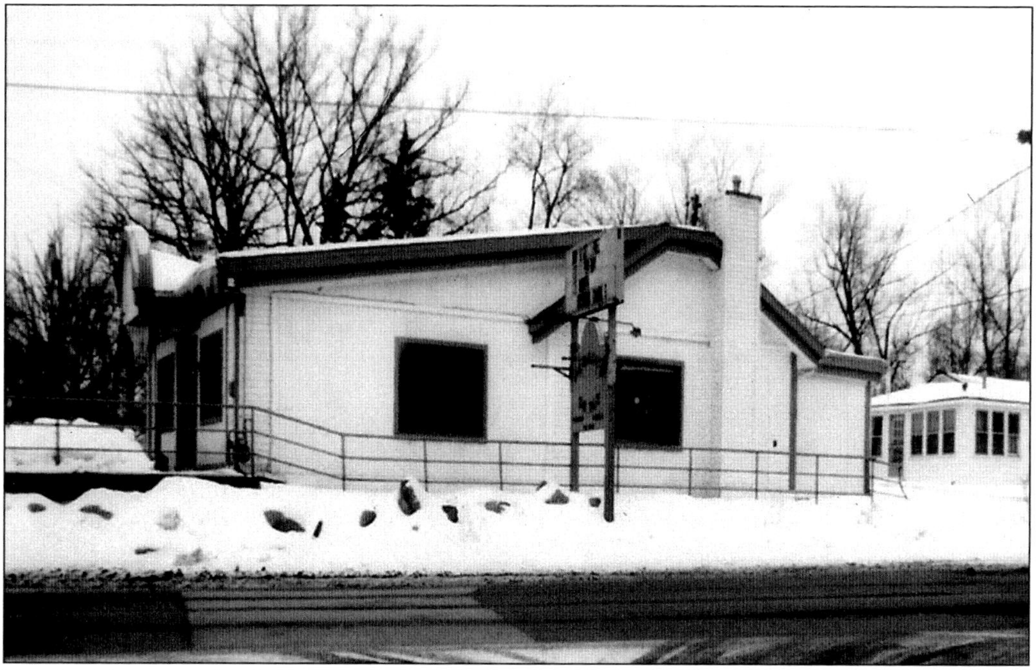

This building was the Burlington Beach Grocery Store. It is located on the northwest corner of Burlington Beach Road and Flint Lake Gateway Road. The building is now occupied by a tanning salon. (Photo by L.G. Eggleston.)

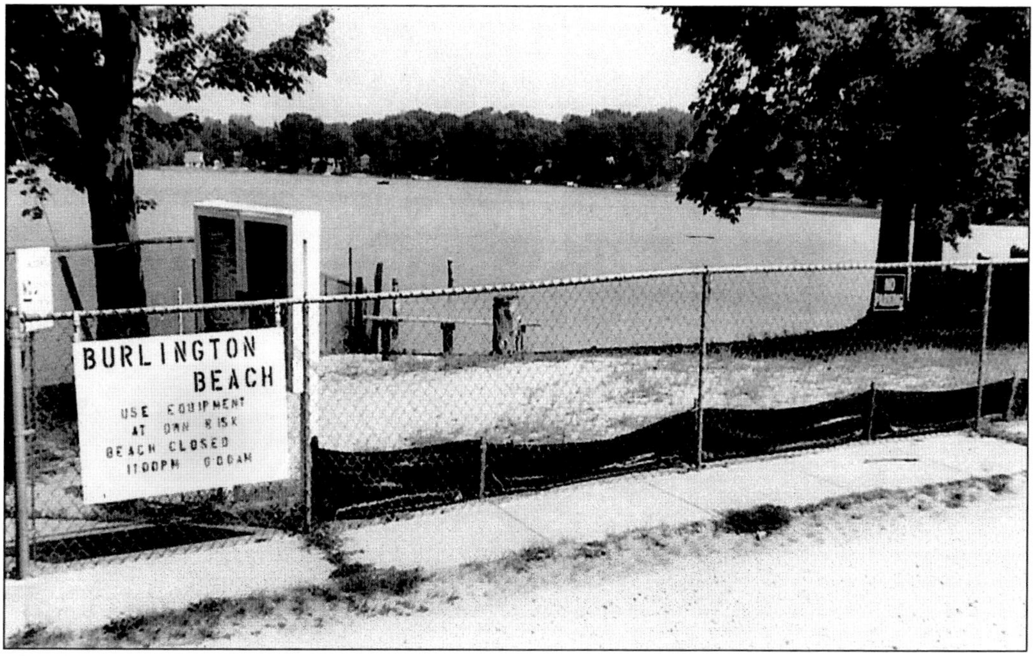

The above photograph is of Burlington Beach as it looks today. Only a small portion of The Willows Resort property remains for swimming. The small beach is private for use only by residents who are members of the beach association and their guests. (Photo by L.G. Eggleston.)

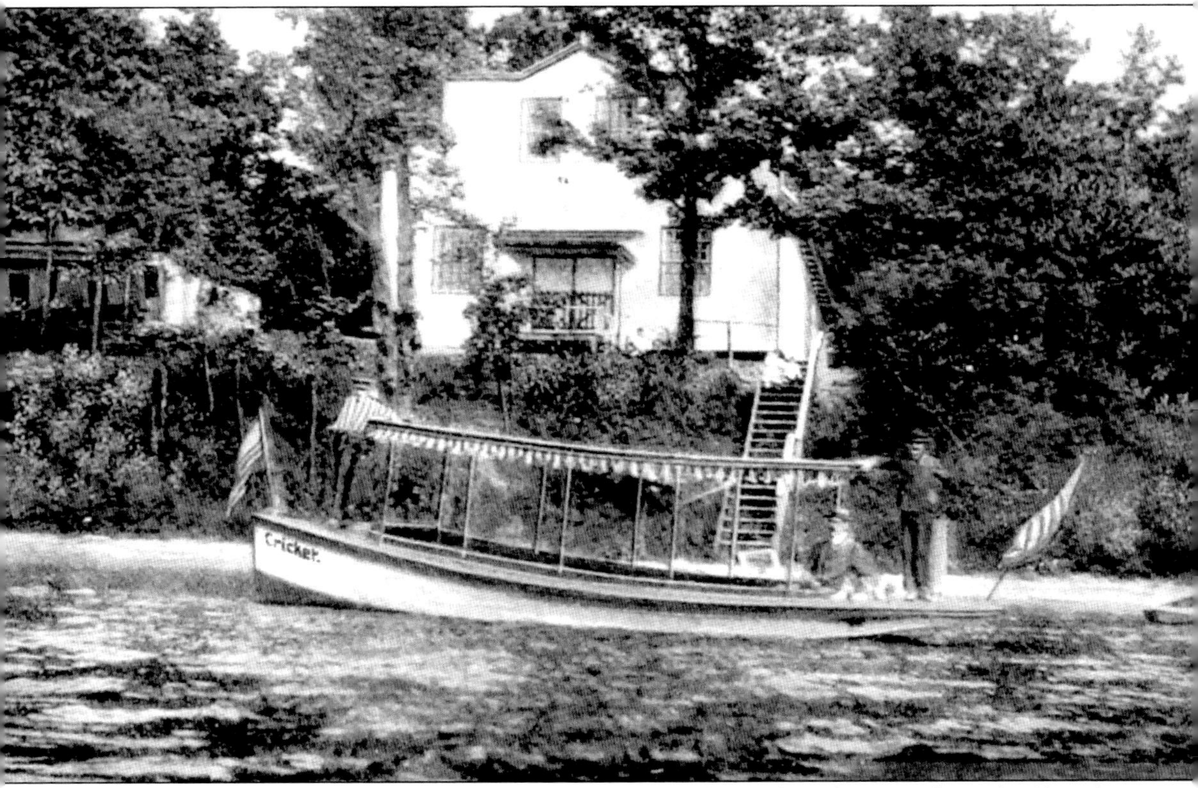

The above photograph is a view of Mr. Lytle's store which stood on the spot where the Sheridan Beach Resort Hotel was built. (Photo courtesy of L.G. Eggleston.)

SHERIDAN BEACH/BLACKHAWK BEACH RESORT Mr. Richard Lytle owned the southeast side of Flint Lake in 1865. He built a fishing camp on the edge of Flint Lake. He built his home on the corner of what is now Blackhawk Beach Road and Calumet. He kept a fleet of fishing boats on the lake for which he charged a rental fee of 25 cents per day.

Mr. Lytle also built a store on the edge of the lake to supply fishermen and campers with supplies. The store was built on the site where the Sheridan/Blackhawk Beach Resort Hotel was later built. Mr. Lytle also built and operated an icehouse south of the fishing camp. It was constructed on the site where the present day water works stands. The property where the icehouse stood was sold to the Flint Lake Pumping Station on March 26, 1886, and later became part of the Valparaiso City water works.

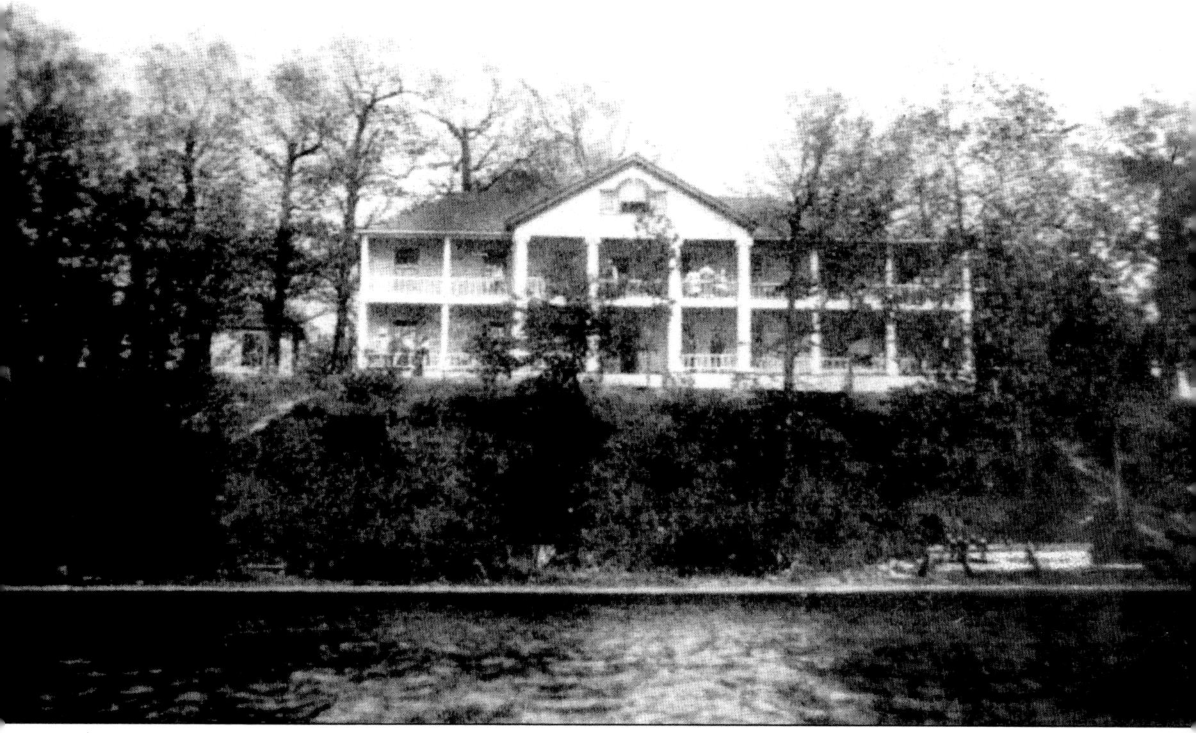

Above is a view of the Sheridan Beach Hotel from the lake, *c*. 1905.

Near the turn of the century Mr. John McQuiston owned the entire eastside of Flint Lake. He built a resort on the lake and named it Sheridan Beach. Mr. McQuiston and his son Sampson built a steam-powered boat, which they rented for pleasure tours of Flint and Long Lakes. There were several other steam powered tourist boats in use on Flint Lake and Long Lake. One of these boats can still be seen by scuba divers. The remains of the sunken boat are approximately 200 feet off the shore where the Sheridan Beach Resort Hotel once stood.

Mr. McQuiston constructed a 50-room resort hotel at Sheridan Beach in 1905. In 1906, a retired manufacturer from Chicago, named Sigmund Freund moved to Porter County. He was so impressed by the natural beauty of Flint Lake that he purchased 47 acres on the east side, which included the Sheridan Beach Resort. He rejuvenated the hotel by adding running water and electricity from a pumping station and a lighting plant, which he constructed, at the resort.

In the spring of 1924 the Kilmer-Frasier Company purchased a large portion of the southeast shore of Flint Lake. On July 4, 1925, the Kilmer-Frasier Company purchased Sheridan Beach Resort from Sigmund Freund and renamed it Blackhawk Beach Summer Resort.

The new owners upgraded the resort and added a toboggan slide, concession stands, roller skating, and expanded picnic areas. The resort became a very popular destination for summer tourists. The hotel was torn down in 1957. (Photo courtesy of Edwin Kuehl.)

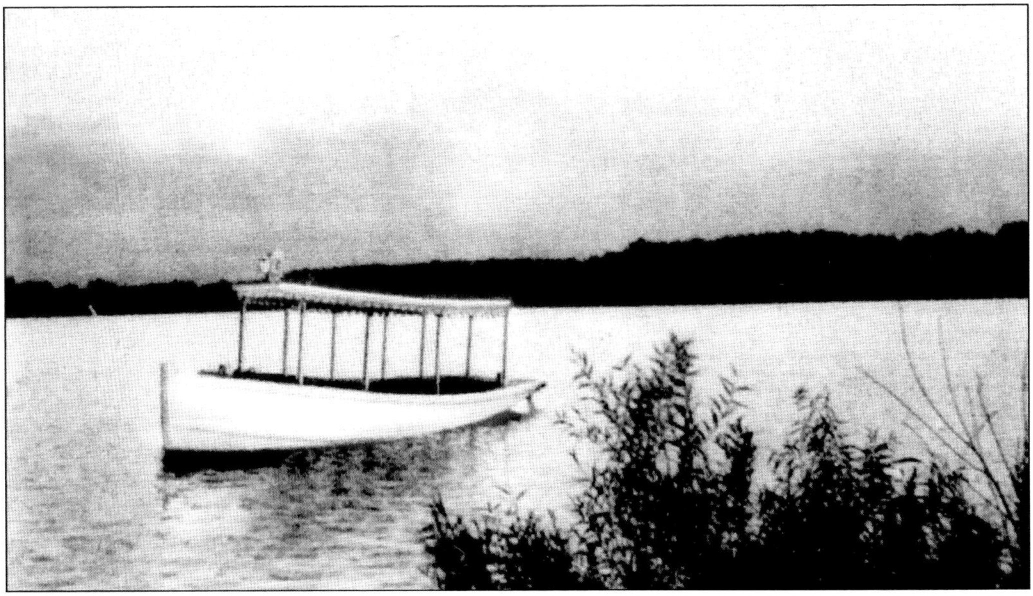

The above photograph is a picture of a ferry boat and pleasure boat of the type built by Mr. McQuiston and his son Sampson. These were used for tours of Flint Lake and Long Lake. (Photo courtesy of L.G. Eggleston.)

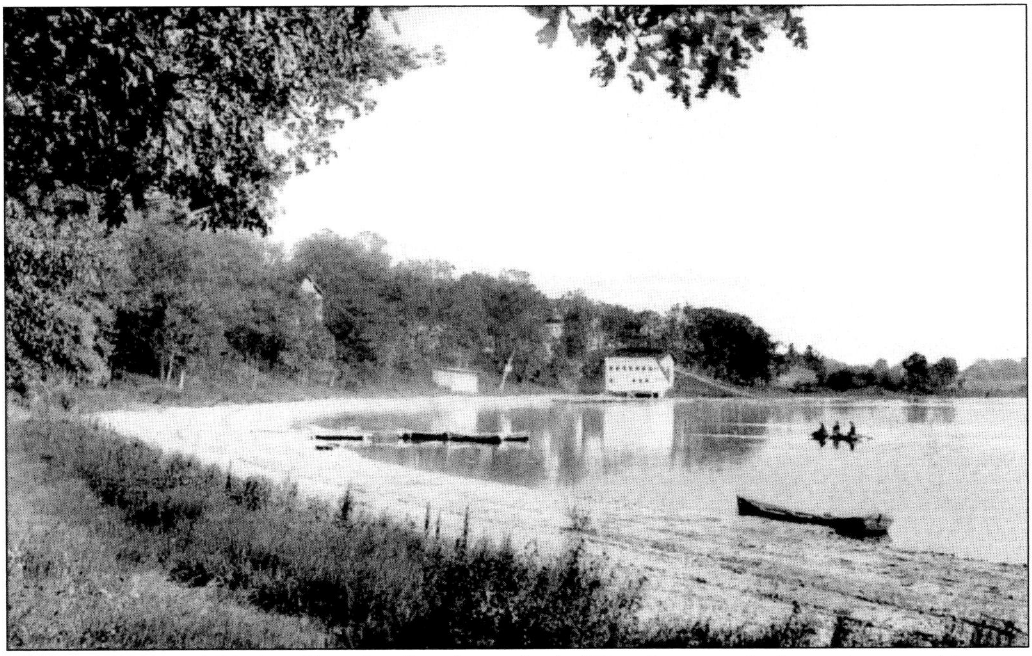

This is a view c. 1905 after Sheridan Beach was built. The photograph shows the rental houses, the hotel, the boathouse, and the icehouse with ramp. (Photo courtesy of L.G. Eggleston.)

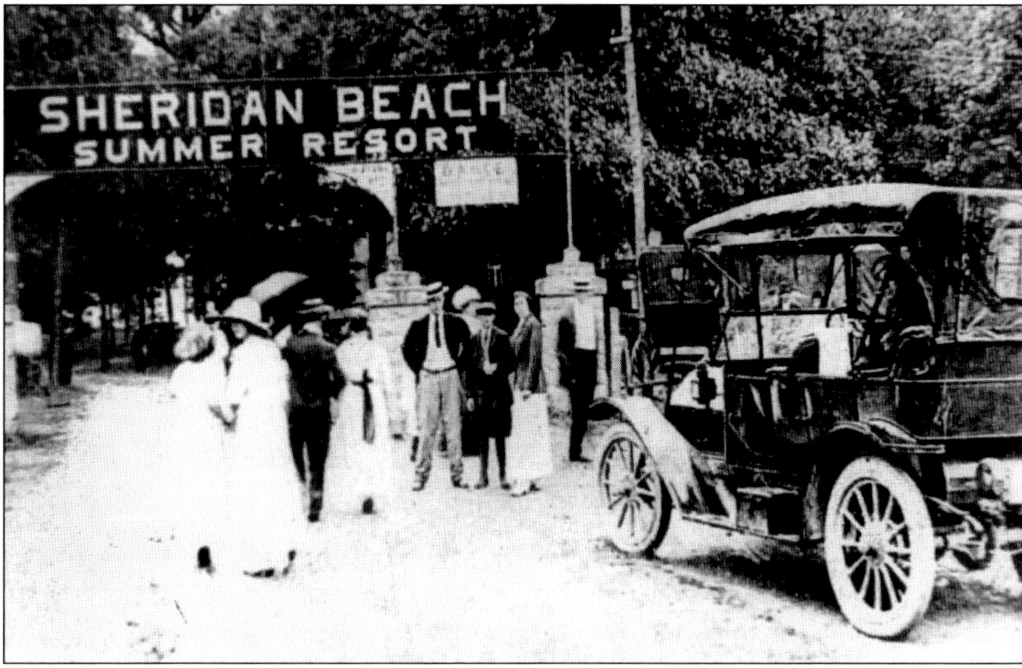

The above photograph is of the entrance to Sheridan Beach Resort as it looked in 1915. (Photo courtesy of L.G. Eggleston.)

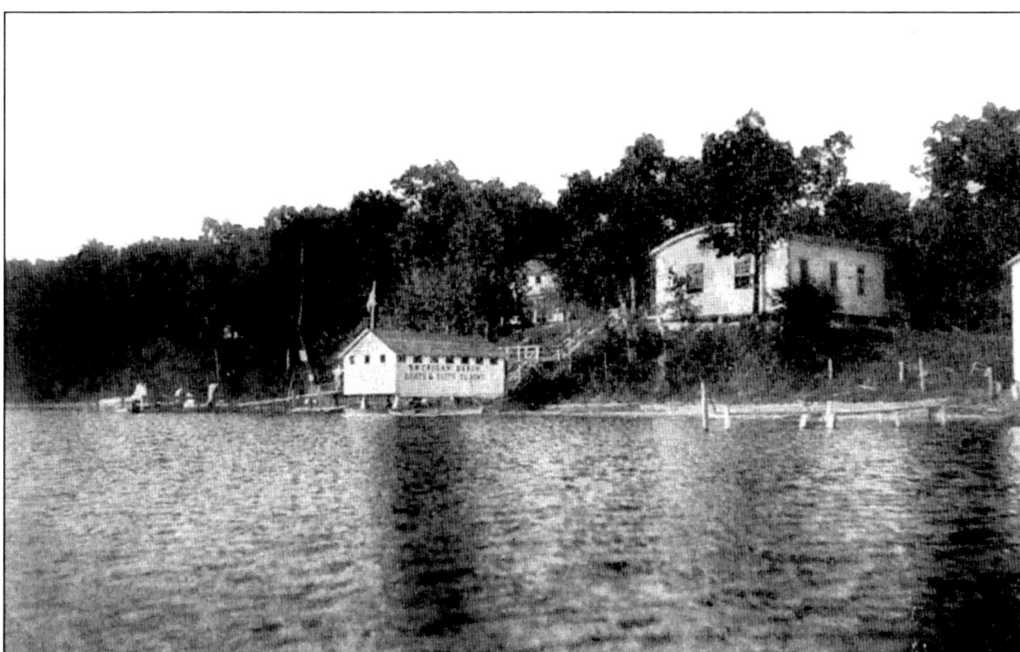

This photograph is of the dance hall and bathhouse at Sheridan Beach, with William Frasier's icehouse partly visible to the right. (Photo courtesy of L.G. Eggleston.)

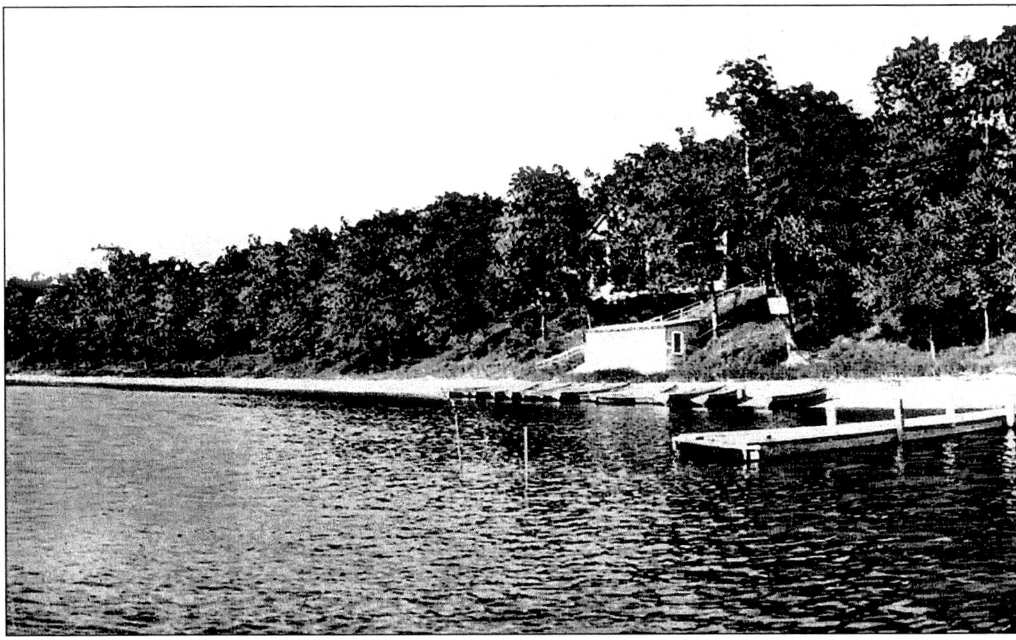

The above photograph of Sheridan Beach was taken in 1906 prior to the renovations being completed by Mr. Freund. (Photo courtesy of L.G. Eggleston.)

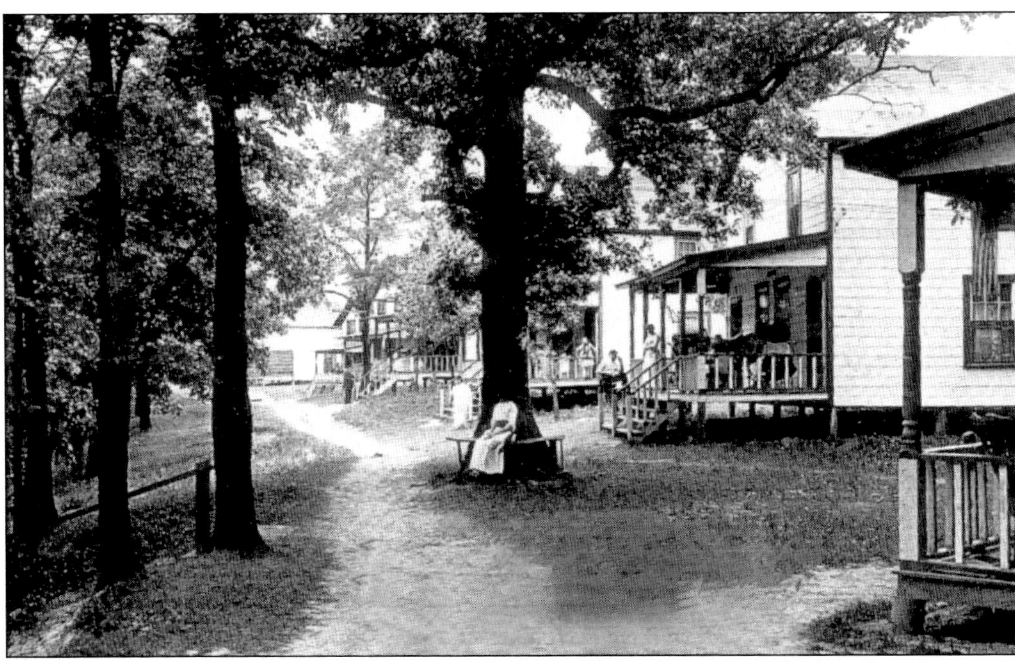

Sigmund Freund built a row of rental units on the lake directly north of the hotel, as seen in the above photograph. (Photo courtesy of L.G. Eggleston.)

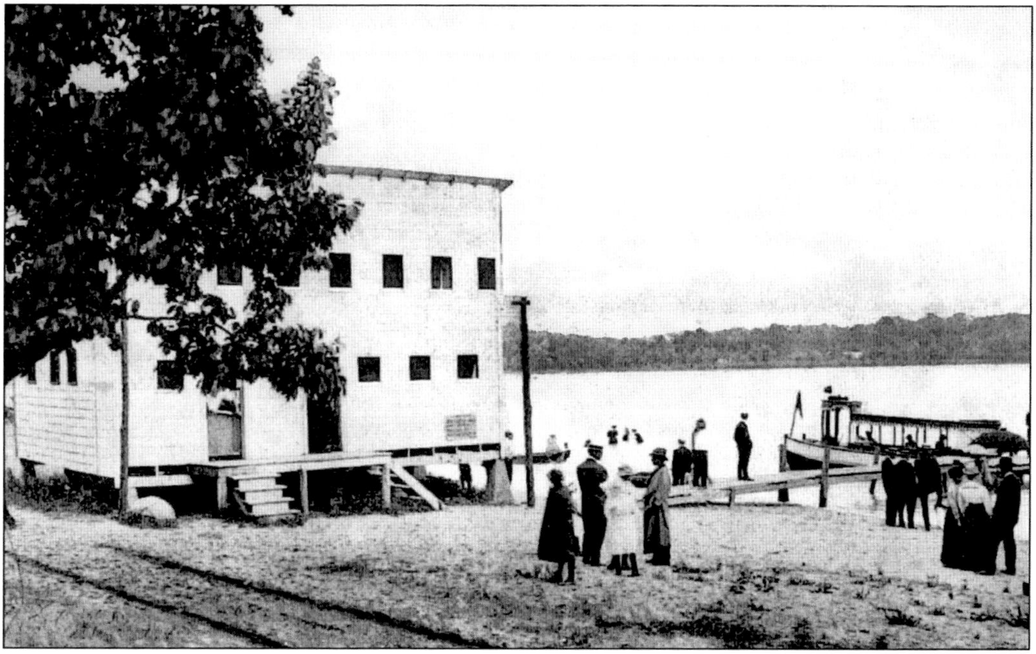

The above scene is a close-up view of the bathhouse and boat landing at Sheridan Beach. The steam-powered boat is the *Cricket*, which was used as a ferryboat as well as for private tours of Flint Lake and Long Lake. (Photo courtesy of L.G. Eggleston.)

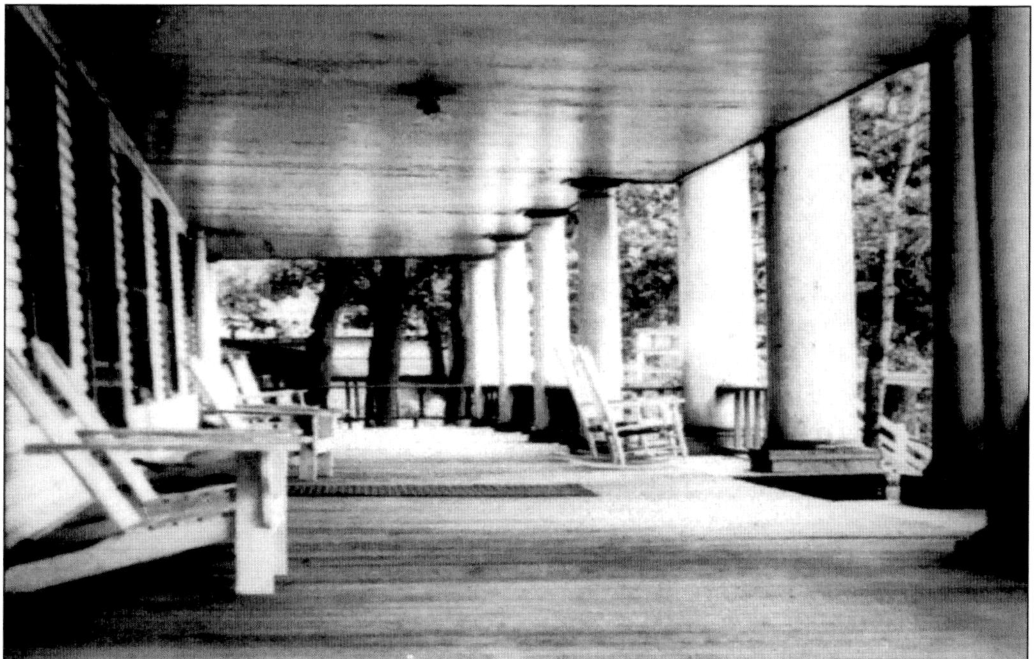

This is a view of the front porch of the hotel at Sheridan Beach. The porch faced the lake and allowed the guests a view of the entire lake area. (Photo courtesy of Edwin Kuehl.)

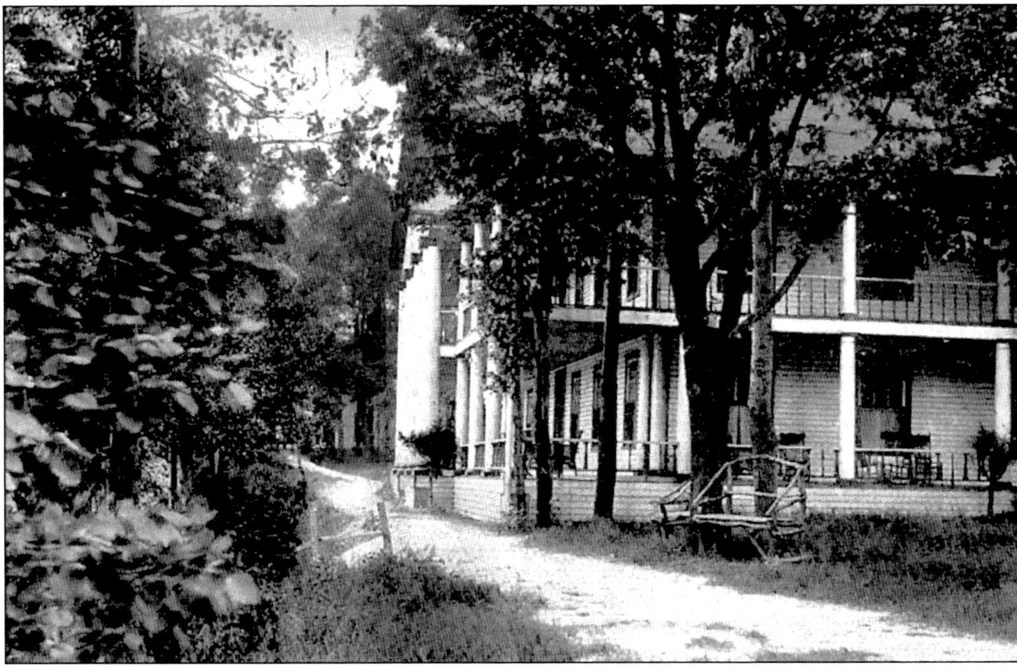

A view of the front of the Sheridan Beach Hotel in the early 1900s prior to the resort being sold and renamed Blackhawk Beach Summer Resort. The new owners constructed a water toboggan slide, which was built next to the stairs going down to the beach. (Photo courtesy of L.G. Eggleston.)

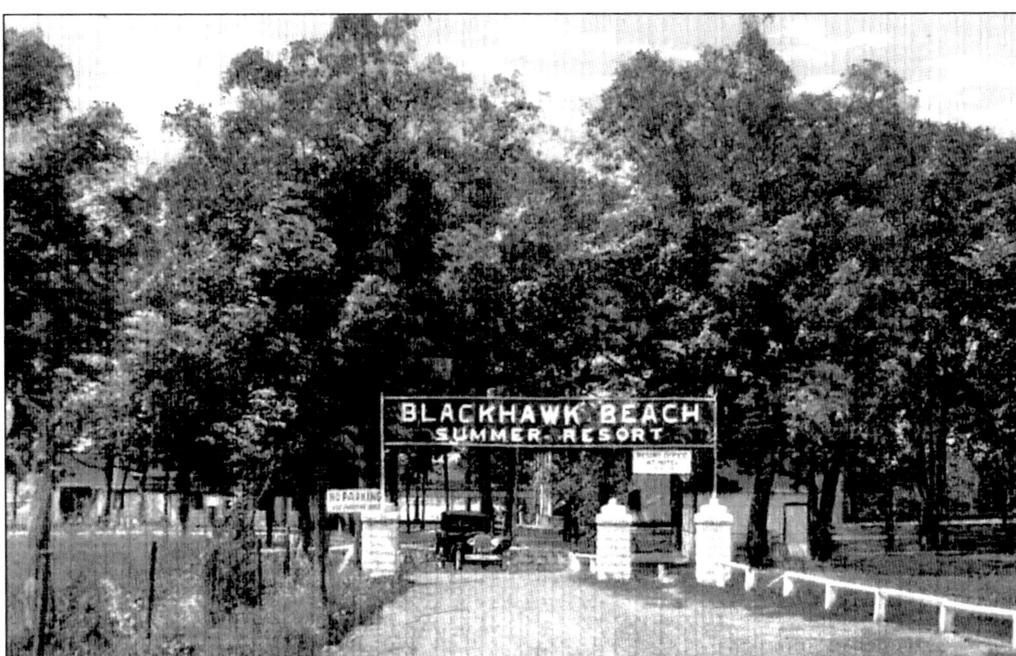

The Blackhawk Beach Summer Resort sign, shown here, replaced the Sheridan Beach Summer Resort sign in 1925. (Photo courtesy of L.G. Eggleston.)

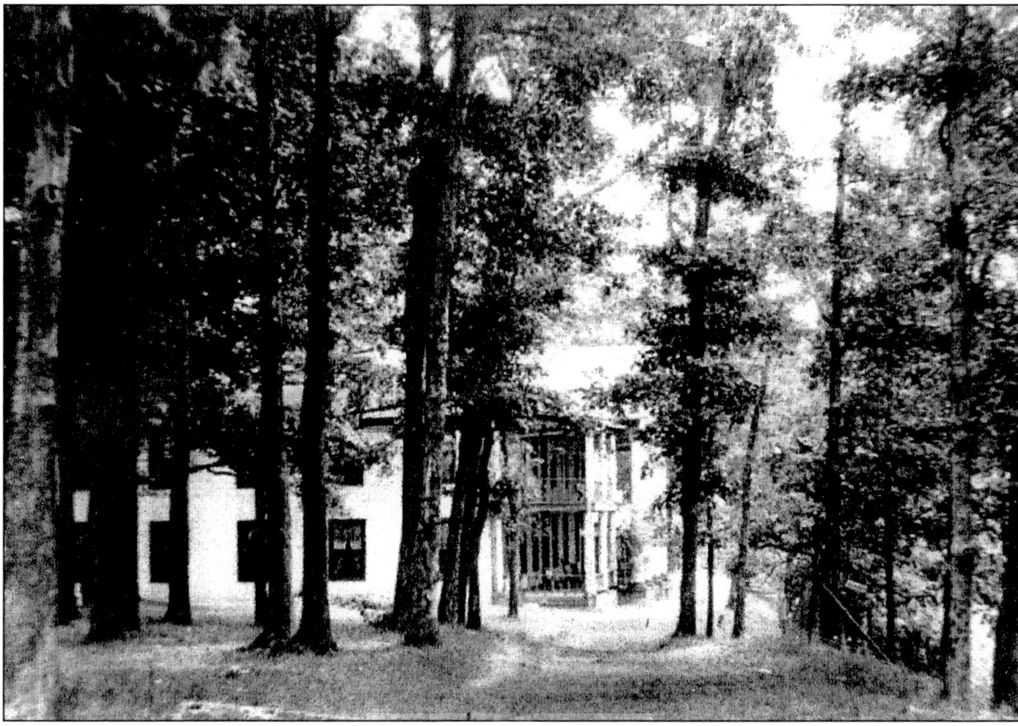

Shown here is the front of the Blackhawk Beach Hotel. This view is looking south along the dirt path between the hotel and the lake. (Photo courtesy of Edwin Kuehl.)

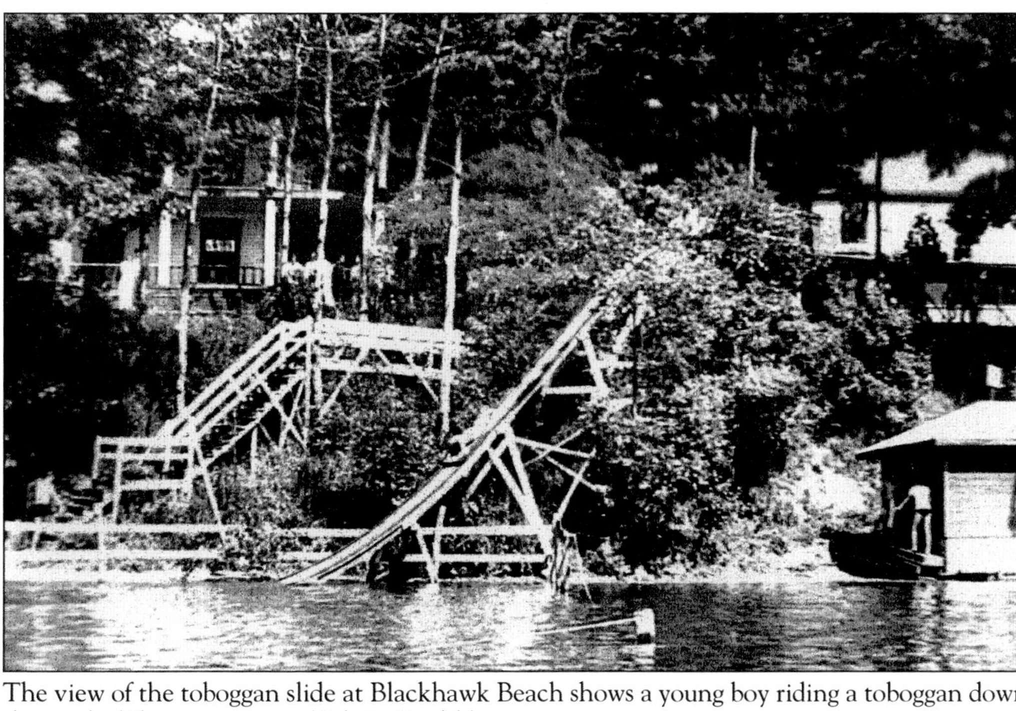

The view of the toboggan slide at Blackhawk Beach shows a young boy riding a toboggan down the track. (Photo courtesy of Edwin Kuehl.)

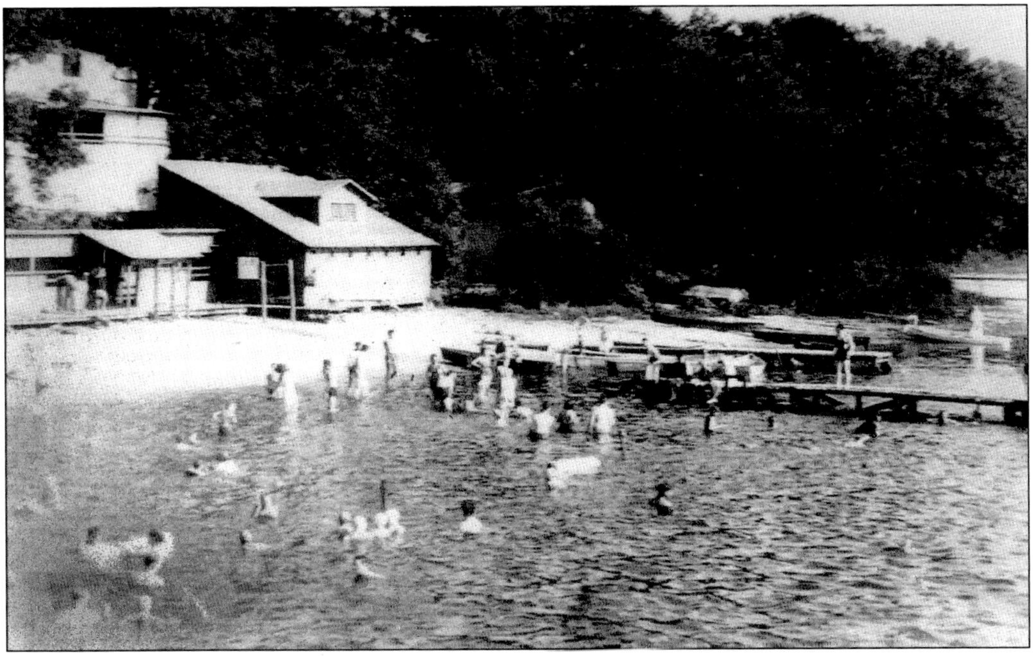

Here is a view of the swimming area at the Blackhawk Beach Resort. (Photo courtesy of Edwin Kuehl.)

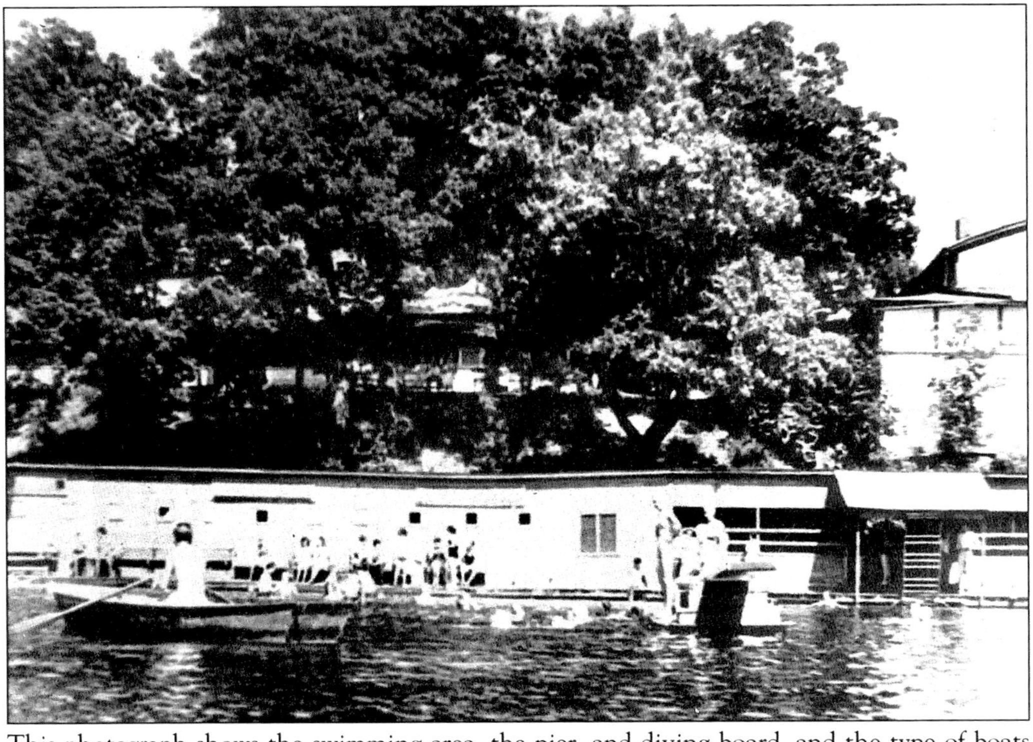

This photograph shows the swimming area, the pier, and diving board, and the type of boats available to tourists. (Photo courtesy of Edwin Kuehl.)

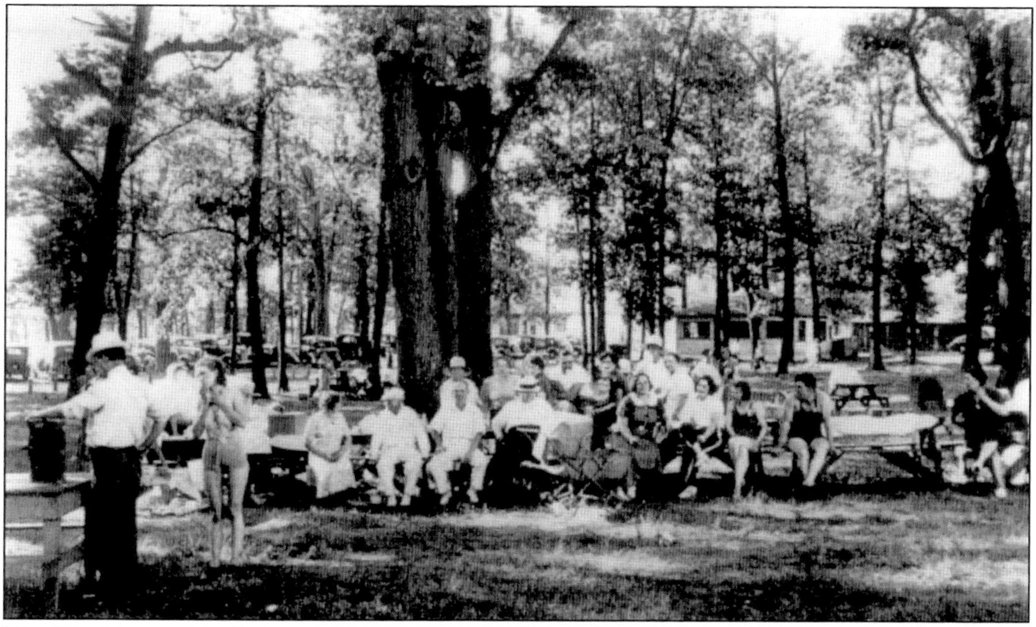

The Blackhawk Beach Resort picnic area, which was directly behind the hotel, is shown here. (Photo courtesy of Edwin Kuehl.)

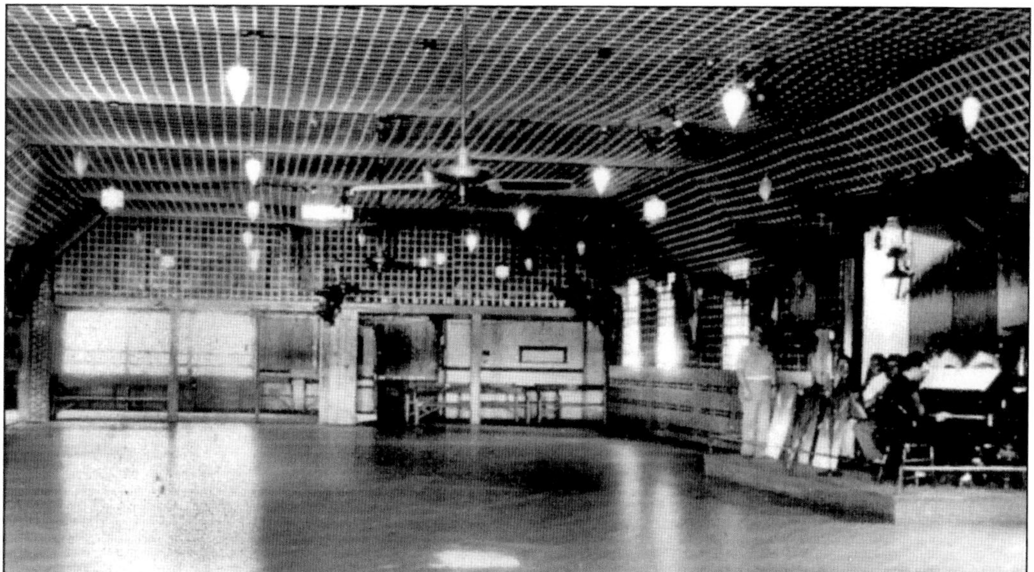

Above is an inside view of the dance pavilion, showing the band rehearsing. The dance floor was used as a roller rink during the day. The pavilion burned down in March 1941. (Photo courtesy of Edwin Kuehl.)

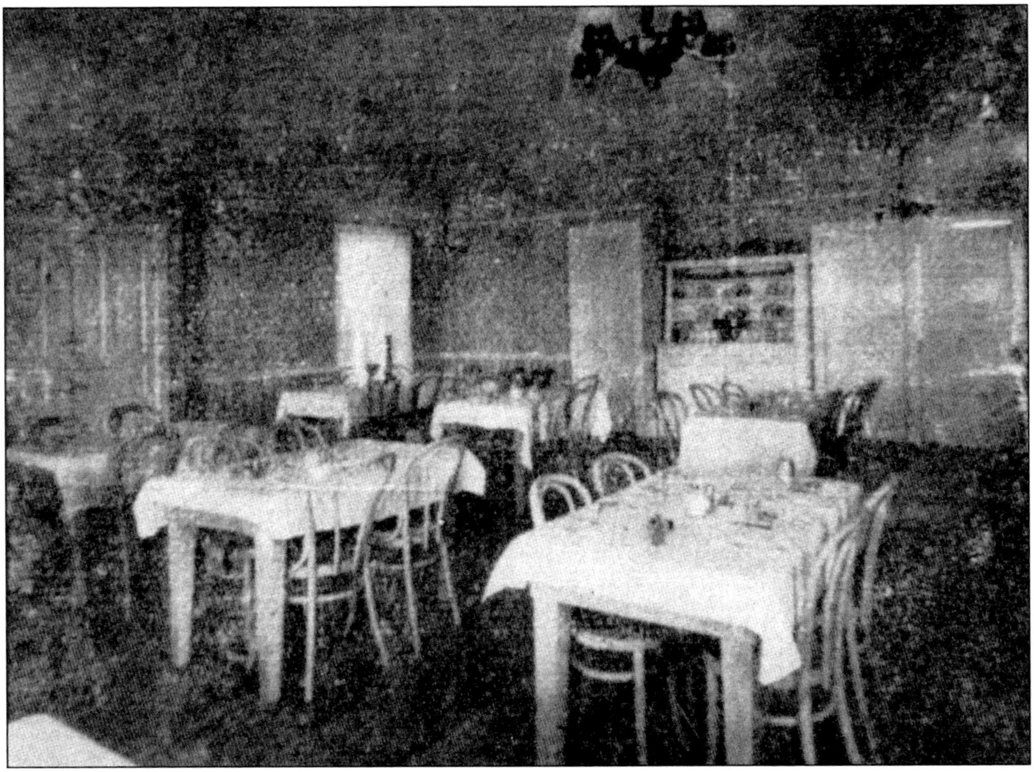

This is an inside view of the Blackhawk Beach dining hall. The building burned down in March 1941 along with the dance pavilion. (Photo courtesy of Edwin Kuehl.)

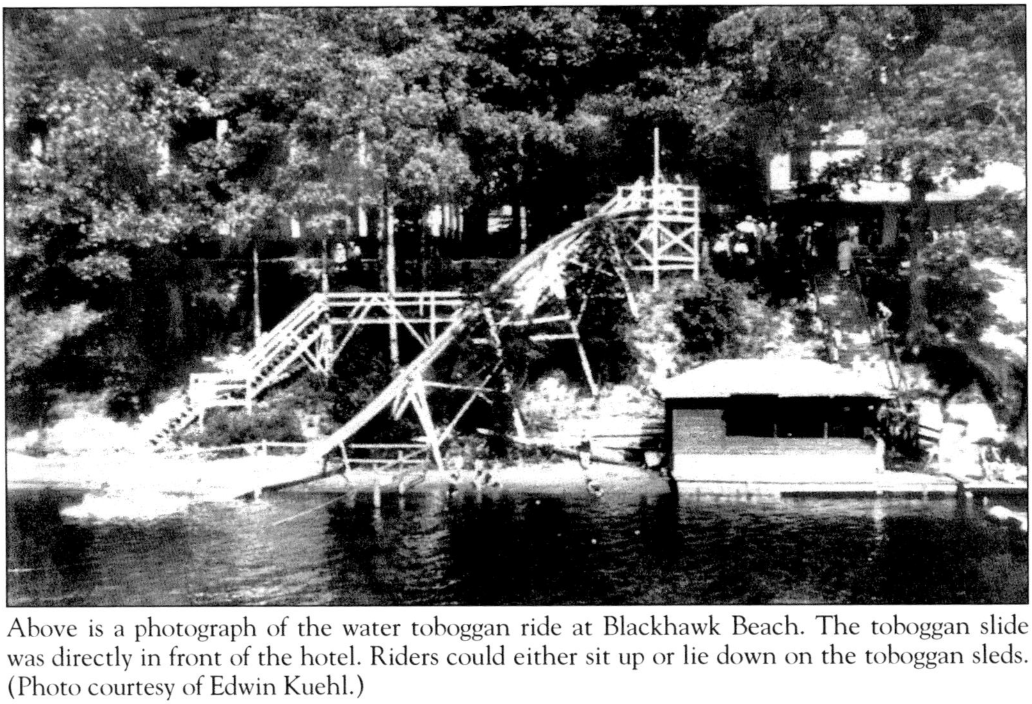

Above is a photograph of the water toboggan ride at Blackhawk Beach. The toboggan slide was directly in front of the hotel. Riders could either sit up or lie down on the toboggan sleds. (Photo courtesy of Edwin Kuehl.)

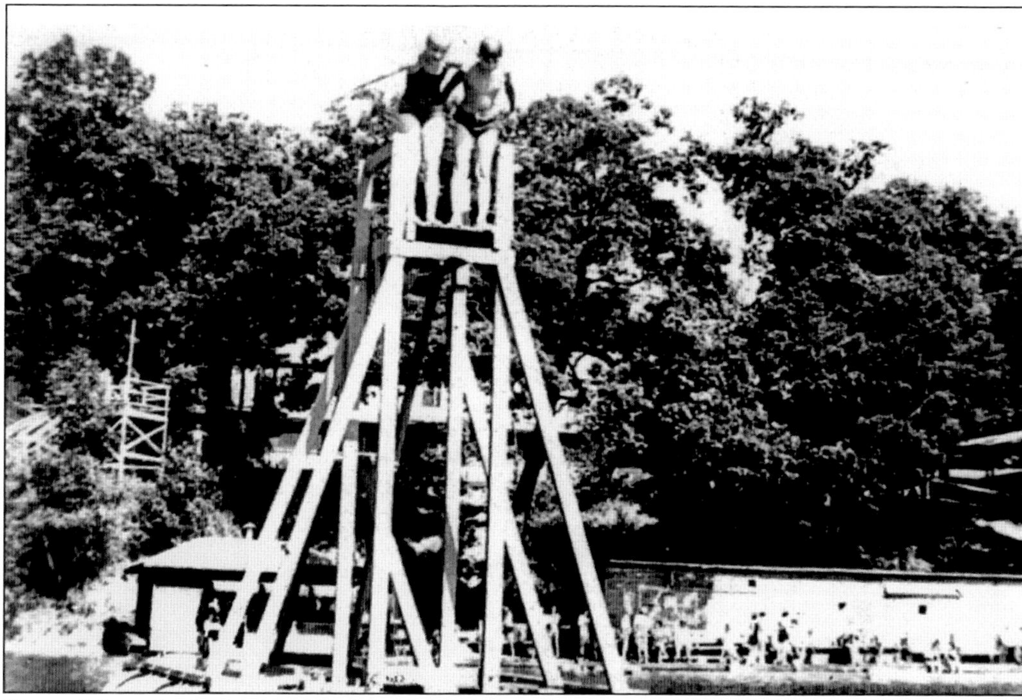

This offshore high dive at Blackhawk Beach sat on 12 metal barrels and was secured in the center to six wooden telephone poles, which went down into the bottom of the lake. This anchoring system provided stability to the structure. (Photo courtesy of Edwin Kuehl.)

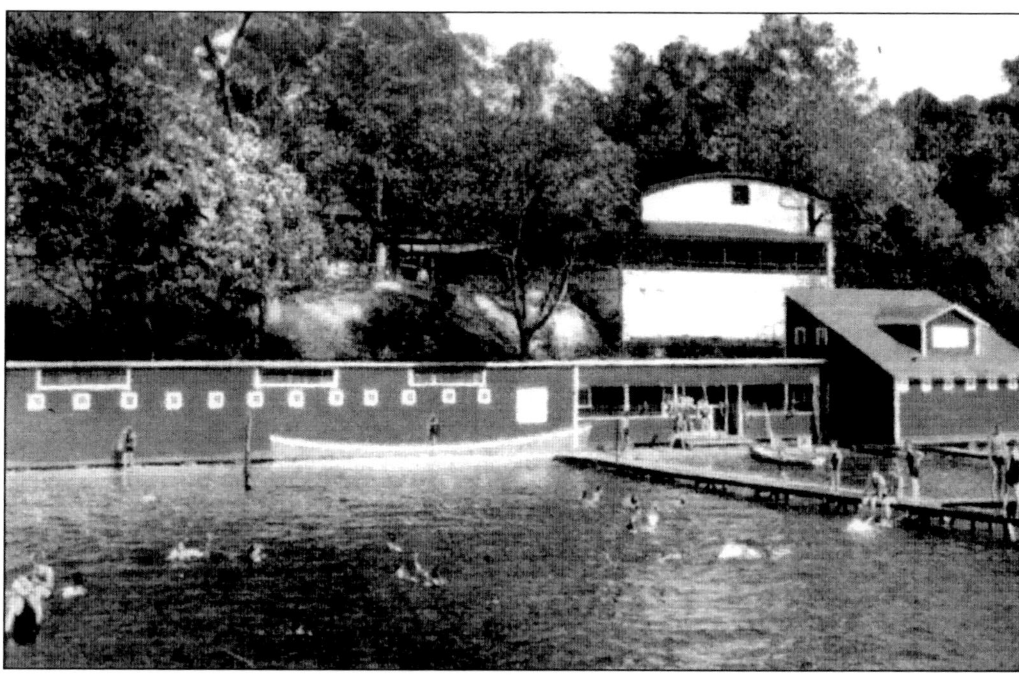

The above photograph is of the swimming area at Blackhawk Beach. (Photo courtesy of L.G. Eggleston.)

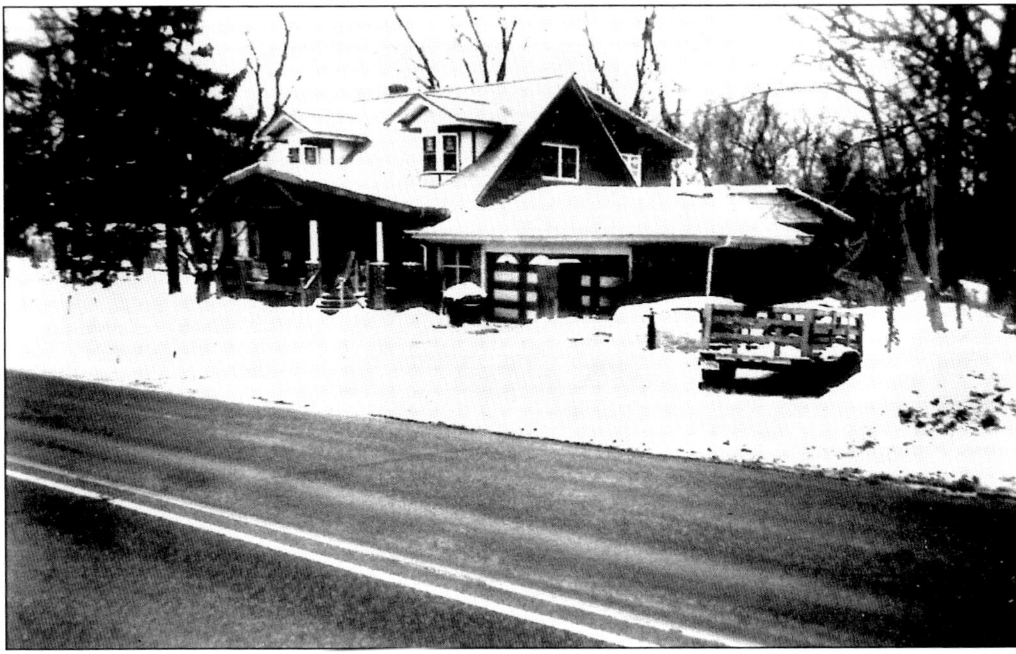

The portion of this building which is now a two car garage was the grocery store which serviced Blackhawk Beach area. (Photo by L.G. Eggleston.)

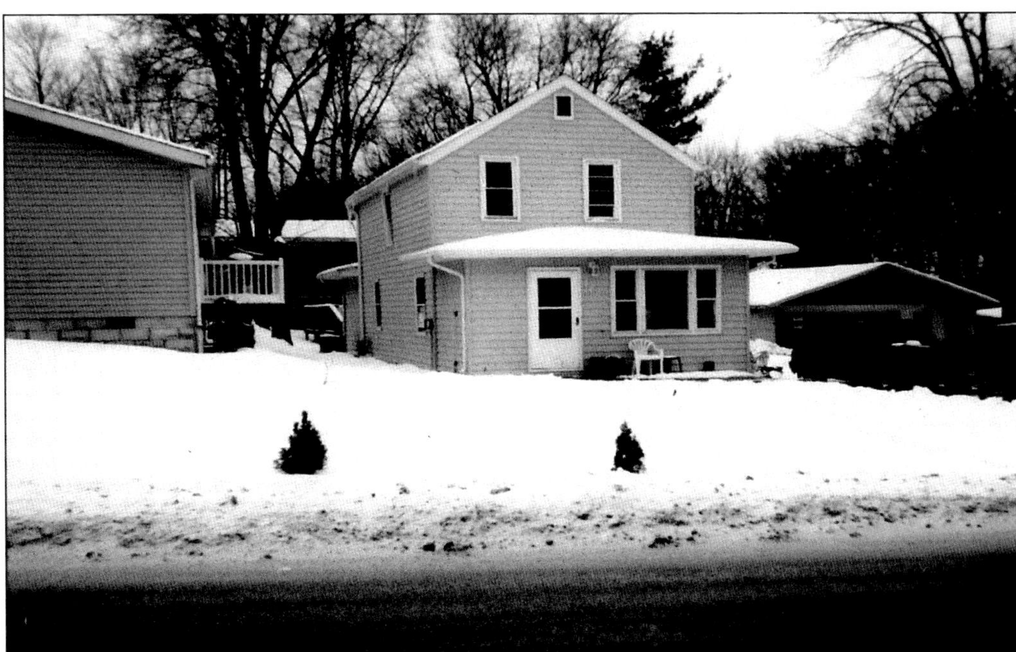

This house is the only remaining house built by Sigmund Freund in 1905. This house was a summer rental cottage next to the Blackhawk Beach Hotel. The house is now a private residence on Edgewater Road. (Photo by L.G. Eggleston.)

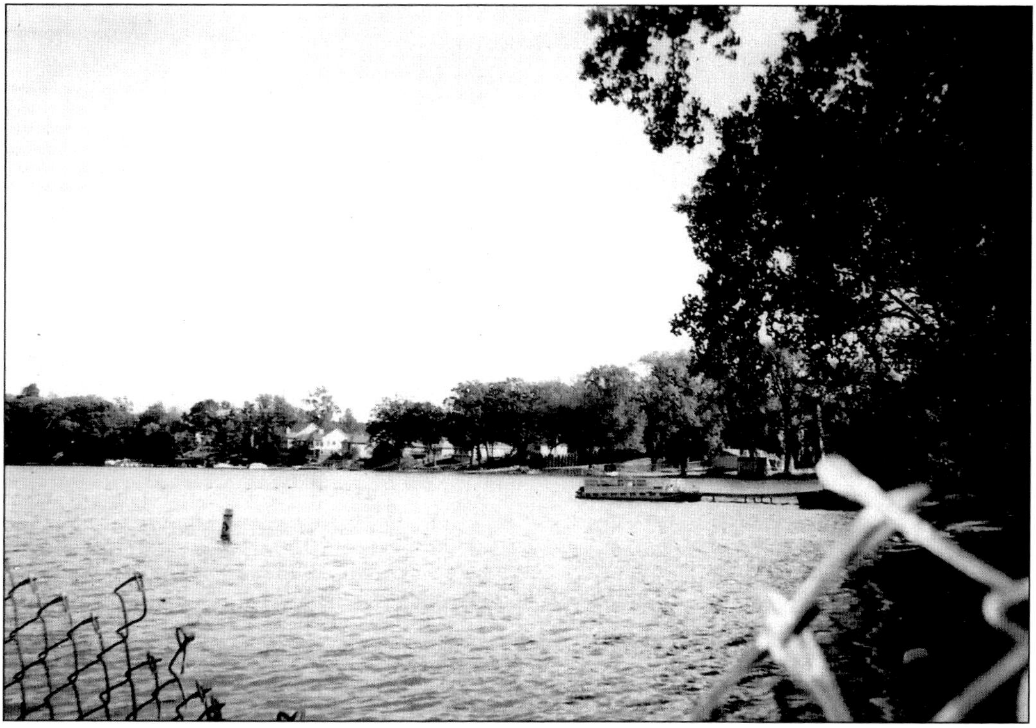

This is a current view from Burlington Beach showing the subdivision where Blackhawk Beach Resort once stood. The entire property has been turned into a private subdivision with no public access to the lake. (Photo by L.G. Eggleston.)

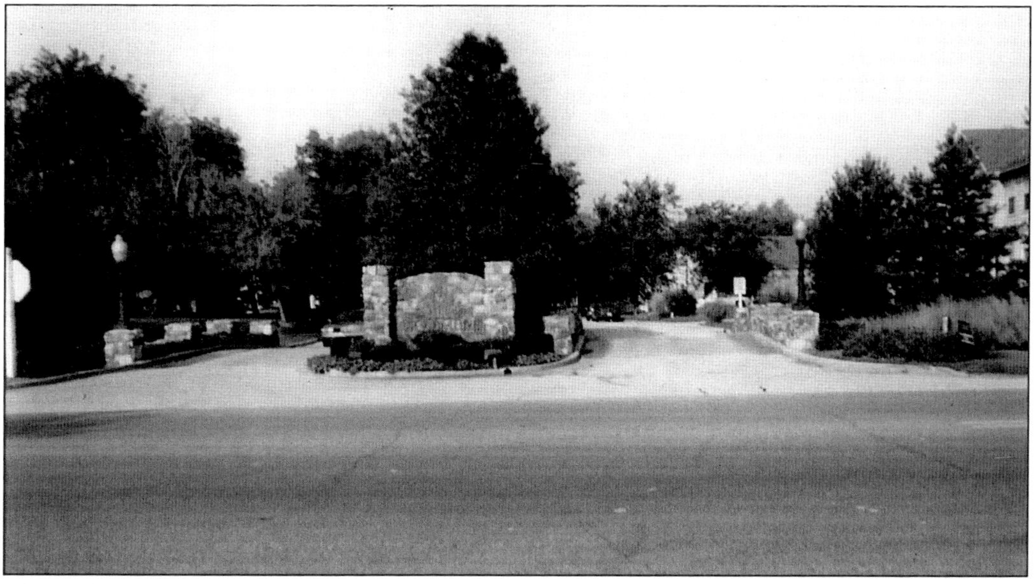

This is the entrance to the subdivision where the Blackhawk Beach Summer Resort once stood. It extends from Calumet Avenue to the shore of Flint Lake (Photo by L.G. Eggleston.)

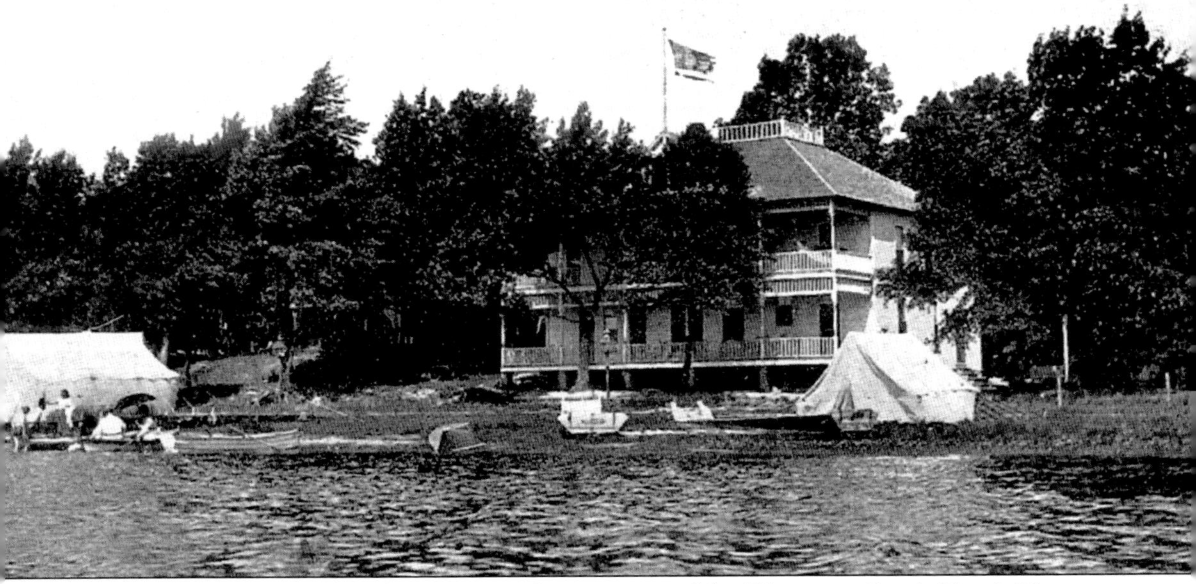

The above photograph, taken in 1911, shows a view of the Edgewater Beach Hotel. The resort hotel was constructed on the site which is now Edgewater Beach Swimming and Picnicking area. Notice the tent campers on the beach. (Photo courtesy of L.G. Eggleston.)

Edgewater Beach Resort

In the year 1890, a gentleman named Howard Dickover purchased the northwest shore of Flint Lake from its owner Mary Clay. Mr. Dickover built a beautiful resort hotel on the edge of Flint Lake and named the area Edgewater Beach. This new resort afforded tourists the pleasures of swimming, boating, fishing, camping, or just relaxing and enjoying the natural beauty of Flint Lake. Summer cabins as well as a few permanent homes sprung up around the resort. Edgewater Beach was a very popular destination for tourists for many years.

Edgewater Beach had an interurban electric railroad station and a grocery store called the Green Lantern. Boat rentals were also available for pleasure or fishing.

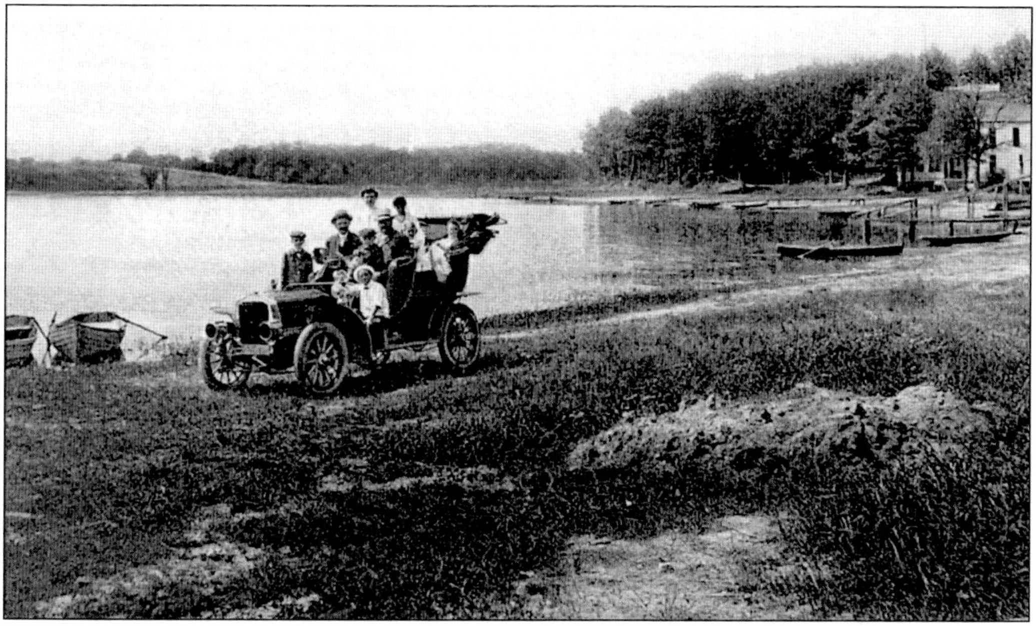

This photograph of a touring car was taken in 1910, on the shore of Flint Lake, east of the Edgewater Beach Hotel. (Photo courtesy of L.G. Eggleston.)

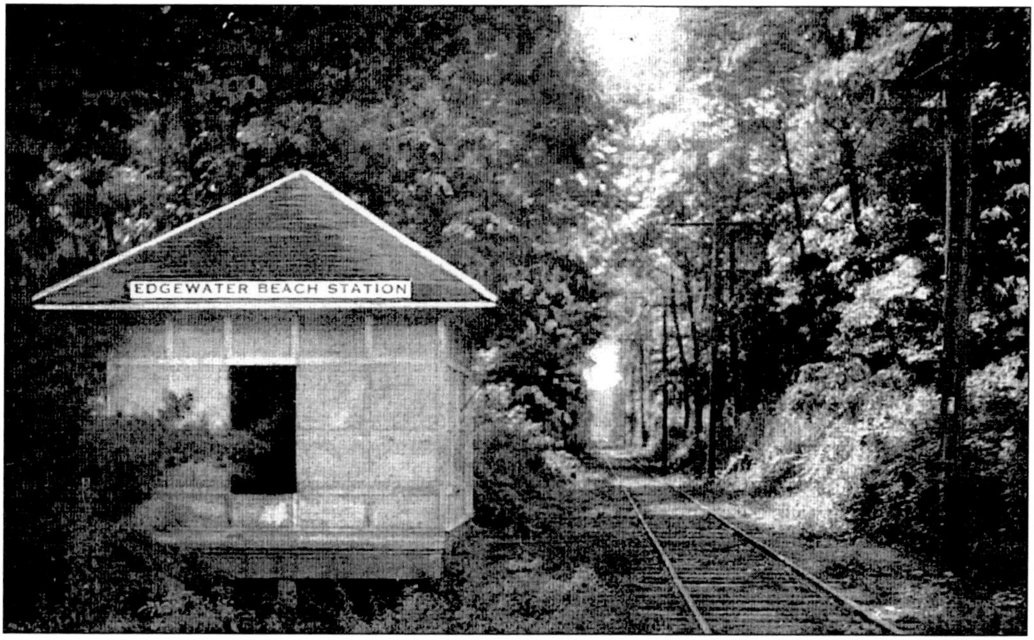

Above is a view of the Edgewater Beach interurban electric railroad station. The station was built in 1910 and was one block north of the Edgewater Beach Hotel. (Photo courtesy of Edwin Kuehl.)

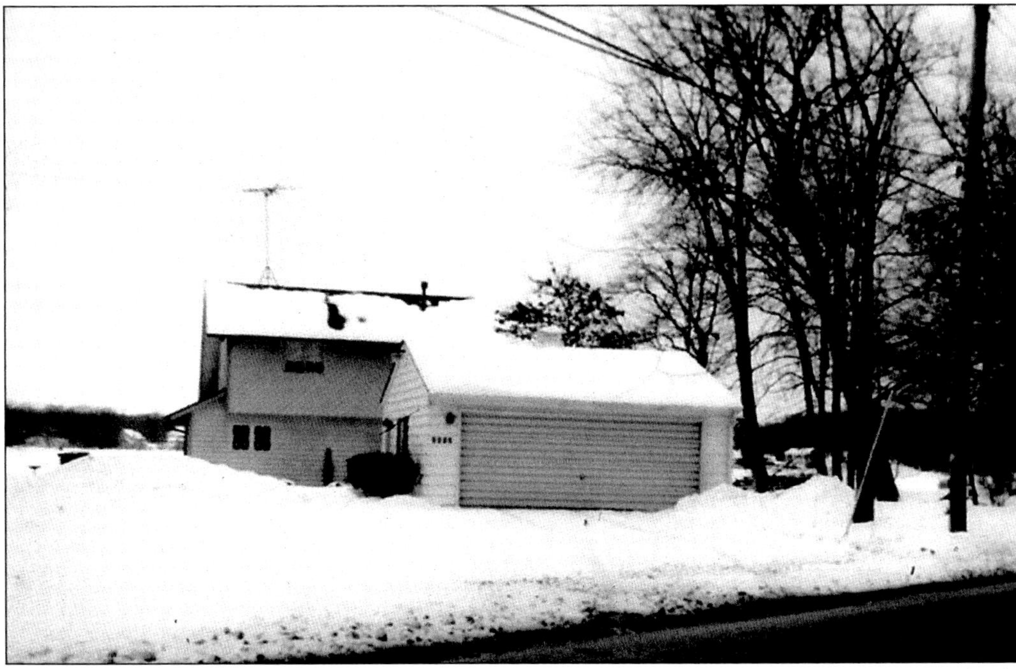

The above site is where the Green Lantern Grocery Store at Edgewater Beach once stood. The name Green Lantern was given to the store by locals because of the green color of the building and the two huge lanterns on each side of the door. A beautiful new private home now occupies the site. (Photo by L.G. Eggleston.)

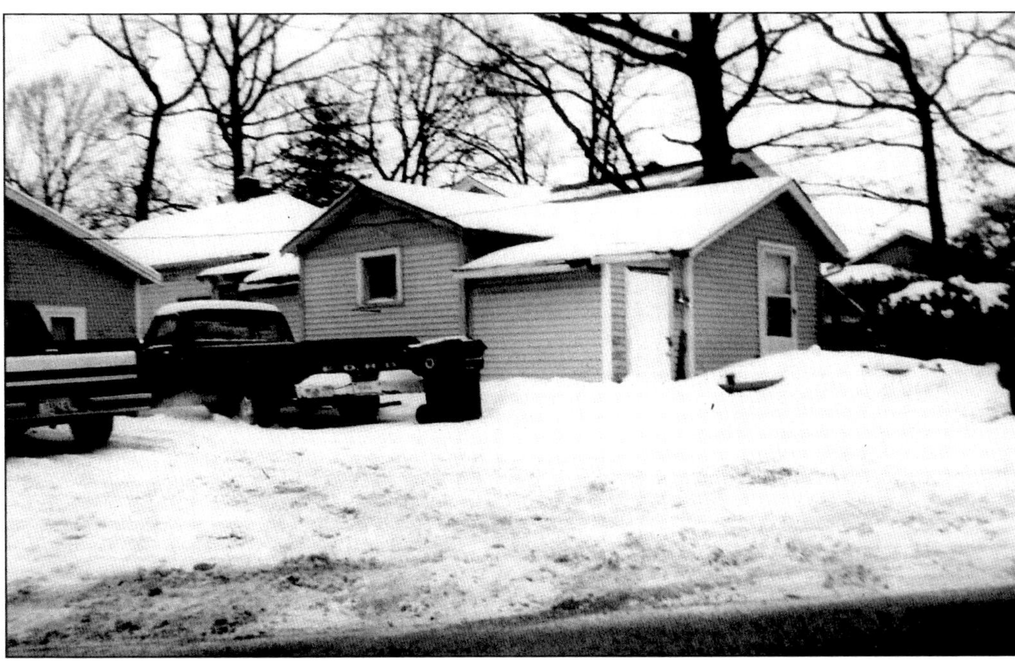

After the Green Lantern store closed, the above building was used as the Edgewater grocery store. The store was run by the Albright family who also rented row boats for fishing. (Photo by L.G. Eggleston.)

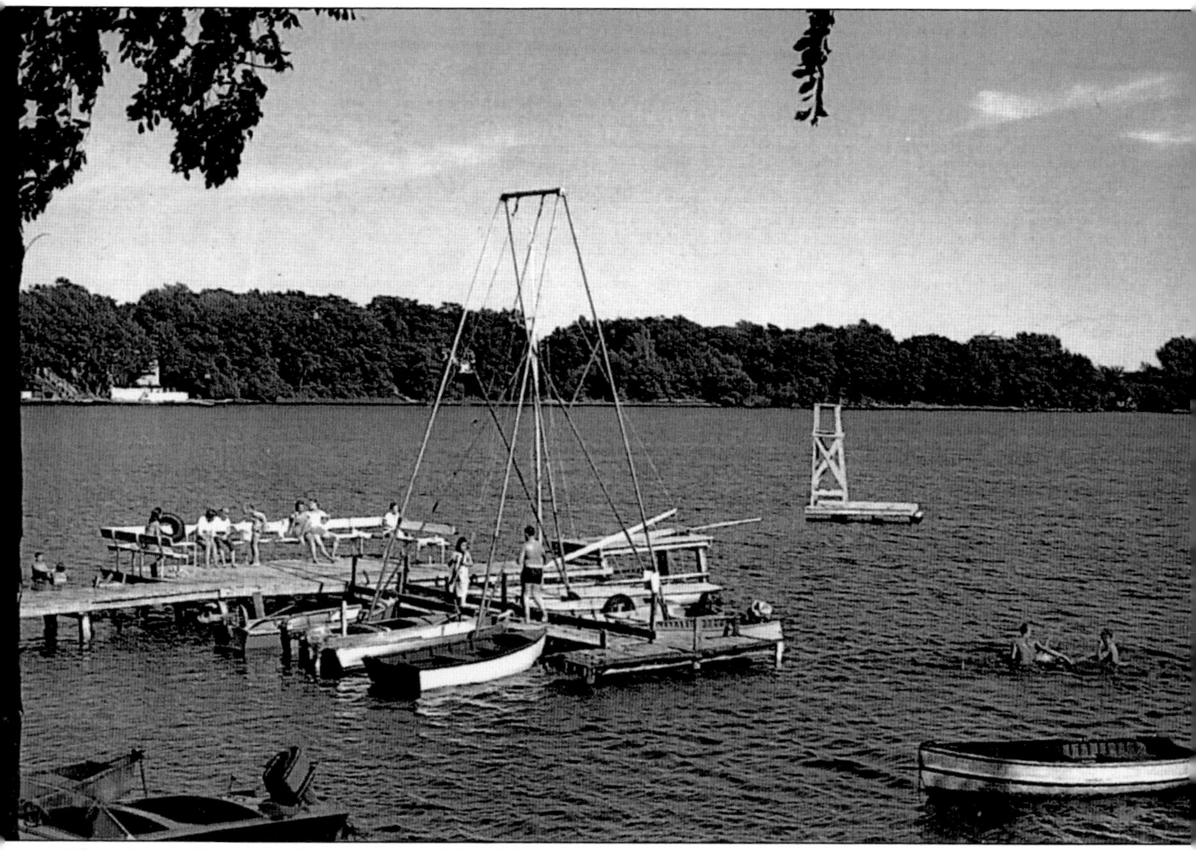

The above photograph is a view of the Edgewater Beach swimming area in the late 1950s. The Edgewater Beach Hotel no longer existed when the above photograph was taken. The property from Edgewater Road to the beach has been converted into a picnic area. The beach is now private with access only to those local residents who belong to the Edgewater Beach association.

The original public roadway, on the west side of the beach area, which allowed public access to the lake has been closed and is now part of Edgewater Beach picnic area.

Most of the summer cottages, which were built around the resort hotel, have been replaced with new permanent homes. Many of the remaining summer cottages are still in use by people from the Calumet Region who enjoy the natural beauty of Flint Lake. (Photo courtesy of L.G. Eggleston.)

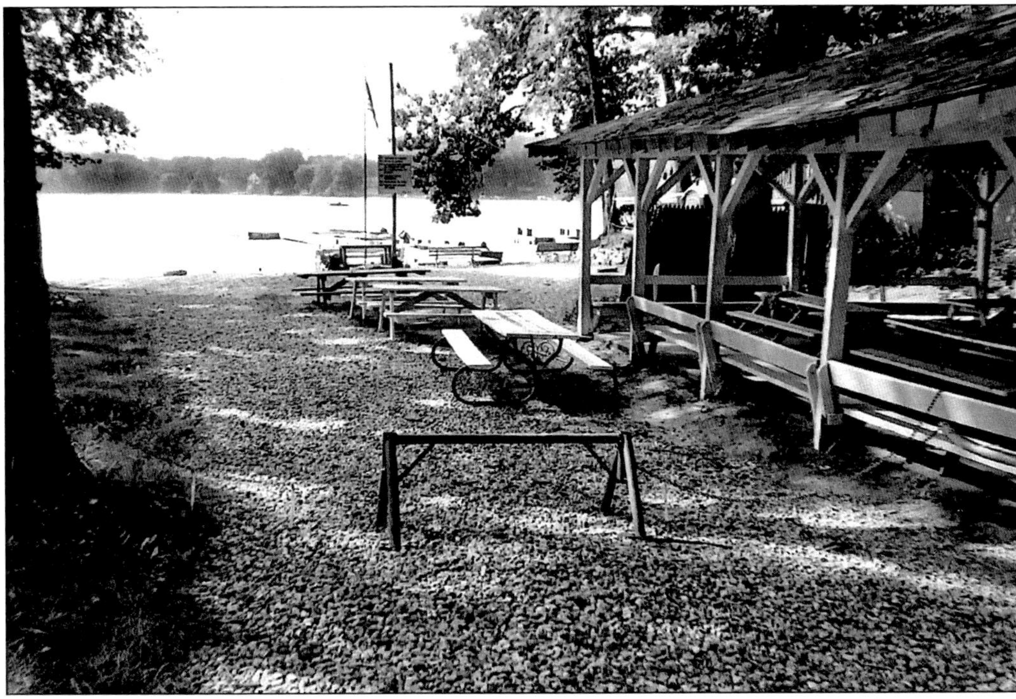

The above photograph is a view of the Edgewater Beach swimming and picnicking area as it looks today. (Photo by L.G. Eggleston.)

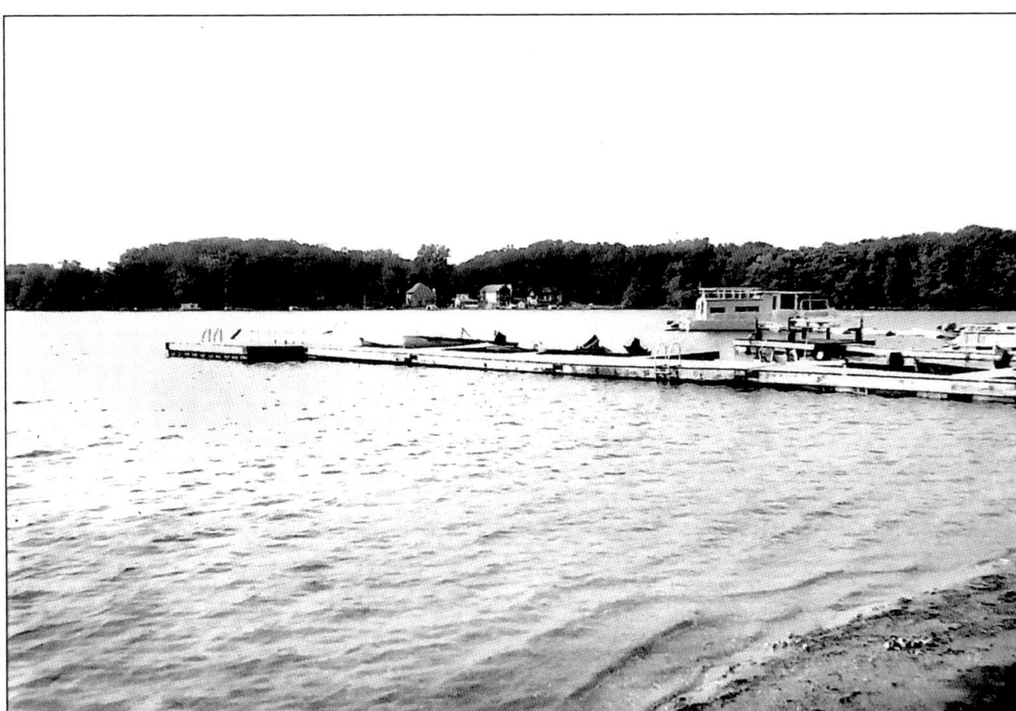

This is a view of the Edgewater Beach swimming area as it looks today. (Photo by L.G. Eggleston.)

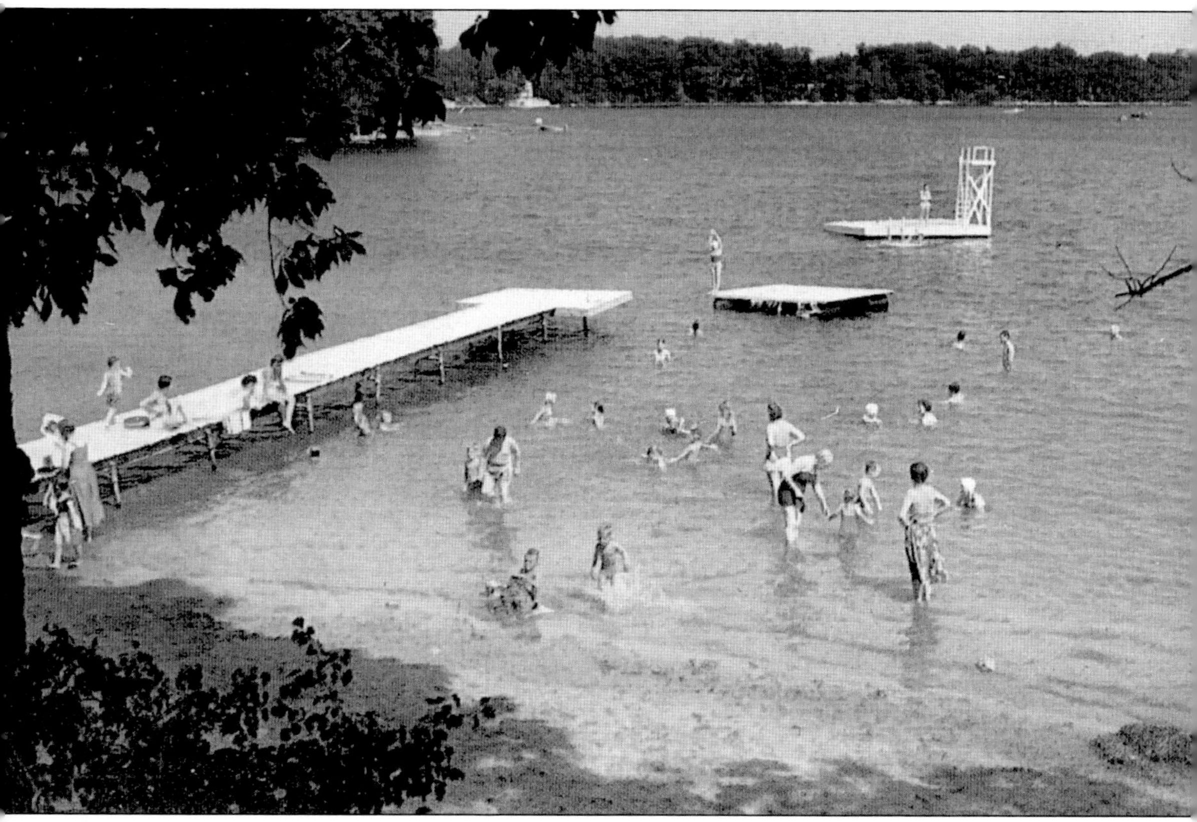

The above photograph shows the swimming area of Hillcrest Beach with its pier, raft, and high dive platform.

Hillcrest Beach was accessible by the interurban railroad and several roads. The channel between the lakes was not bridged until 1923. The electric train trestle was on the north end of the channel overlooking Long Lake and was built in 1910.

A resort hotel was constructed for tourists near the interurban station. The hotel was one block from the railroad station and two blocks from the beach property. (Photo courtesy of L.G. Eggleston.)

HILLCREST BEACH RESORT In the early 1900s, a beautiful swimming, picnicking, and camping area was established on the northwest corner of Flint Lake immediately past the channel which connects Flint Lake and Long Lake. The picnic and camping area was a shaded park that sloped down to the sandy beach. Because this area was located on a hill the beach became known as Hillcrest Beach.

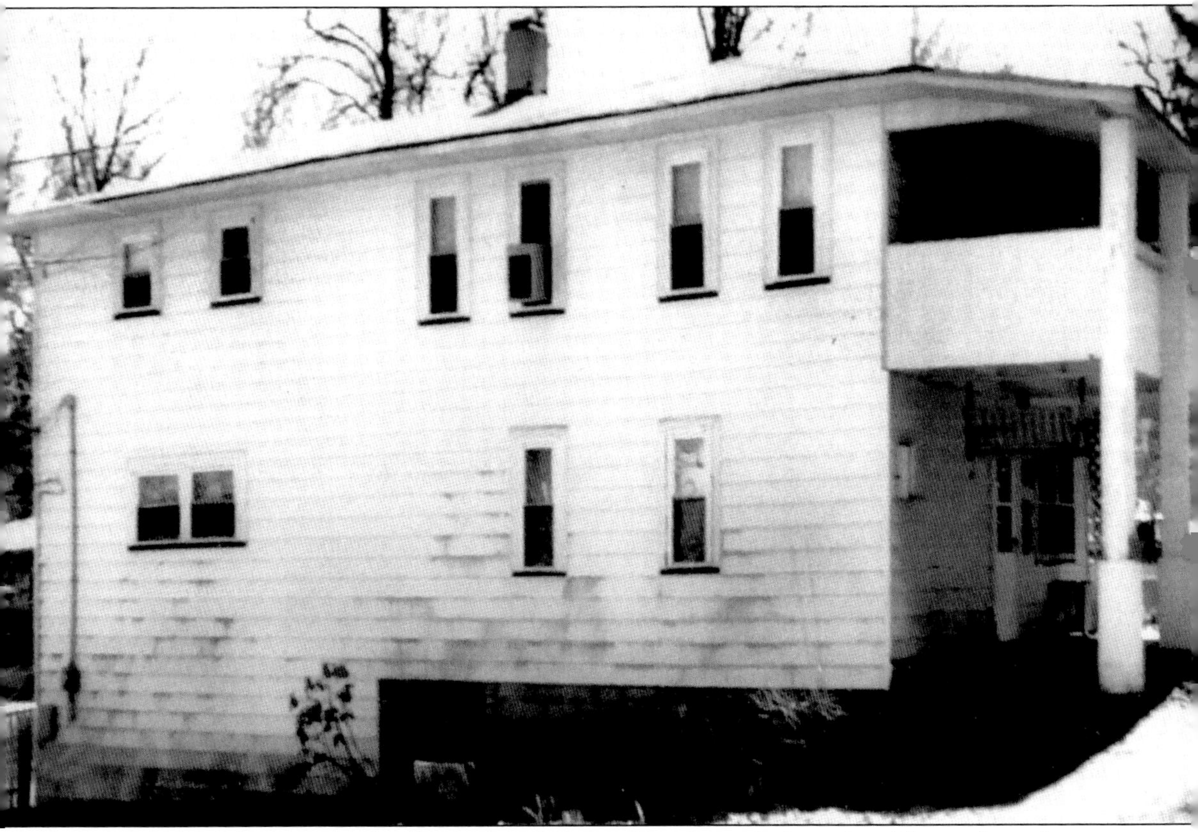

Above is a photograph of Hillcrest Beach Resort Hotel as it looks today. This is the only resort hotel on Flint Lake still standing. The hotel is on May Street and has been converted into a private home.

Many summer cottages as well as permanent homes were erected around the beach area. The area experienced a new growth when the channel was bridged in 1923 and Edgewater Road was extended beyond the channel as Grandview.

The park at Hillcrest Beach is now private with admission only to residents who belong to the beach association and their guests.

The interurban electric railroad depot, which serviced Hillcrest Beach, stood at the north end of Urban Lane overlooking Long Lake and the Long Lake Resort. The Long Lake station however, was one mile west, where the tracks crossed Anderson Road, which is now 600 N.

Hillcrest Beach had its own grocery store and soda fountain. The store was located one-half block west of the beach on Grandview and Leisure Drive. The grocery store was on the main floor of the building. Later a soda fountain and patio were constructed on the lower level facing Grandview. (Photo by L.G. Eggleston.)

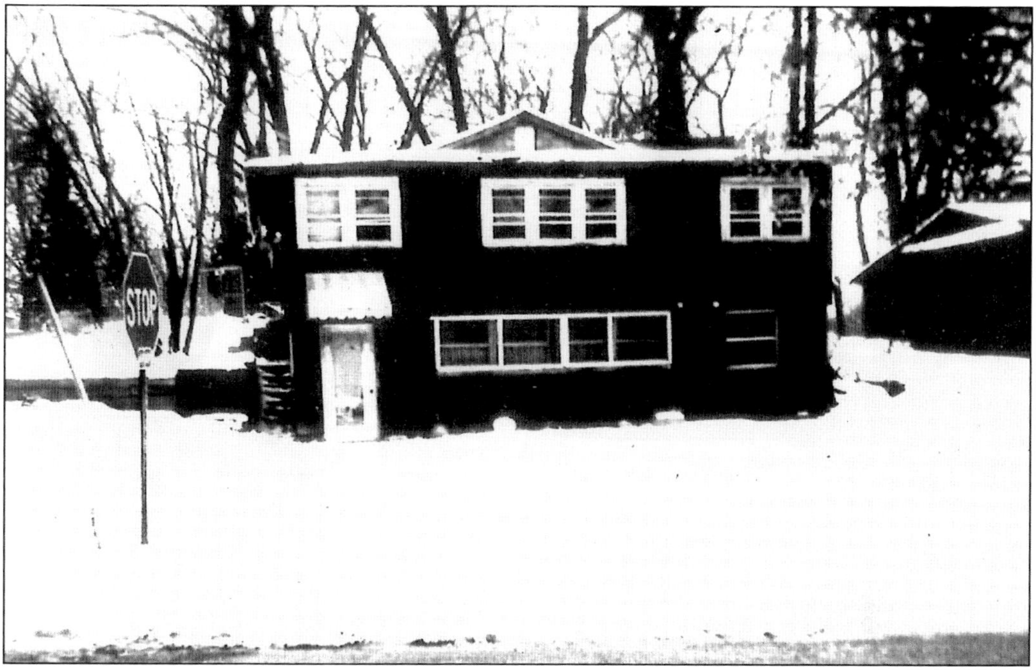

This building once housed the Hillcrest grocery store and soda fountain. (Photo by L.G. Eggleston.)

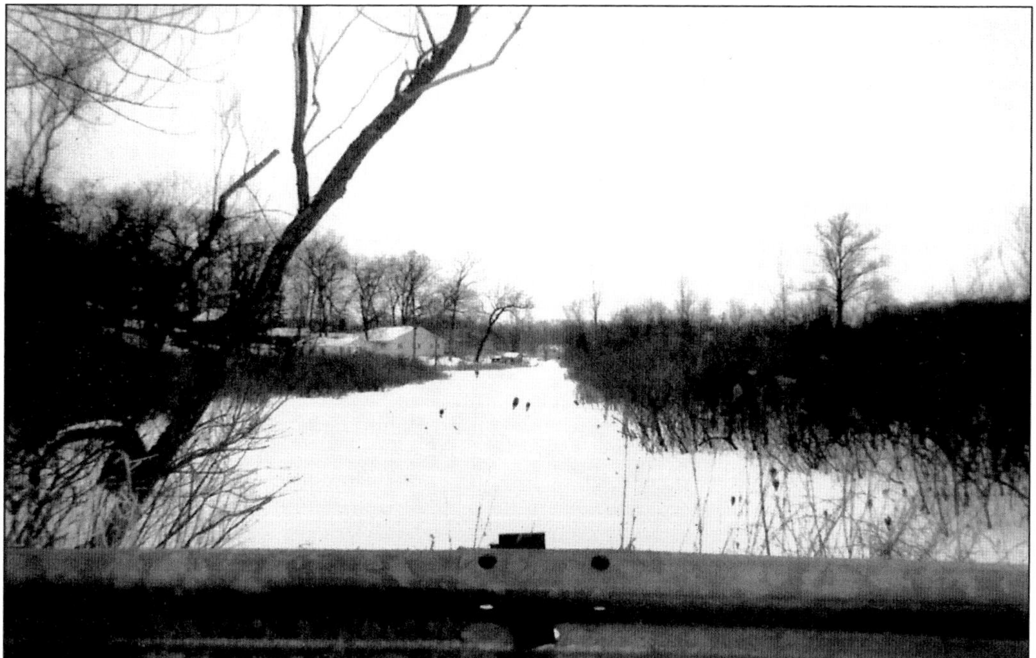

Prior to 1923 this channel, which runs between Flint Lake and Long Lake, gave access to both lakes for fishing and pleasure boating. The channel was bridged in 1923. (Photo by L.G. Eggleston.)

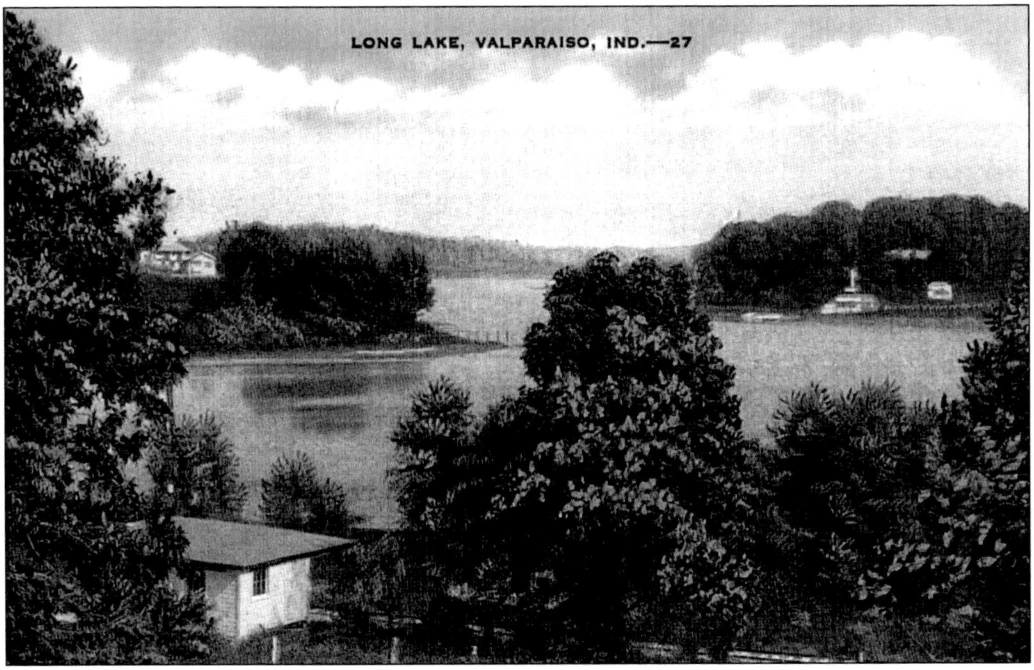

This photograph shows the Hillcrest Beach interurban station at the north end of Urban Lane with Long Lake in the background. It was one block to the store and two blocks to the beach. (Photo courtesy of L.G. Eggleston.)

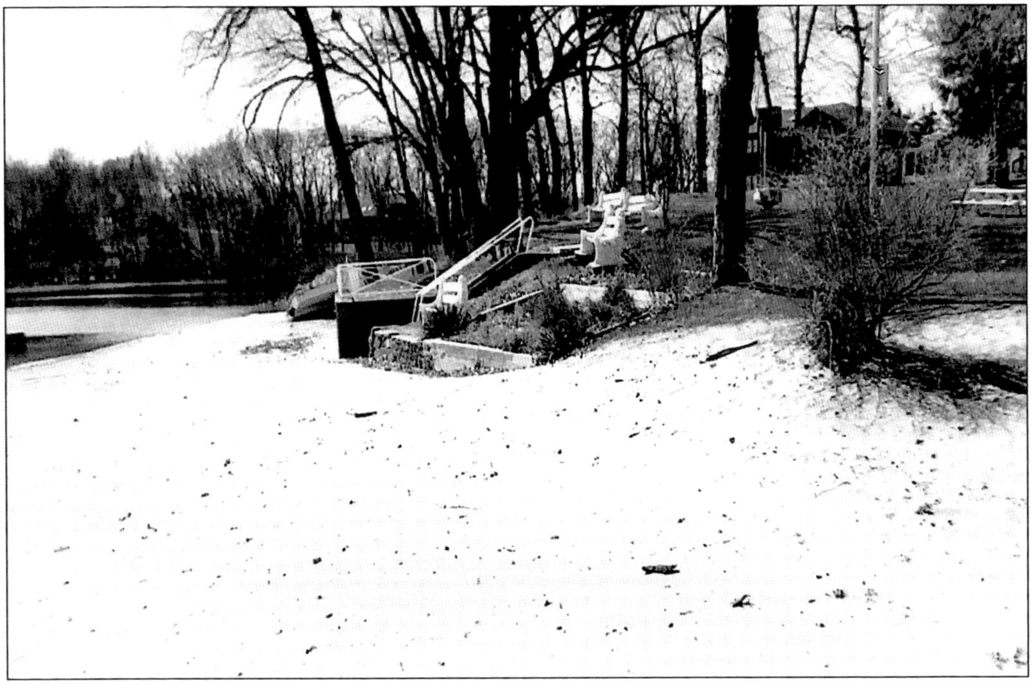

The above photograph is a view of Hillcrest Beach as it looks today. (Photo by L.G. Eggleston.)

Four

Fishing and Boating Lakes

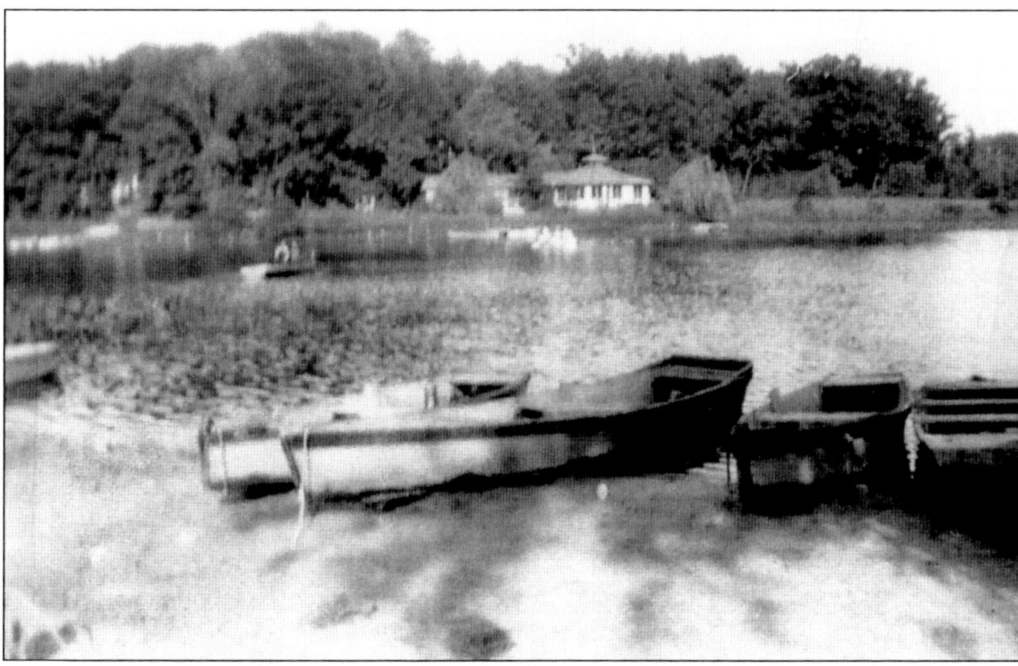

Long Lake Resort The above photograph shows a view of the Long Lake Resort Hotel and beach house. This photograph was taken in 1937. Long Lake is a 95-acre lake fed by the same underground system, which feeds Flint Lake, Bullseye Lake, Spectacle Lake, and Wauhob Lake.

The resort was very popular for fishing, boating, swimming, or just relaxing

The interurban electric railroad station was one block west of this site. The station was at the east-end of Anderson road, which is now 600 N, and runs from Campbell Street to Long Lake. Those tourists who arrived on the train would take a boat across this narrow part of the lake to reach the resort.

From the east side of Long Lake one could come by auto from Highway 49 (now Calumet) west on Edgewater Road and north on East Long Lake Road. (Photo courtesy of Edwin Kuehl.)

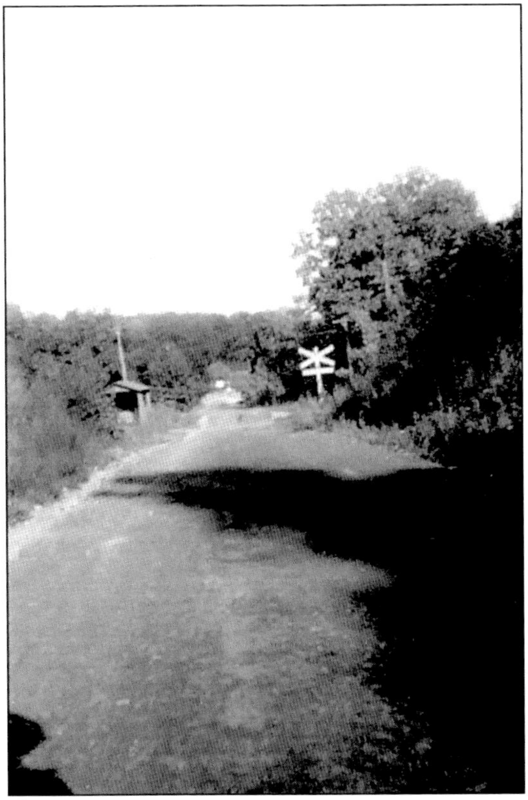

This is a 1937 view of the interurban electric railroad station on Anderson road, now 600 N, which served the Long Lake Resort Hotel. (Photo courtesy of Edwin Kuehl.)

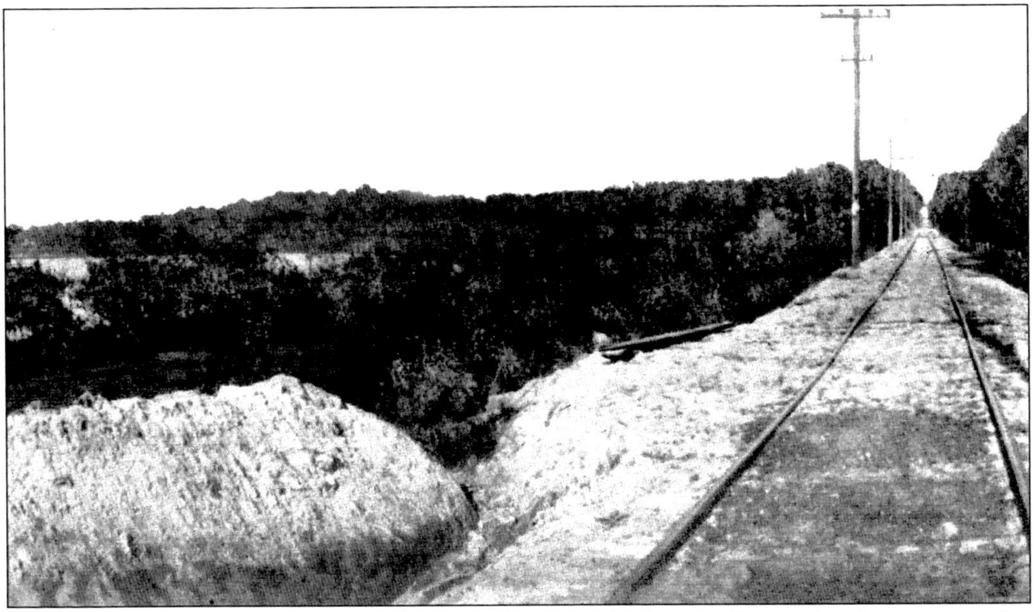

Above is a view of the interurban electric railroad tracks from Hillcrest Beach station to the station on Anderson Road, which serviced the Long Lake Resort. These tracks ran along the south end of Long Lake. (Photo courtesy of Edwin Kuehl.)

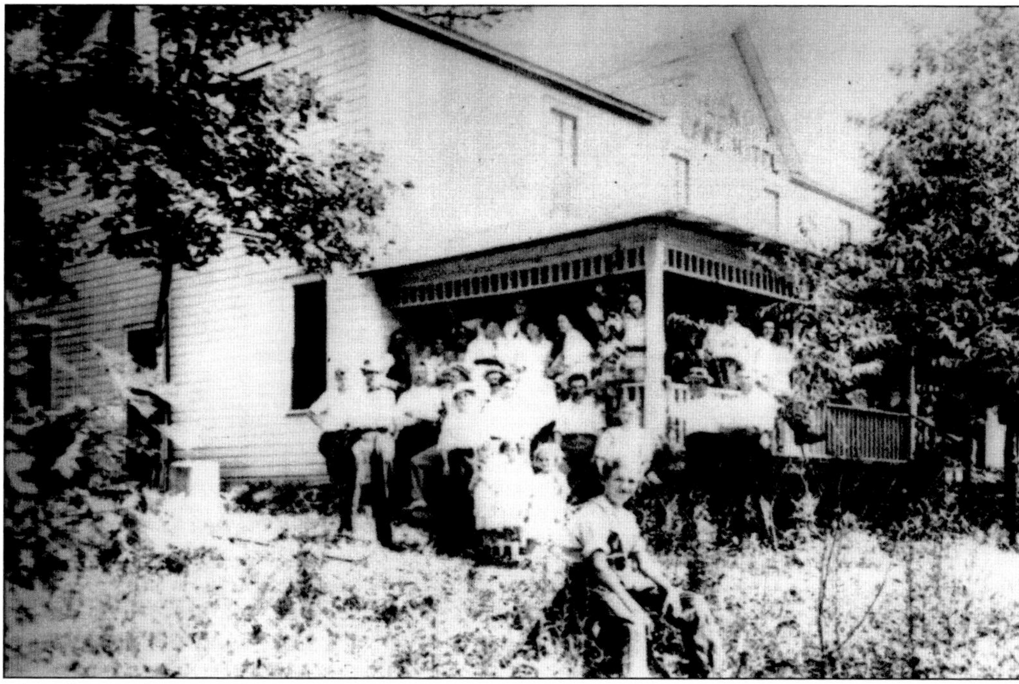

The above photograph shows visitors enjoying the view of Long Lake from the porch of the Long Lake Resort Hotel. (Photo courtesy of G. Bradley Publishing, Inc.)

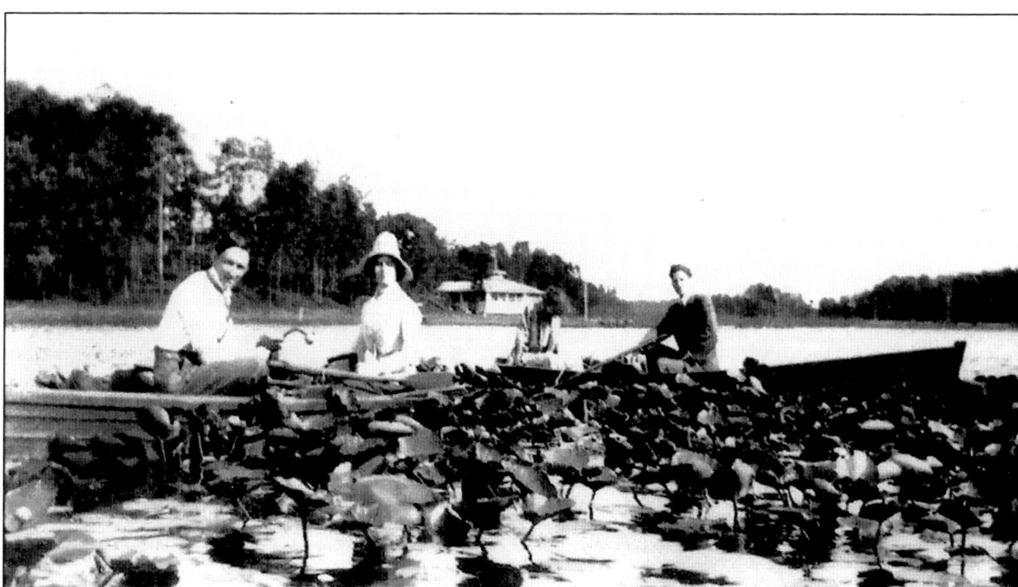

Boaters in the above photograph are enjoying the beauty of Long Lake. The Long Lake Resort can be seen in the background. (Photo courtesy of Porter County Historical Society.)

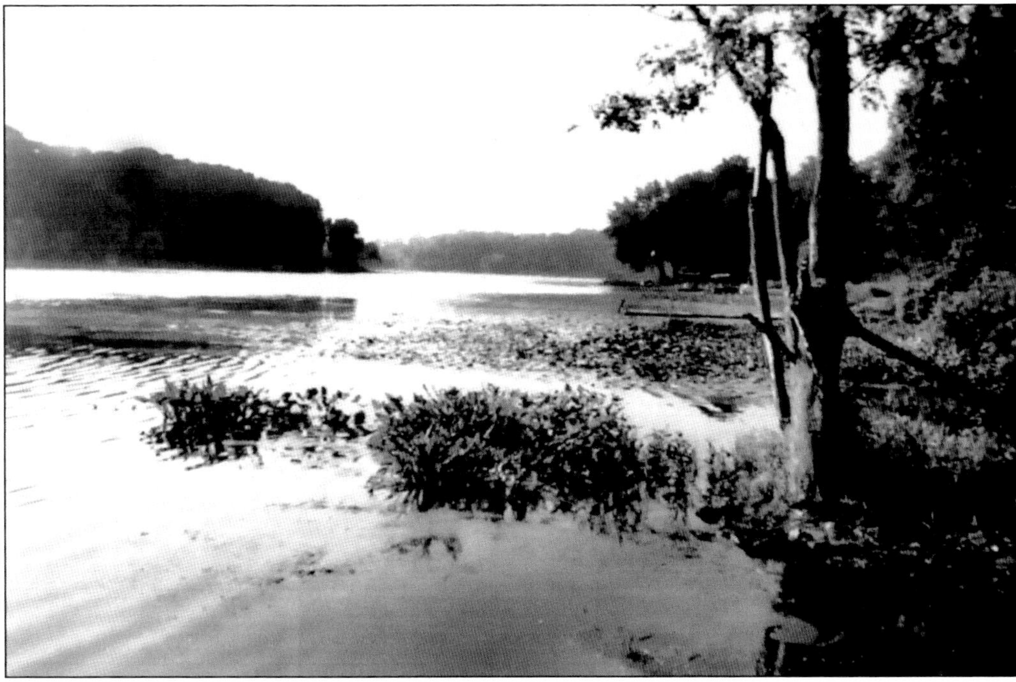

Above is a view of Long Lake looking south from the public access area which is two-tenths of a mile north on West Long Lake Road. The public access area has a boat launching ramp, parking lot, and restroom facilities. (Photo by L.G. Eggleston.)

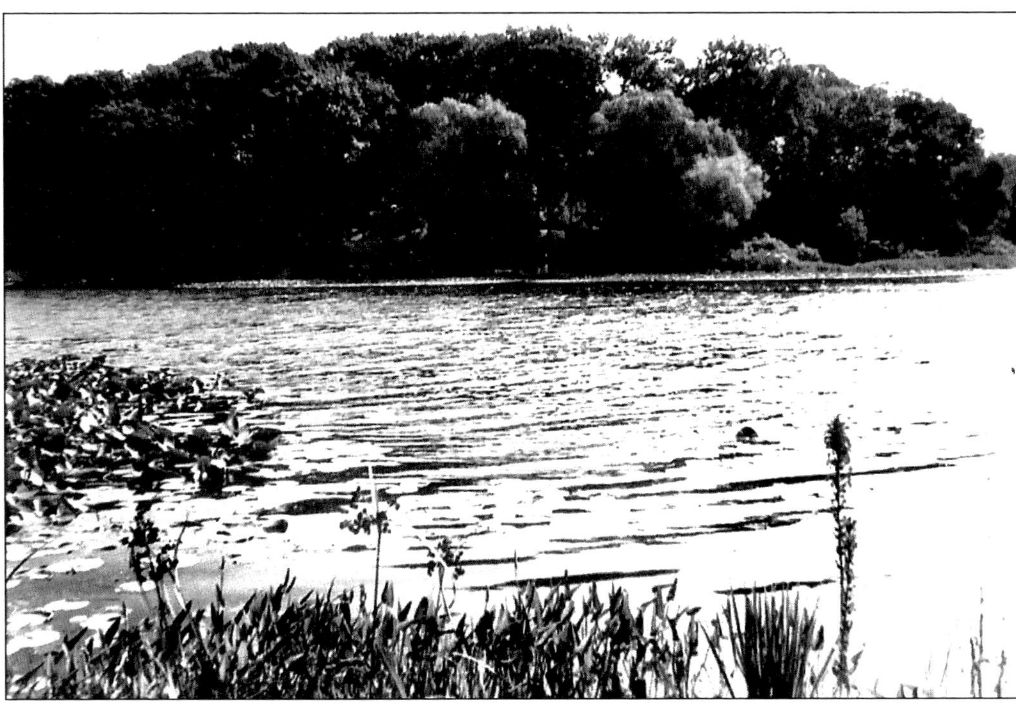

The shoreline on the other side of the lake is the site where the Long Lake Resort once had its beach house and piers. Only the hotel remains standing. (Photo by L.G. Eggleston.)

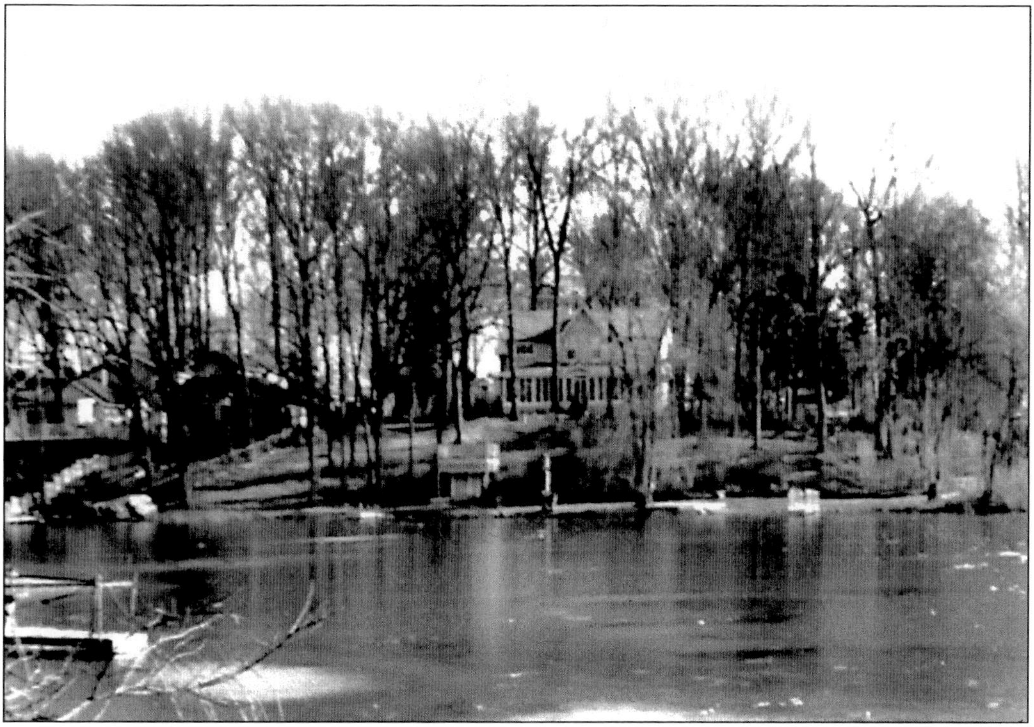

The above photograph shows the Long Lake Resort Hotel as it appears today. The resort no longer exists and the hotel has been converted into a private home. (Photo by L.G. Eggleston.)

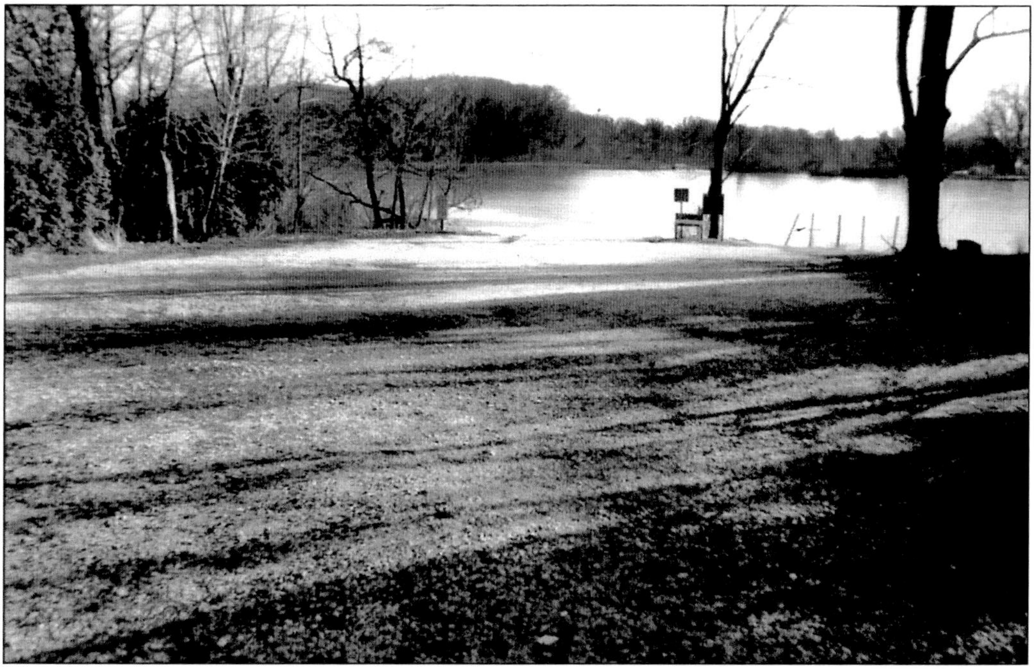

The above photo shows the public access area for Long Lake. (Photo by of L.G. Eggleston.)

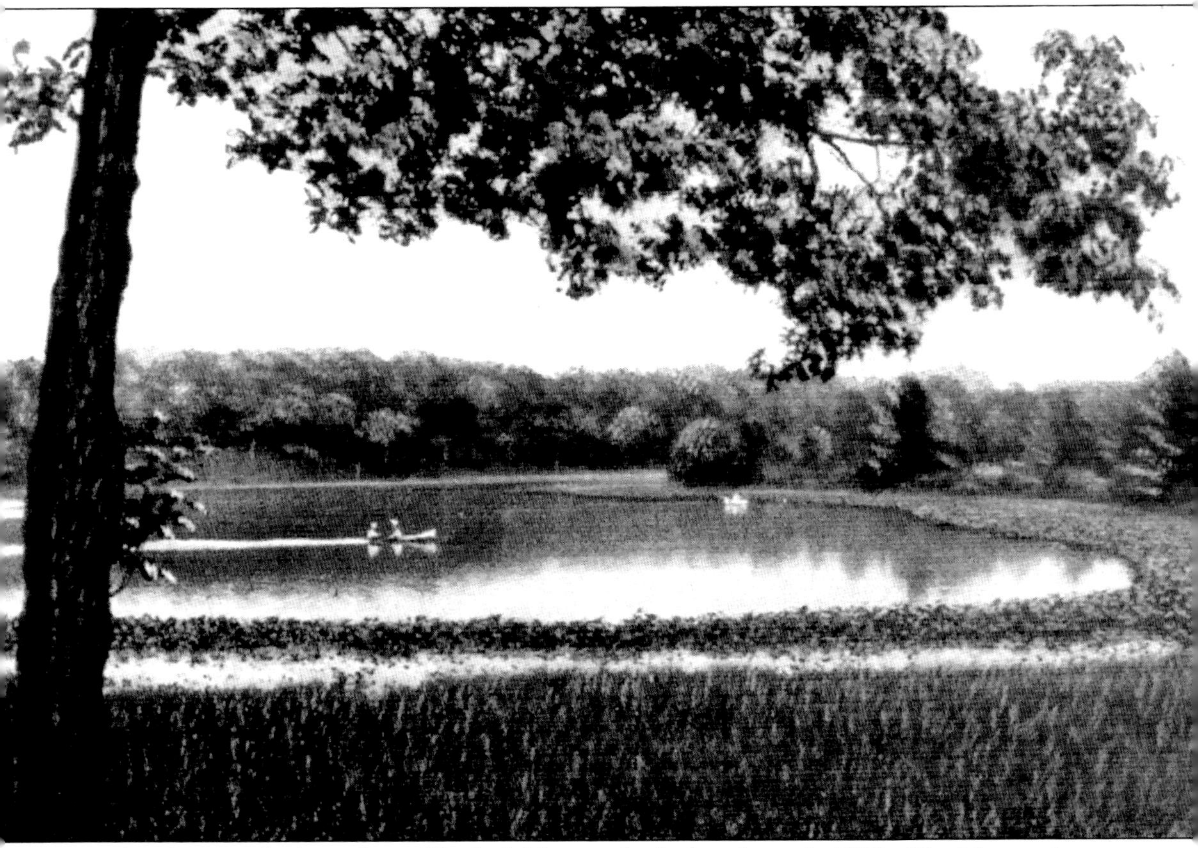

The photograph above shows Wauhob lake as it looked in the early 1900s. The lake was known as a good fishing and boating lake. The lake is still as beautiful as it was then. The south and west sides of the lake have never been developed.

Wauhob Lake Wauhob Lake was originally called Van Loon Lake. The lake was purchased by the U.S. Government in 1826 and later sold to the Dillingham Family. Mr. William (Billie) Wauhob acquired the land when he married Betsy Electra Dillingham on January 28, 1837. William then renamed the lake Wauhob Lake, as it is know today.

The interurban electric train ran along the west side of Wauhob Lake as it proceeded north from Long Lake. The interurban station was located on the west side of the lake. A deep cut through the north-west hill on the lake shore was made for the railroad as it proceeded to Woodville Junction. This cut was called the Wauhob Cut and is still visible from Wauhob Lake Road, which is now 700 N, and from the new highway 49.

Wauhob Lake, a 21-acre lake, is fed by an underground spring. (Photo courtesy of L. G. Eggleston.)

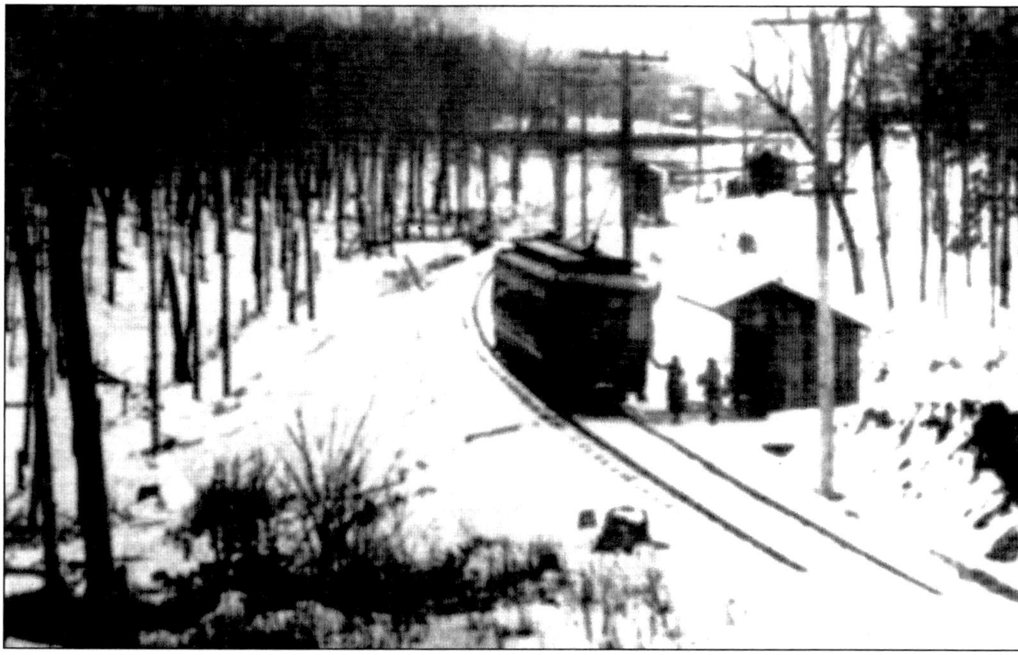

This photograph shows the interurban electric train stopped at the Wauhob Station, which was below the Wauhob cut. (Photo courtesy of Porter County Historical Society.)

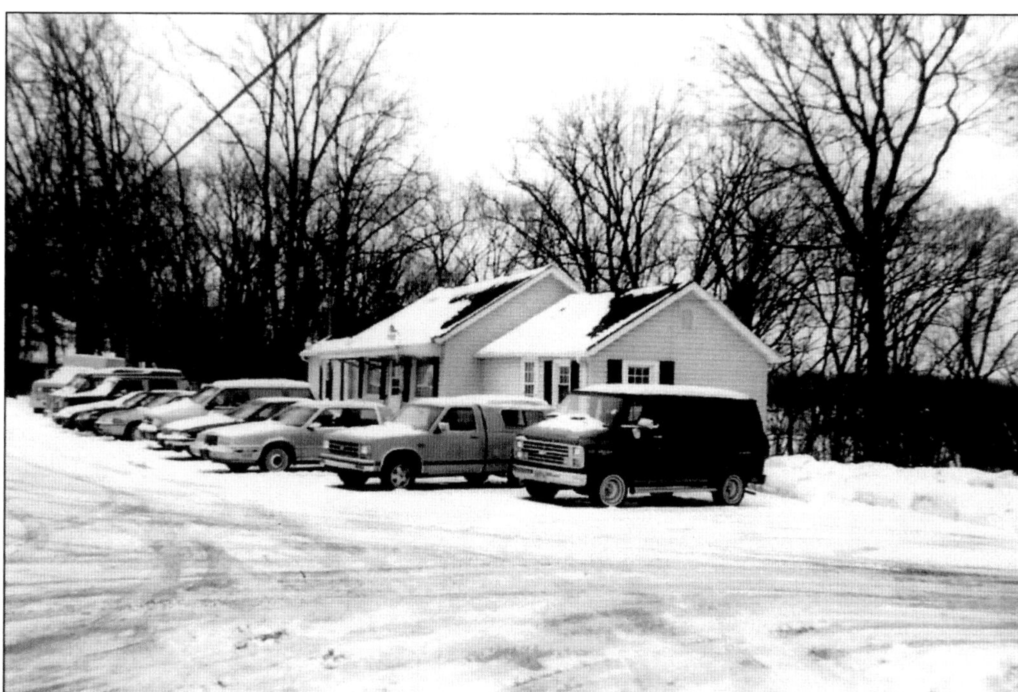

The Wauhob grocery store shown here was two blocks from the lake and is located on Calumet Avenue (Old Highway 49). The building now serves as a used car lot. (Photo by L.G. Eggleston.)

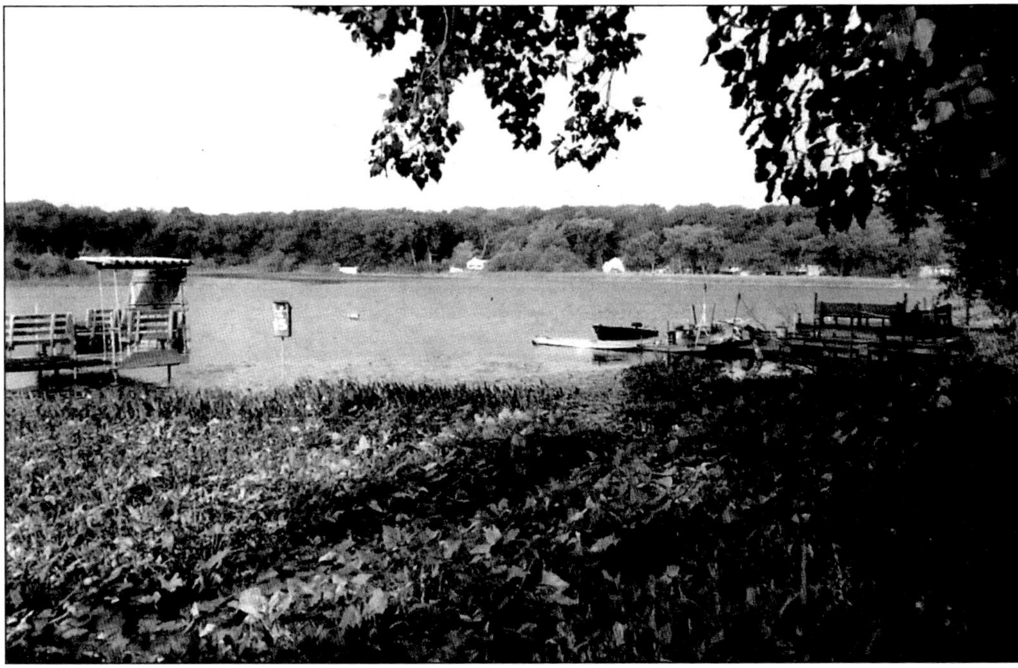

Here is a view of Wauhob Lake as it looks today. The lake is as beautiful as it was before the area was settled. (Photo by L.G. Eggleston.)

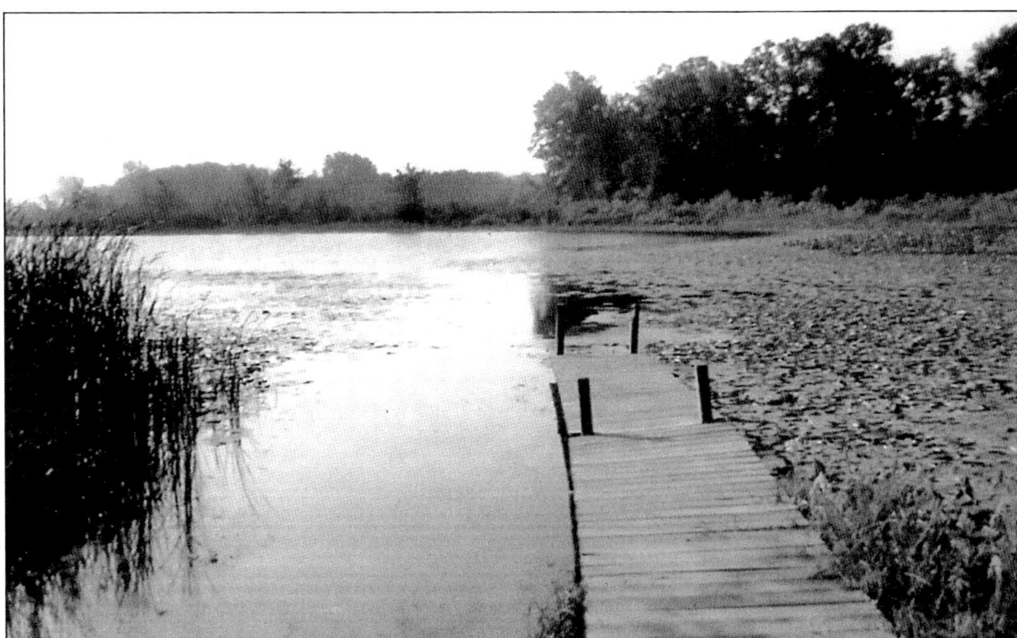

This photograph of Wauhob Lake is from the boat rental area on the west side. The south and west sides of the lake have never been developed. (Photo by L.G. Eggleston.)

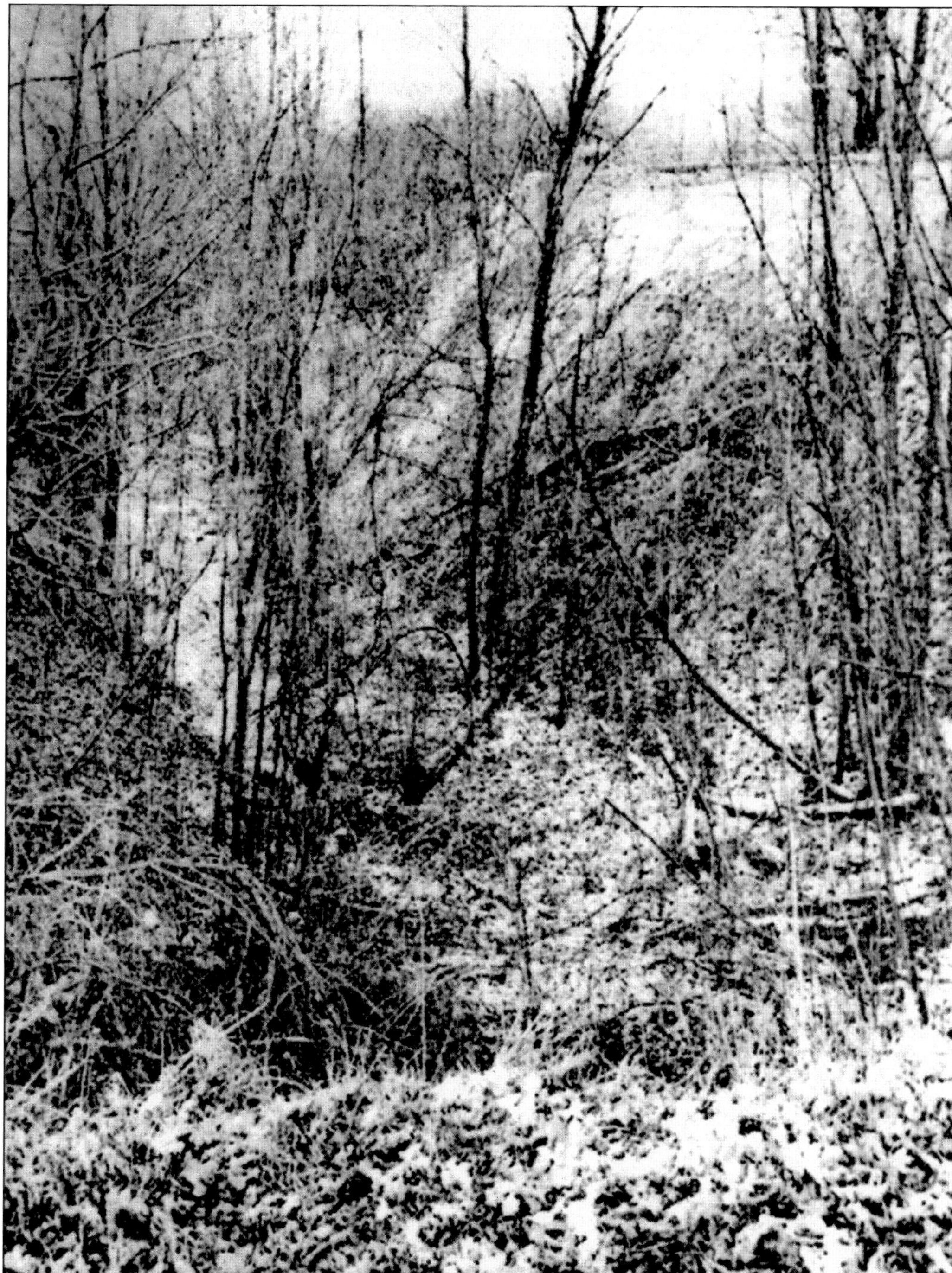

There were no resort hotels or recreation facilities built on Wauhob Lake. The lake was used mainly for fishing and boating. There were several summer cottages built on the east and north sides of the lake. Most of these summer cottages have since been converted into permanent year round homes. The above photograph shows the remains of the Wauhob cut. (Photo courtesy of the *Vidette Messenger*.)

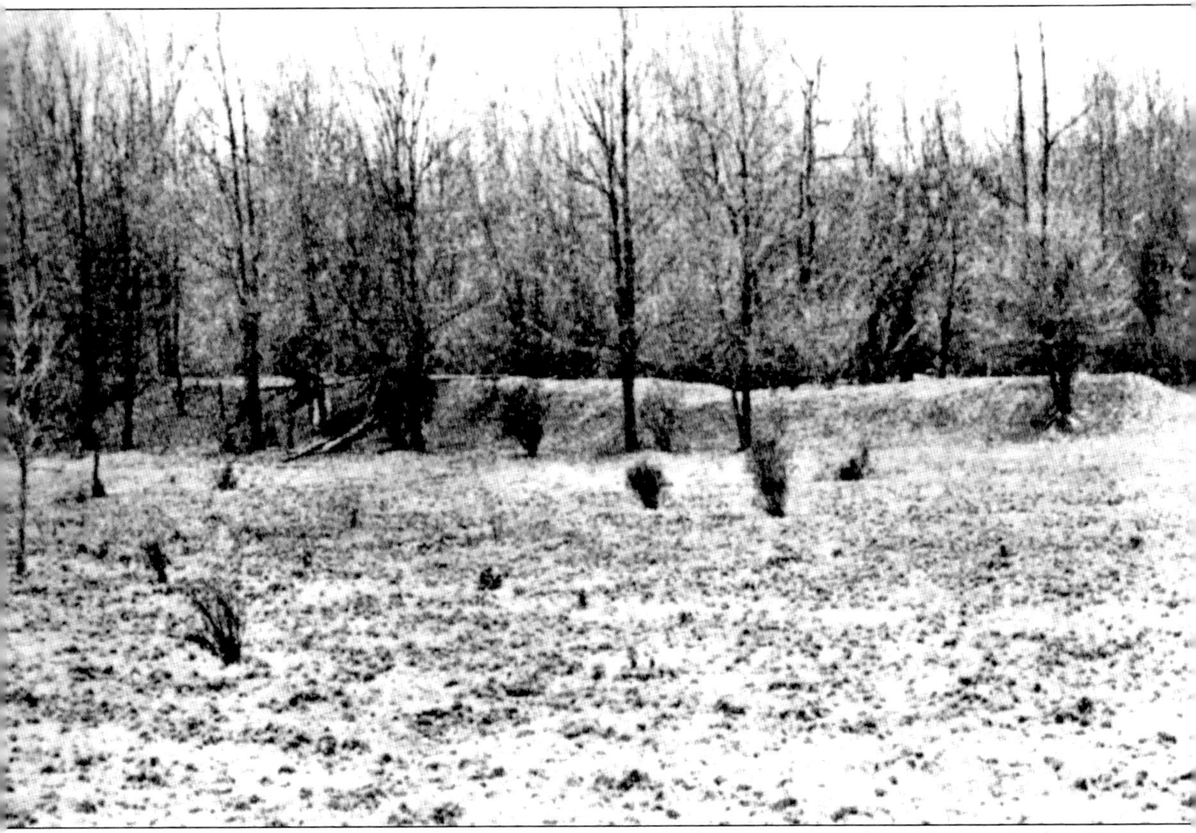

The above dirt trestle, which was part of the Gary-Valparaiso Interurban Electric Railroad, is still visible. It is located between Indiana 49 and the Wauhob Cut in Liberty Township. (Photo courtesy of the *Vidette Messenger*.)

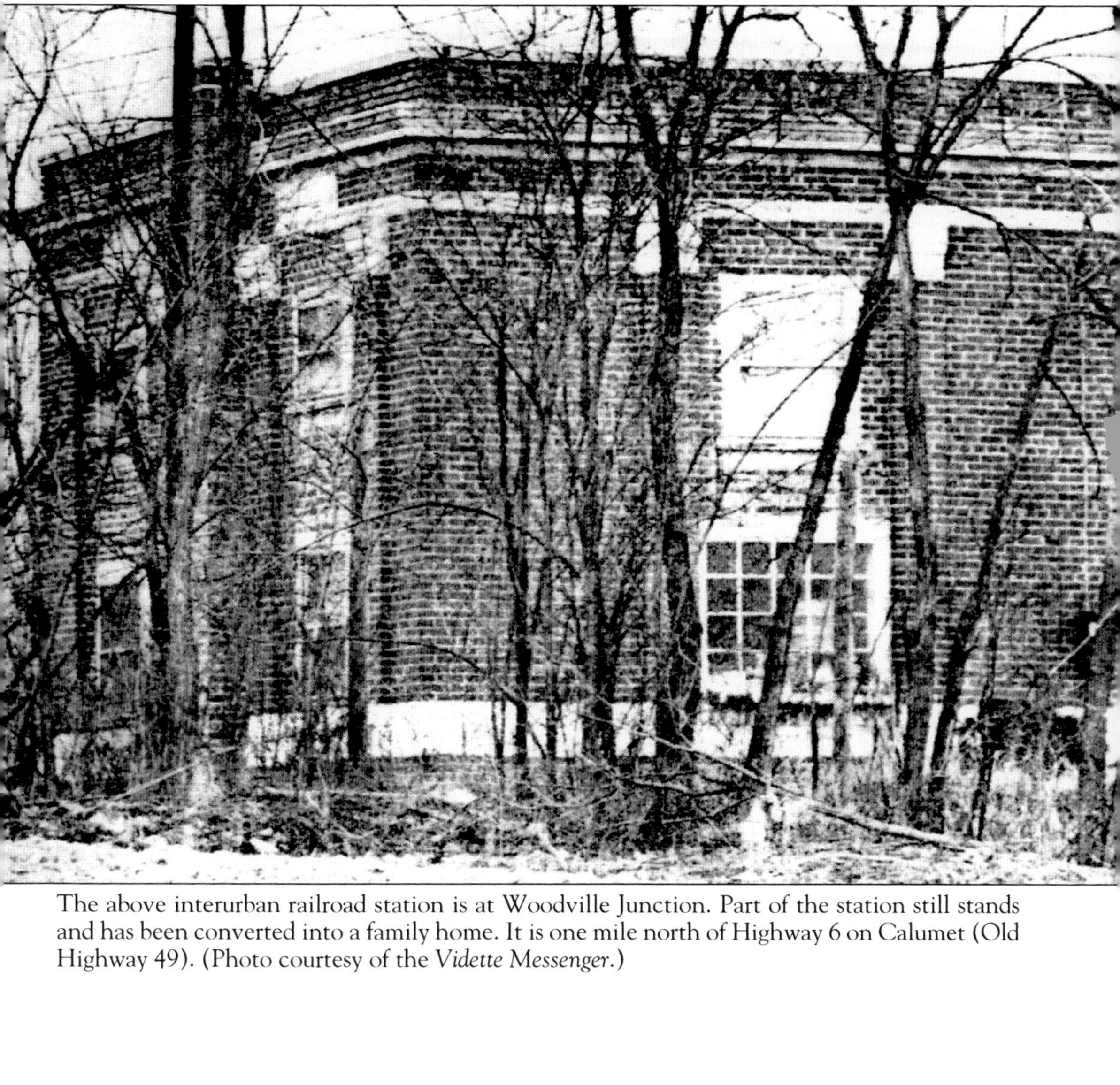

The above interurban railroad station is at Woodville Junction. Part of the station still stands and has been converted into a family home. It is one mile north of Highway 6 on Calumet (Old Highway 49). (Photo courtesy of the *Vidette Messenger*.)

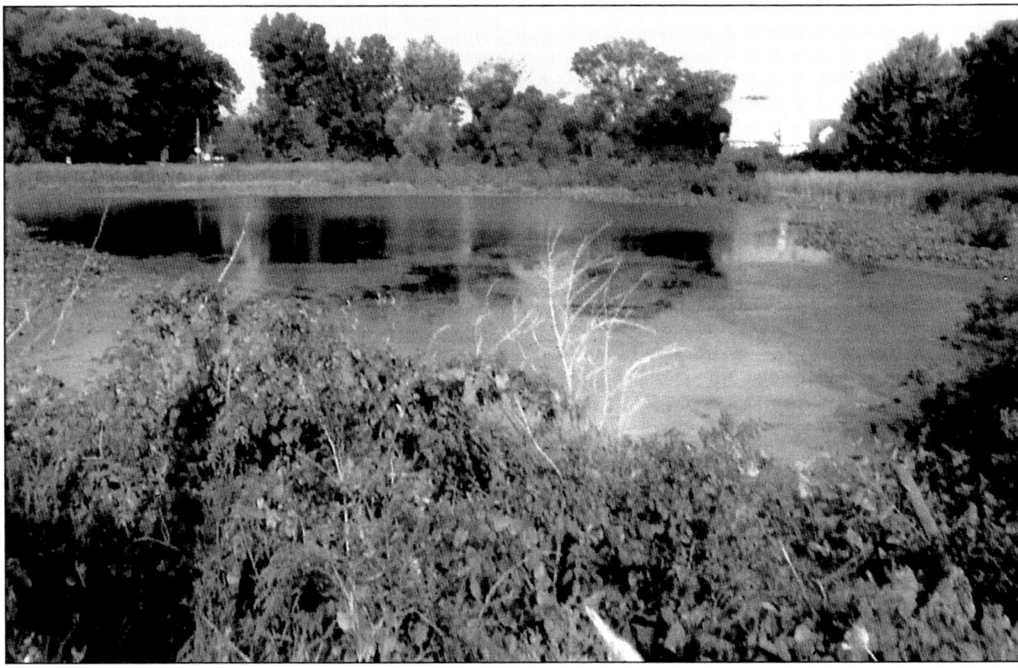

Bullseye Lake as it looks today. The photograph was taken from the north-west corner of Bullseye Lake Road and Calumet. (Photo by L.G. Eggleston.)

BULLSEYE LAKE Bullseye Lake is located at the north-west corner of Calumet (Old Highway 49) and Bullseye Lake Road and on the north side of Valparaiso. The lake was named for its round shape.

Early Indian legend says the lake is bottomless and is the dark place where evil spirits dwell. As the area became settled, the myth of a bottomless lake continued to grow as many unusual things happened around the lake.

The first of these events occurred on August 26, 1839. It was a bright Sunday morning and Mr. Thomas Brim decided to drive his team and buggy into the shallow water of the lake to soak his loose wagon wheels and thus make them tight again. As he entered the water the horses and buggy and Mr. Brim all disappeared and were never seen again.

Over the years, reports were made of many cows and farm animals that went to the lake to drink, slipped and sank into the bottomless pit.

Two brothers named Barnes decided to test the legend of the lake by pushing a buggy into the west end of the lake. They acquired an old discarded wagon from a local woman named Mary Buell and took it to the lake. They backed it into the lake and it quickly disappeared from view.

In 1870, Mr. Marion Kinne measured the depth of the lake from a boat and determined that it was only 40 feet deep. In 1889, an Indiana State geologist named Mr. Blatchley surveyed the lake and reported that it was 200 feet deep.

In 1912, the State of Indiana had the lake measured in 16 different spots and found that the lake bottom slopes from all sides to a point about three fourths of the way west where it is fed by an underground river. The so-called bottomless pit is only the opening into the underground river.

Chemicals and a red dye were poured into Bullseye Lake as a geological experiment. Within a few days the dye was visible in the waters of Flint Lake, Long Lake, Mink Lake, and Wauhob Lake. This verified the path of the underground river.

After its construction in 1910, the interurban electric railroad ran past the east side of Bullseye Lake and along the west side of Highway 49 (now Calumet).

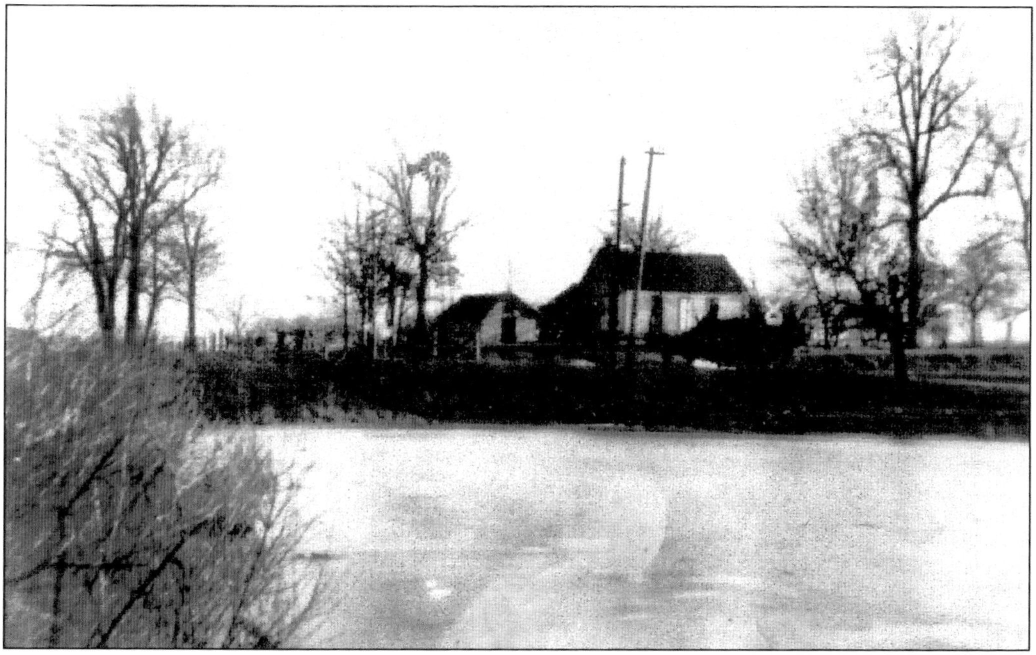

The above photograph was taken in 1917 and shows the interurban tracks and crossing sign where it passed Bullseye Lake Road. The farm shown was on the east side of the lake. (Photo courtesy of Edwin Kuehl.)

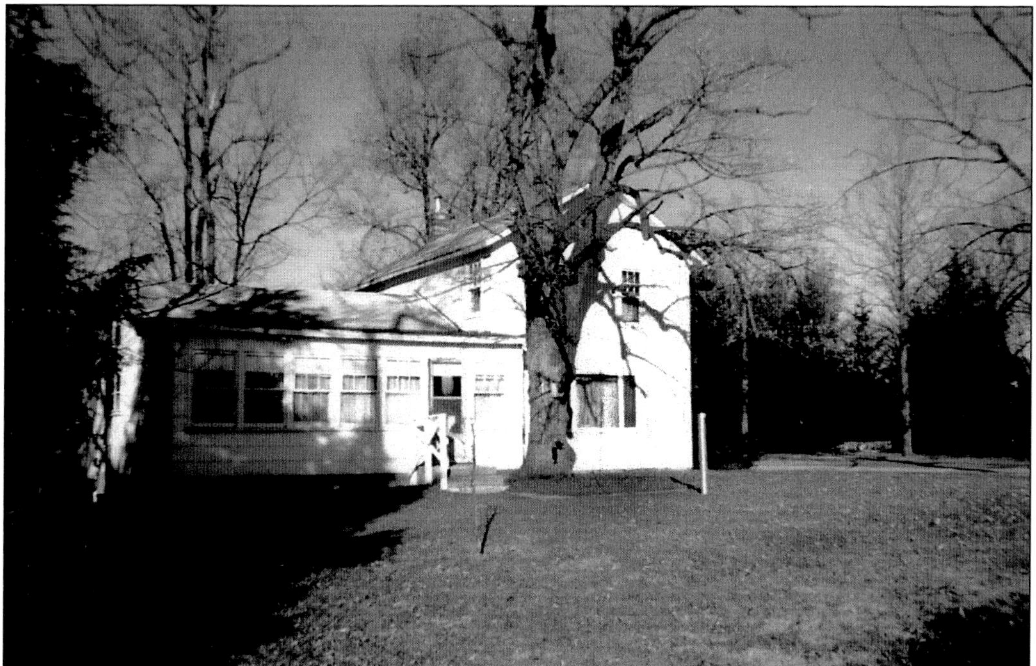

The above photograph shows the original farmhouse of the north side of Bullseye Lake. (Photo by L.G. Eggleston.)

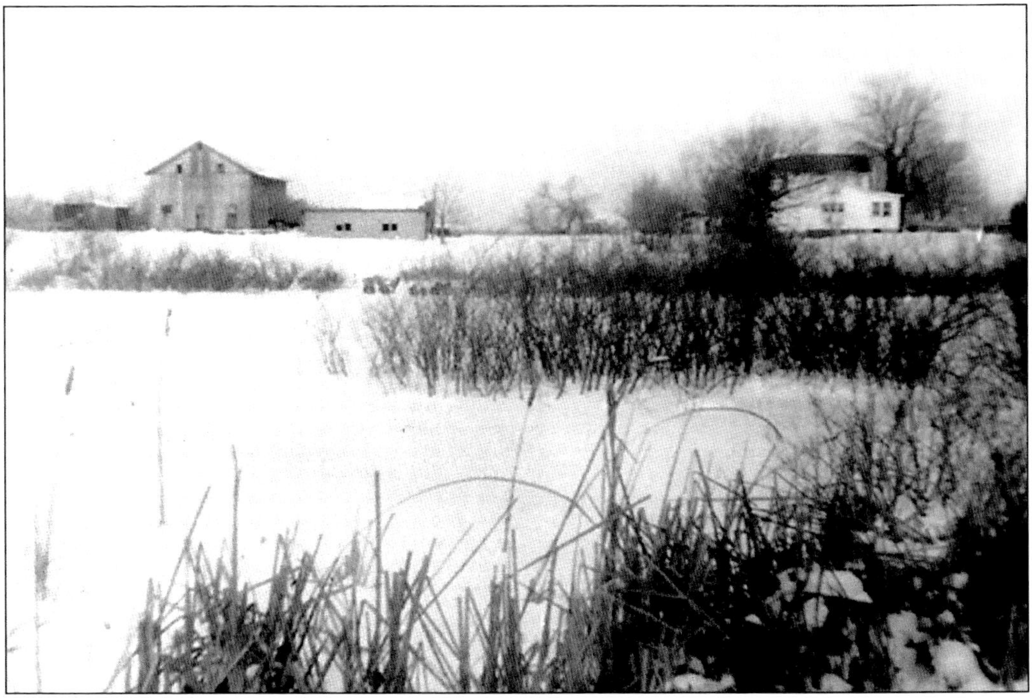

This view looking across Bullseye Lake shows the original farm on the north side of the Lake (Photo courtesy of Edwin Kuehl.)

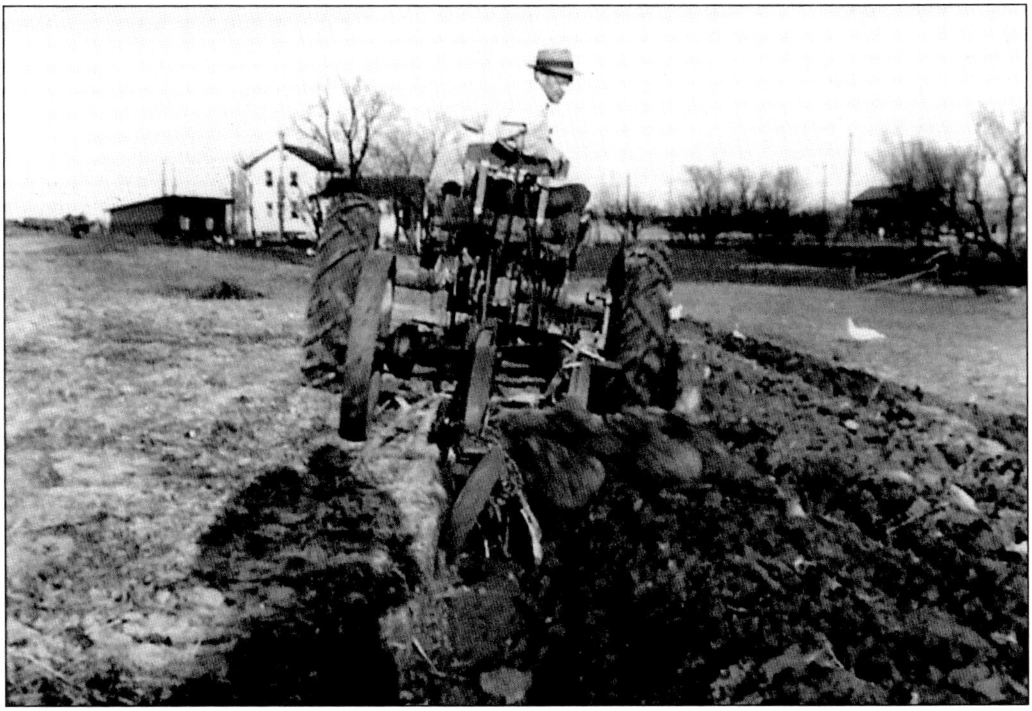

Above is a photograph of Mr. Edwin Kuehl Sr. plowing the farmland on the north shore of Bullseye Lake. (Photo courtesy of Edwin Kuehl.)

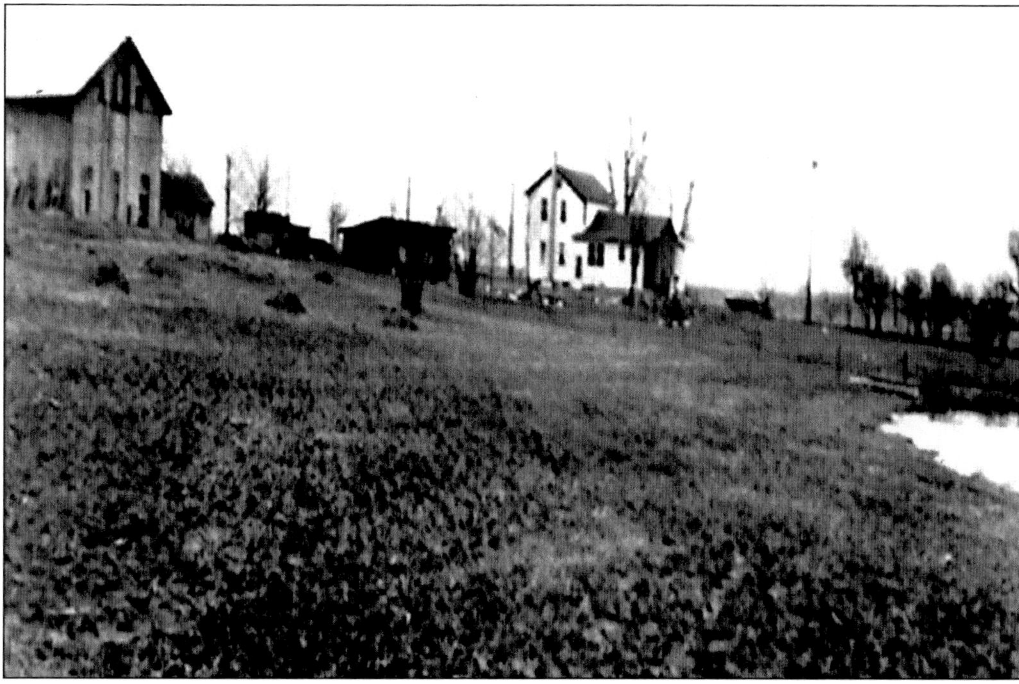

This view of Bullseye Lake Farm shows the farm and the edge of the lake from the west. (Photo courtesy of Edwin Kuehl.)

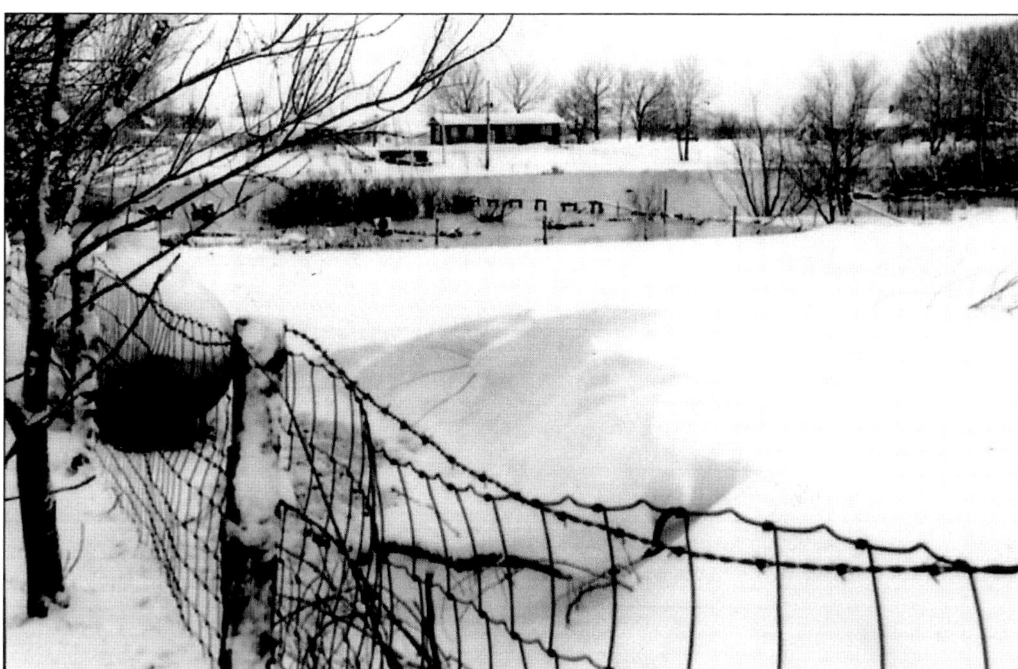

The above photo is a view of Bullseye Lake in the winter. The lake was a good place to ice skate and was also a favorite spot for ice fishing. (Photo courtesy of Edwin Kuehl.)

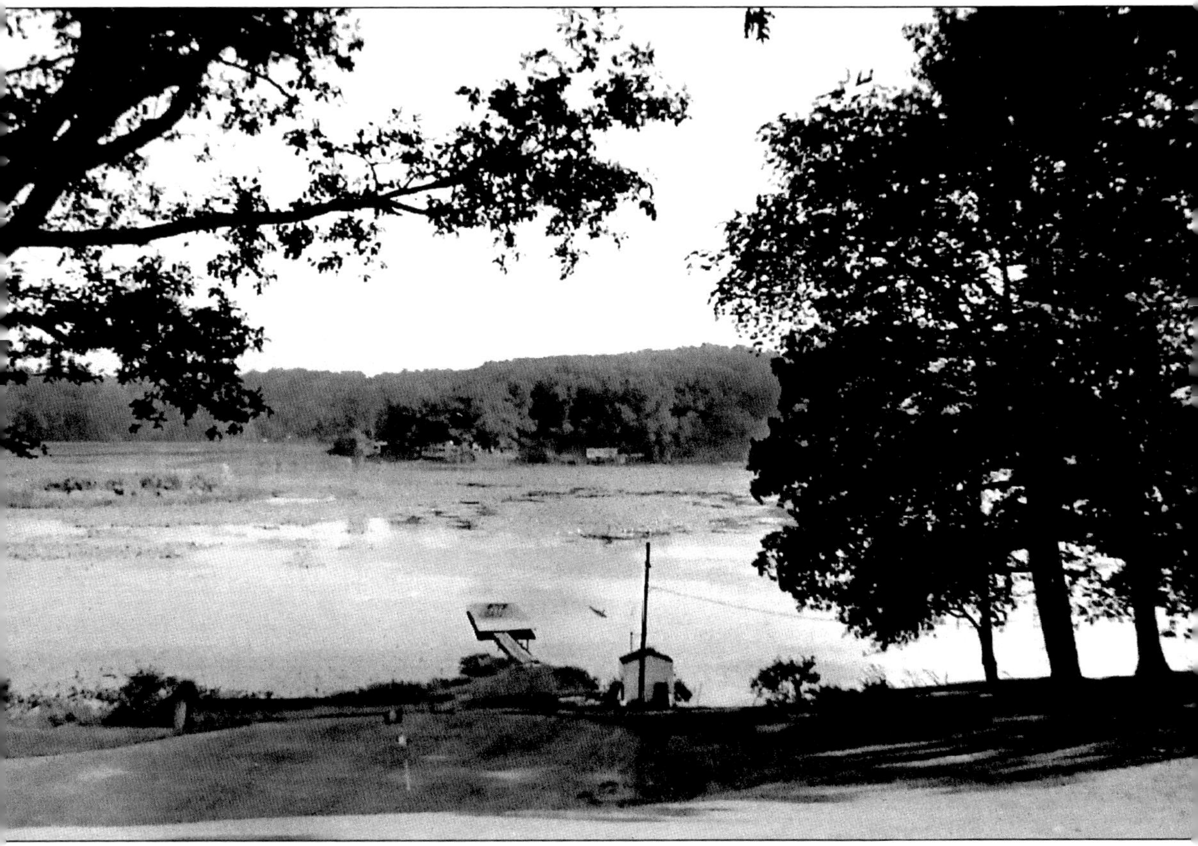

This view is of Mink Lake looking north across part of the golf course. The campground can be seen in the background on the north shore of the lake. (Photo by L.G. Eggleston.)

MINK LAKE Mink Lake is located approximately five miles north of Valparaiso on Old Highway 49, which is now Calumet. It is a small lake and was named by early settlers for its abundance of mink. Many people trapped and raised mink in the area up to the late 1940s.

A golf course borders the lake on two sides while a campground and wilderness area surrounds the other two sides. A nine-hole golf course was built in 1950 around the south end of the lake. This course is very popular with Porter County golfers.

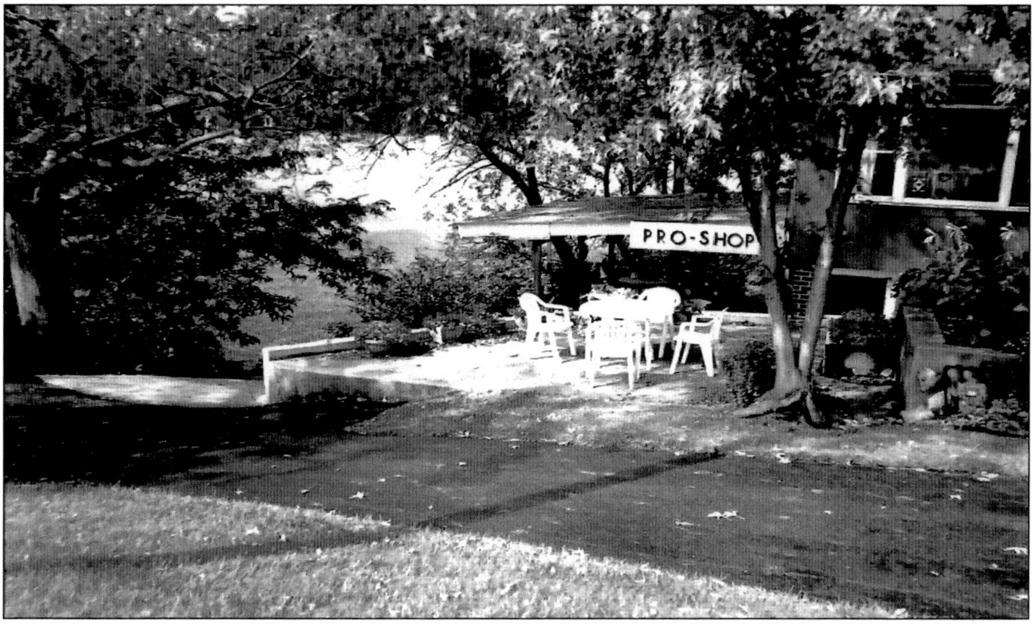

This photograph is of the pro-shop at Mink Lake Golf Course on Calumet. It was opened for business in 1950. (Photo by L.G. Eggleston.)

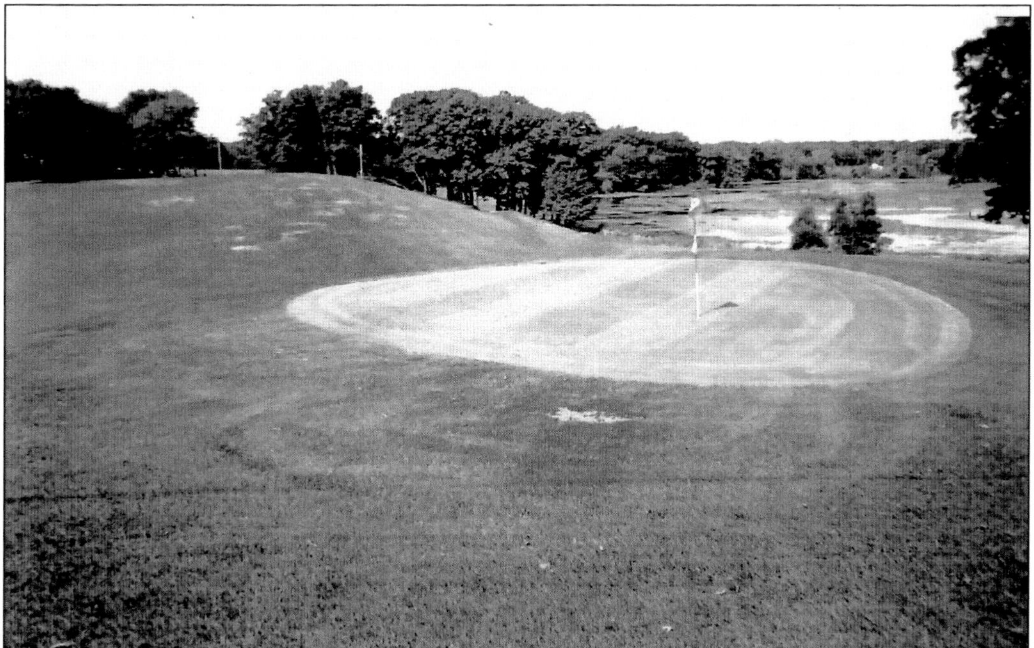
The above is a view of Mink Lake from the 9th green at Mink Lake Golf Course. (Photo by L.G. Eggleston.)

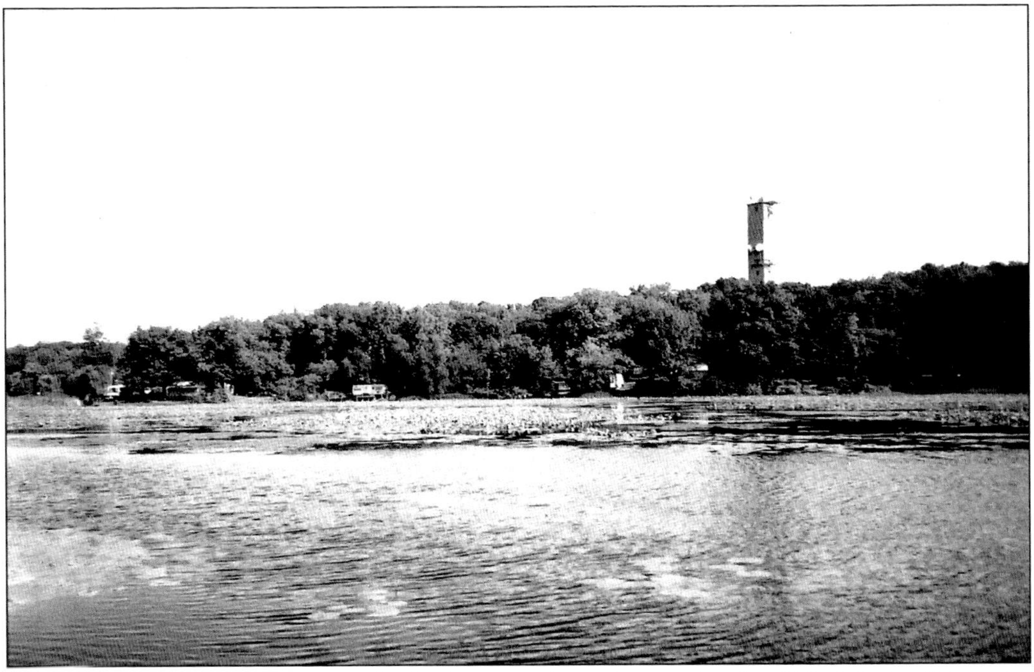

Above is a view of the campground, which was built on the north side of Mink Lake. (Photo by L.G. Eggleston.)

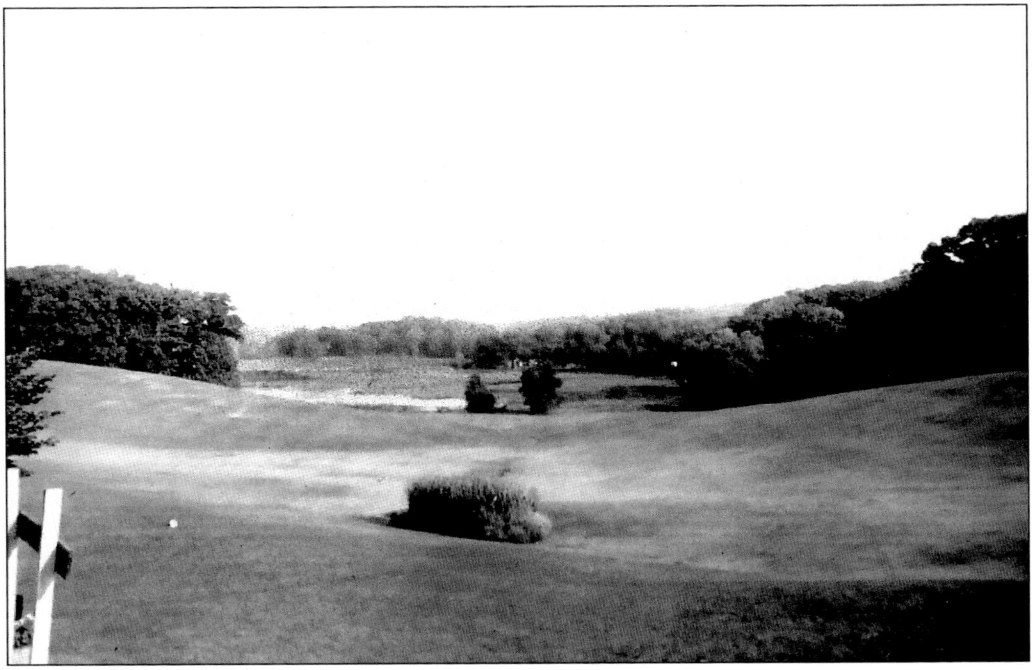

This photograph shows a view of the Mink Lake Golf Course and Mink Lake from the 1st tee. (Photo by L.G. Eggleston.)

Five

THE INTERURBAN ELECTRIC RAILROAD

The interurban electric railroad operated from Valparaiso to Gary. The railroad opened on July 4, 1910 with its first run from Valparaiso to Flint Lake. The fare was ten cents for the three-mile ride. Frank Cowdrey was the engineer and Charles Shunk was the conductor on the first run.

On opening day 3,500 people gathered for the celebration. The desire of such a crowd to ride the train on opening day was such that the railroad added a steam work engine with flat cars to help haul the crowd.

The railroad eventually wound its way through the lake area of northern Porter County. Stations were erected at Burlington Beach, Sheridan Beach, Edgewater Beach, Hillcrest Beach, on Anderson Road at Long Lake, Wauhob Lake, and Woodville Junction. At Woodville Junction the railroad split with one set of tracks going to La Porte and the other to Chesterton and Gary.

The railroad operated 18 years and 4 months. The last train to run on the tracks completed the 16-mile stretch between Valparaiso and Gary at 3:00 p.m. on October 23, 1938. There were no crowds or fanfare for this final run and the railroad quietly closed and became part of history. The only remnants of the railroad are the areas where old trestles are still visible such as the Wauhob Cut in Liberty Township and the station at Woodville Junction which has been converted into a family home.

The interurban electric railroad had a great influence on the growth and development of the lake-area and resorts of Northern Porter County.

The original name of the Valparaiso Interurban Railroad was Valparaiso and Northern Railroad. The railroad was founded on August 25, 1908, and cost $10,000 to build. The individual sections of the railroad were opened as follows:

Valparaiso to Flint Lake	July 4, 1910
Chesterton to Goodrum	February 18, 1911
Flint Lake to Woodville	October 7, 1911
Woodville to Goodrum	February 17, 1912

The railroad ran two trains each hour.

On January 28, 1913 the Valparaiso and Northern Railroad merged with the Gary Interurban Railroad and became the Gary and Valparaiso Railroad.

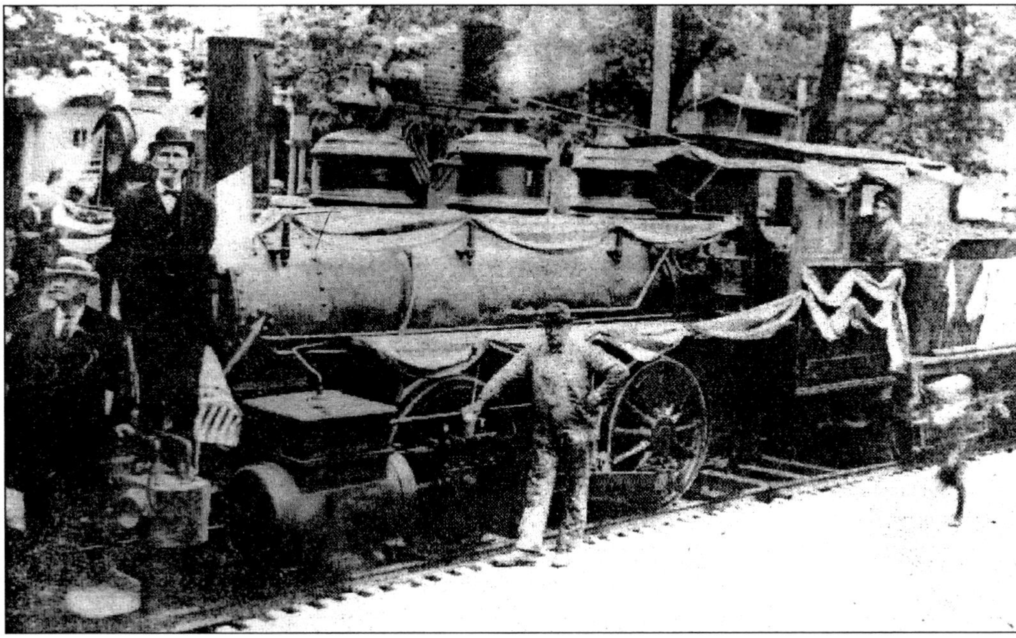

This photograph shows the steam engine that was used to accommodate the crowds who wanted to ride on the first day of operation of the interurban electric railroad in Valparaiso. (Photo courtesy of the *Vidette Messenger*.)

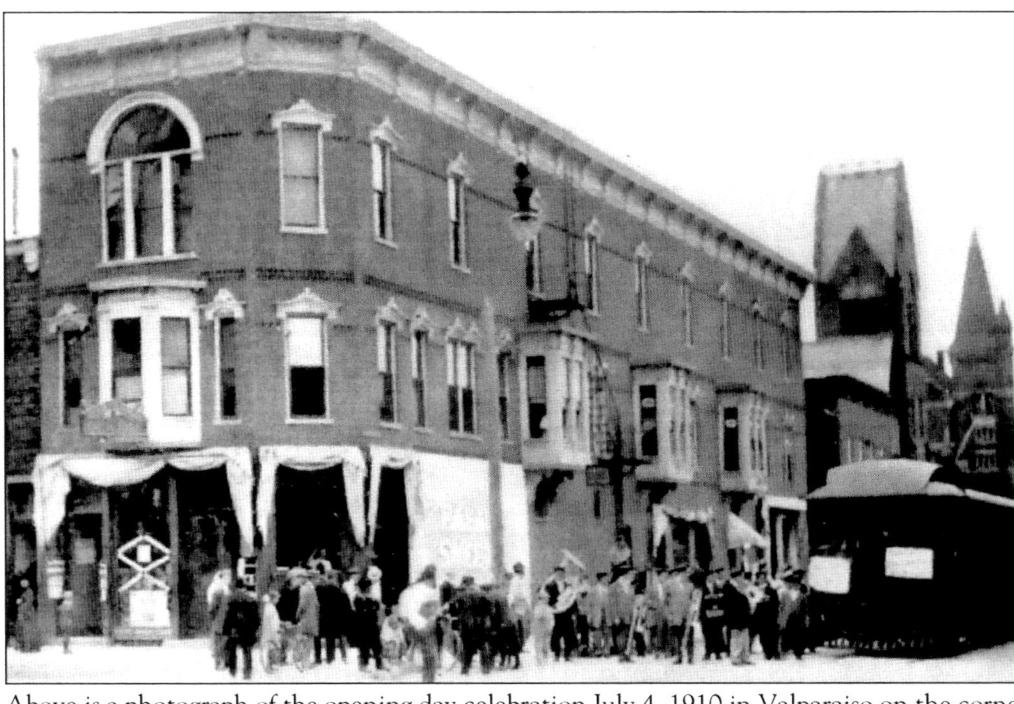

Above is a photograph of the opening day celebration July 4, 1910 in Valparaiso on the corner of Lincolnway and Franklin Street. The store to the left is now Binders Jewelers. (Photo courtesy of L.G. Eggleston.)

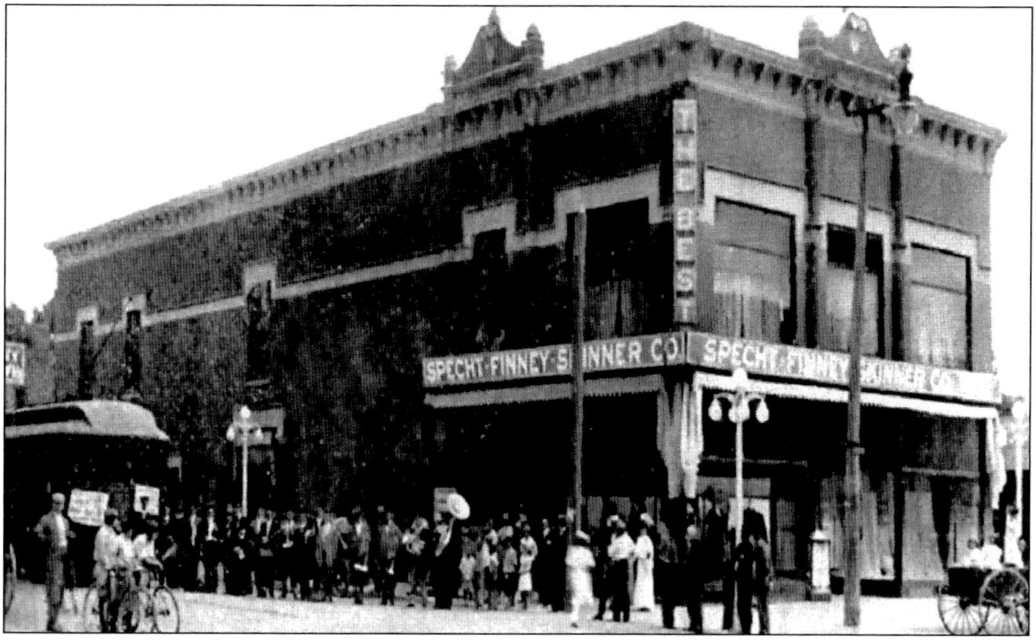

This photograph of the opening day celebration is of the north-east corner of Lincolnway and Franklin Street. The store to the right is now the site of Bank One. (Photo courtesy of L. G. Eggleston.)

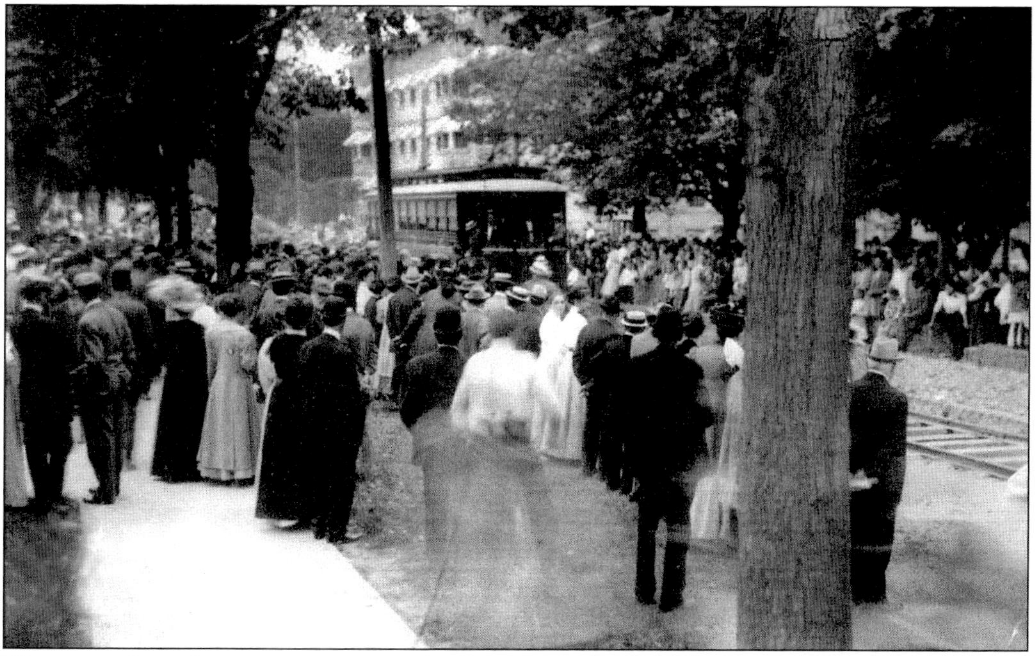

The interurban electric train passing the Pioneer Apartments building on Franklin Street on July 4, 1910 is shown in the above photograph. (Photo courtesy of L. G. Eggleston.)

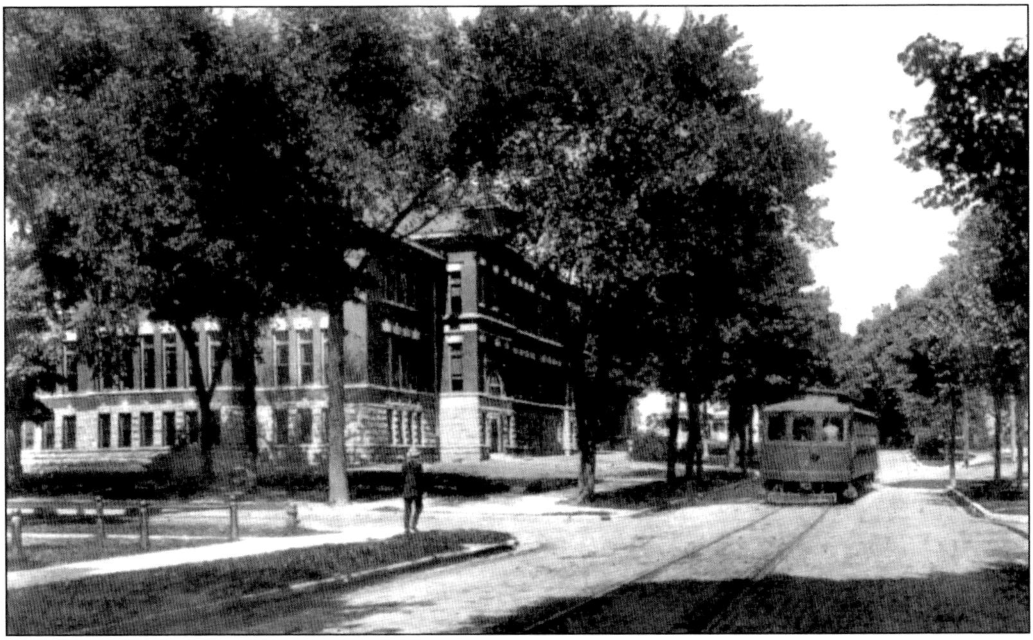

The interurban electric train passing Valparaiso High School on Franklin Street in 1910 is shown above. (Photo courtesy of L.G. Eggleston.)

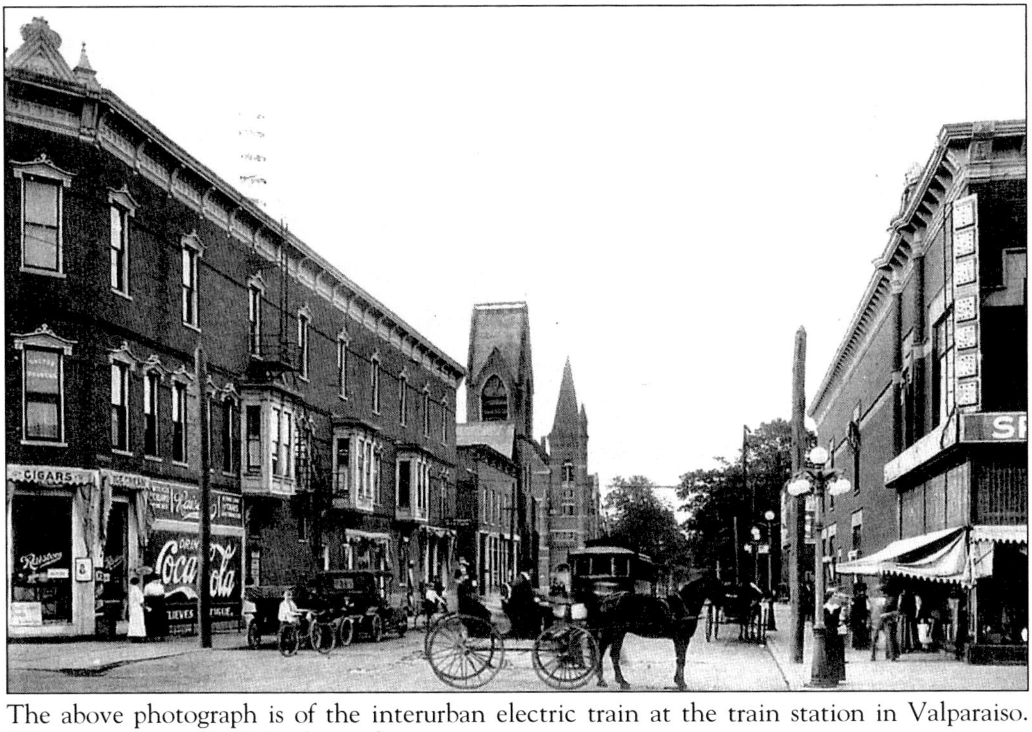

The above photograph is of the interurban electric train at the train station in Valparaiso. (Photo courtesy of L.G. Eggleston.)

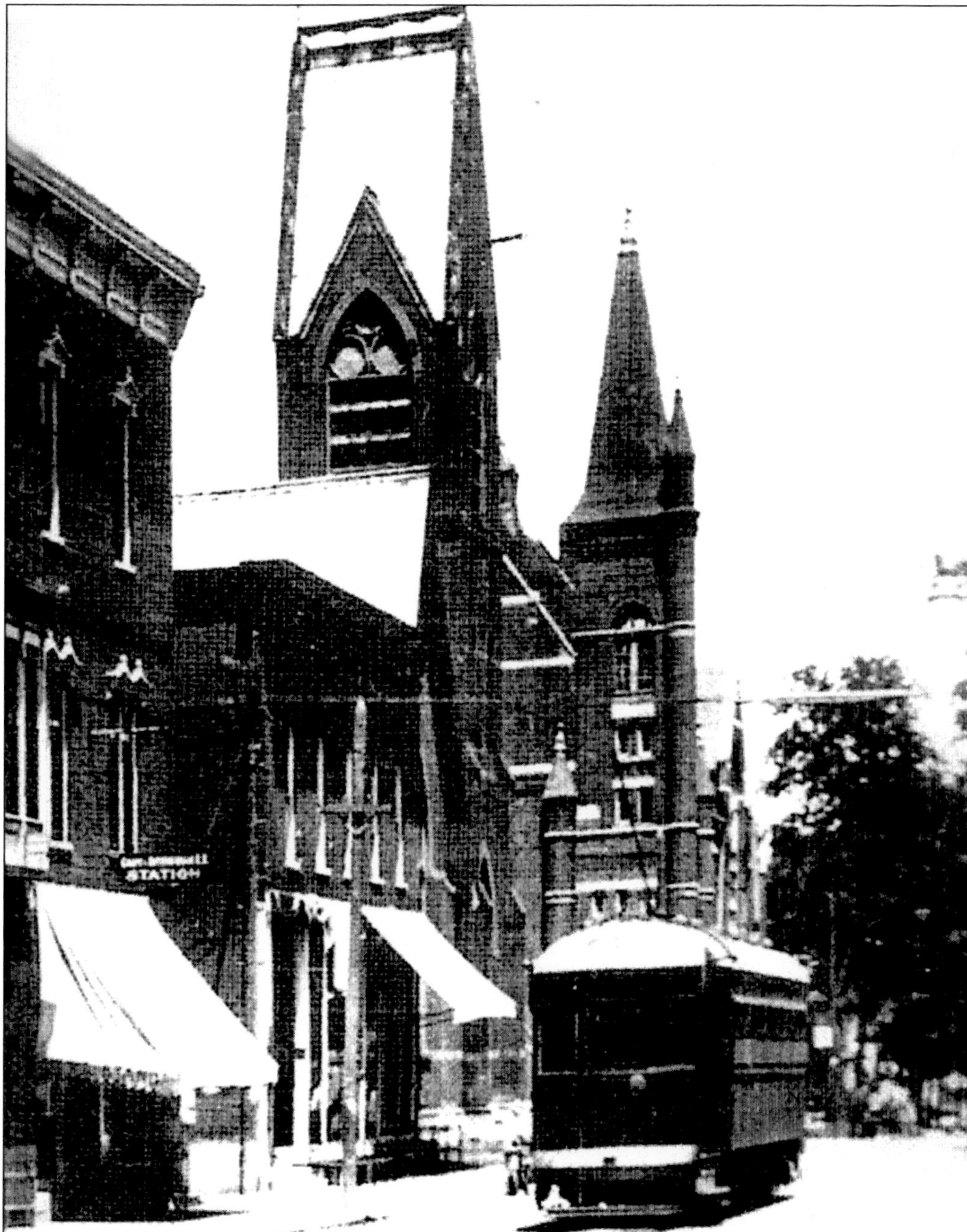

The interurban railroad tracks ended at Lincolnway on Franklin Street. The train backed down onto Jefferson Street (where the Valparaiso Public Library now stands) to turn around. Most of the track is reportedly still under Franklin Street. The cracks in the pavement in front of the Pioneer Apartments show where the tracks supposedly are still in place.

The canopy to the left in the above picture is the Gary and Valparaiso Interurban Railroad Station in Valparaiso. The station was on Franklin Street one half-block north of Lincolnway. (Photo courtesy of G. Bradley Publishing, Inc.)

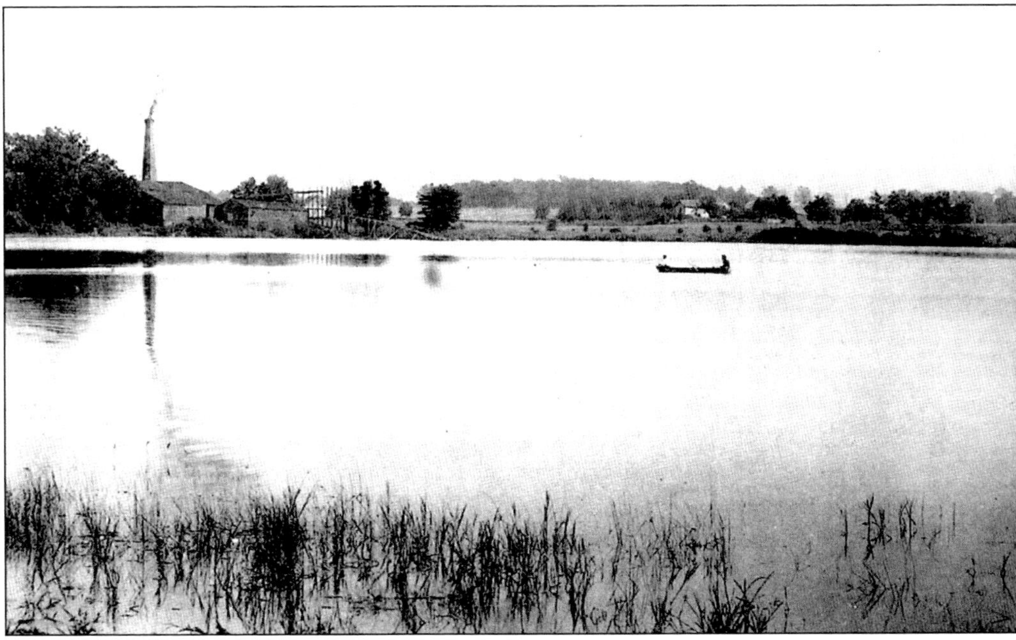

The above photograph is a view from Flint Lake showing the interurban tracks going past the water works. (Photo courtesy of L.G. Eggleston.)

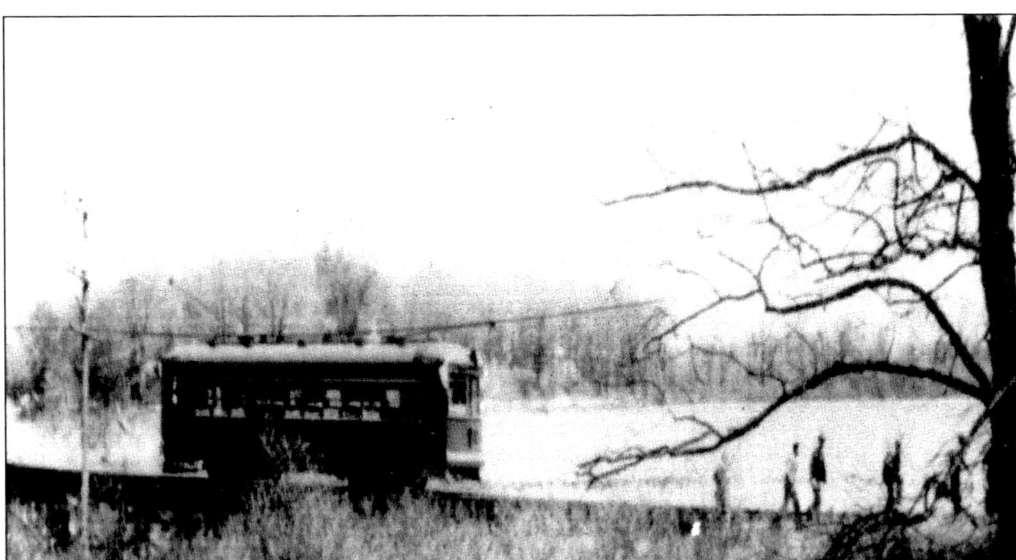

The interurban electric train passing the east side of Flint Lake near the town of Flintville and the water works is shown in the above photograph. (Photo courtesy of L.G. Eggleston.)

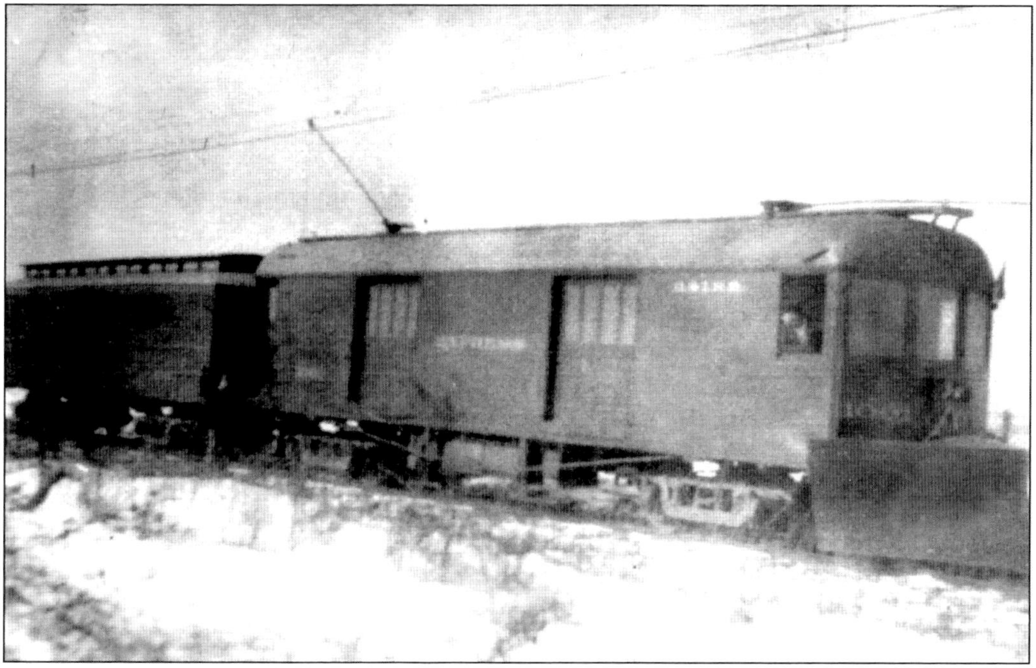

The interurban freight cars with snow plow are shown above. (Photo courtesy of Edwin Kuehl.)

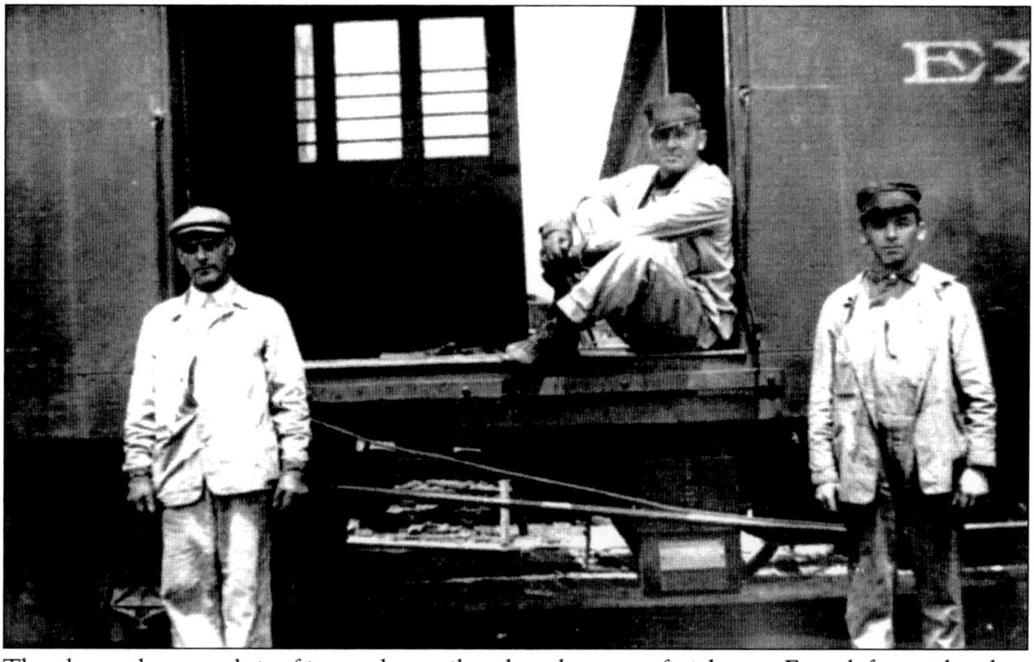

The above photograph is of interurban railroad workers on a freight car. From left to right, they are: Walter Mack, Ray Berlin, and William Belmont. (Photo courtesy of Edwin Kuehl.)

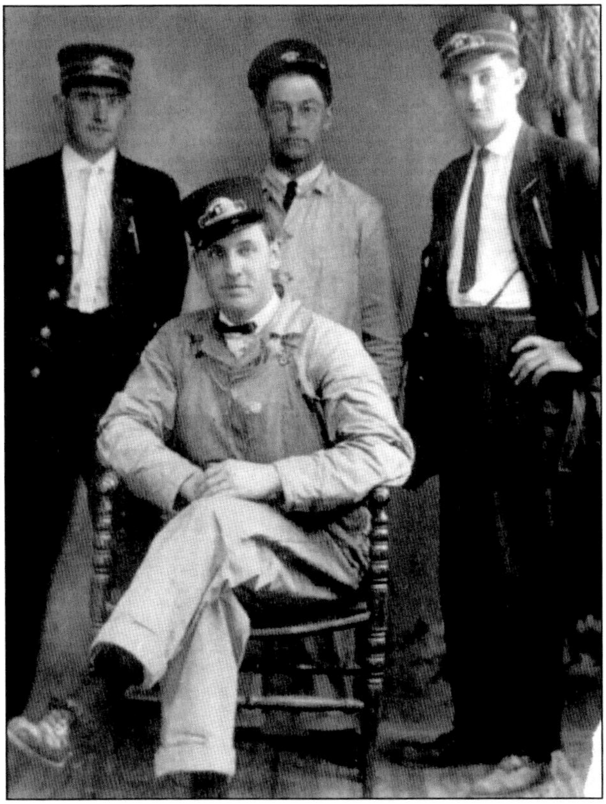

This photograph is of the crew of the interurban electric railroad. From left to right they are: William Belmont, Ray Berlin, Walter Mack and Ray Berlin Jr. (Photo courtesy of Edwin Kuehl.)

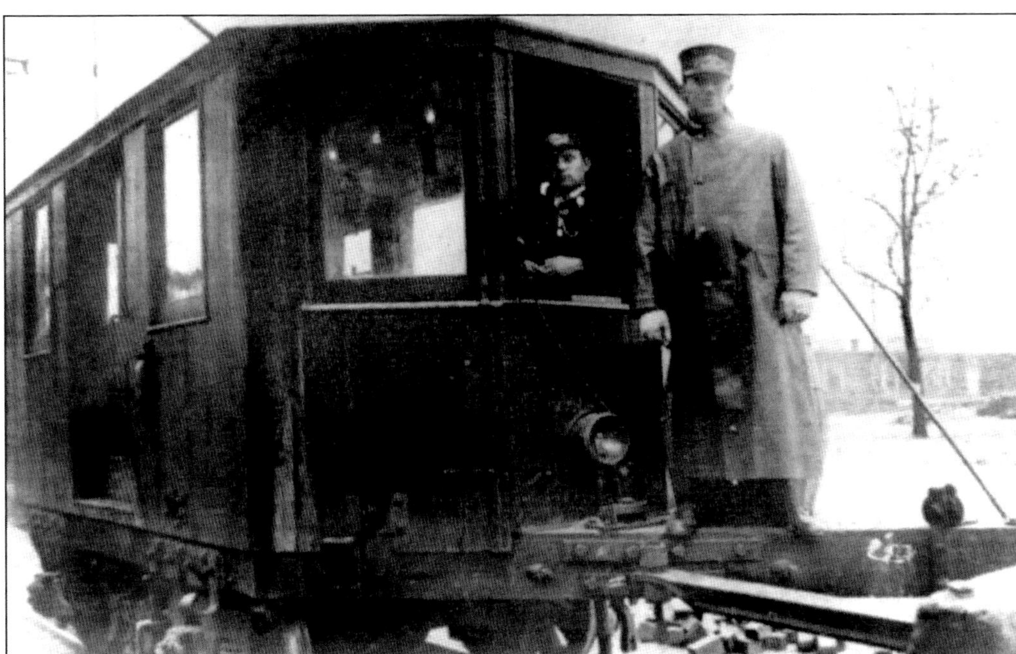

The interurban work engine is shown here. (Photo courtesy of Edwin Kuehl.)

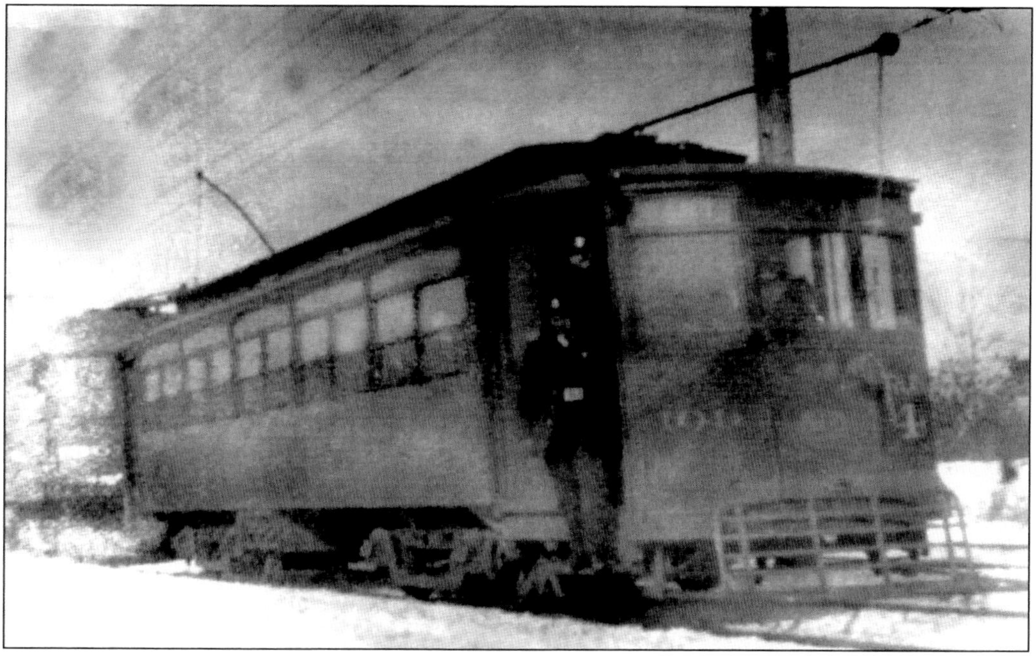

The interurban passenger car is shown here. This photo shows the electric lines and connector above the train car. (Photo courtesy of Edwin Kuehl.)

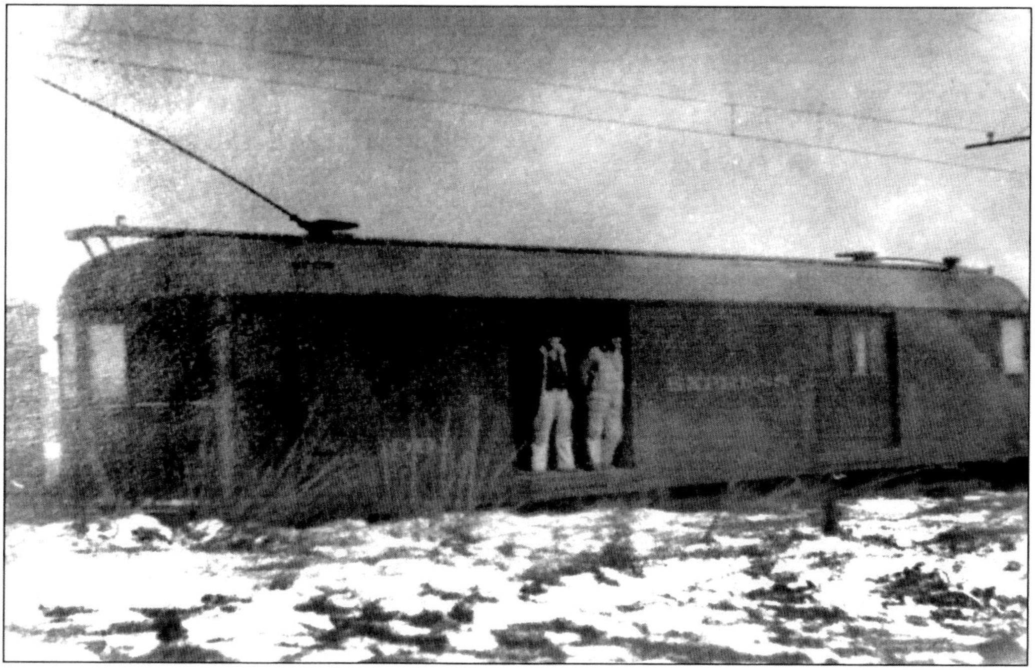

An interurban electric railroad freight car is shown here. (Photo courtesy Edwin Kuehl.)

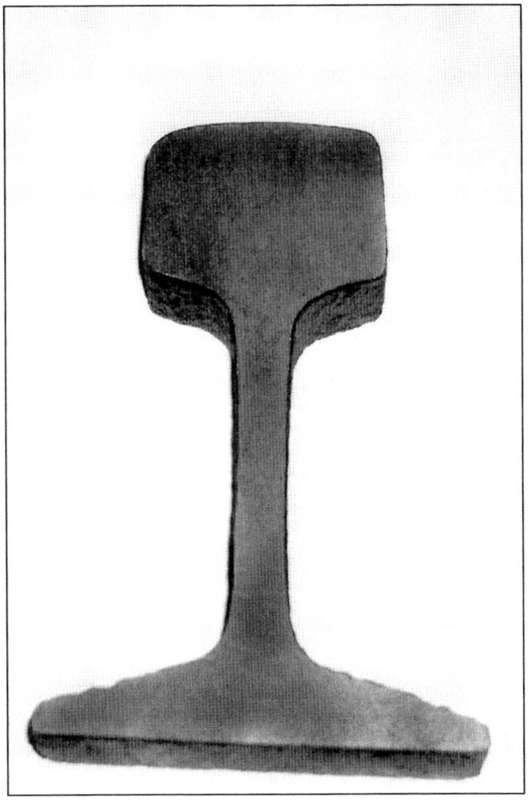

The photograph was made from an actual cross section of the track used on the Gary-Valparaiso Interurban Electric Railroad. The track was 4 inches wide at the bottom, $2^1/_4$ inches wide at the top and stood $4^1/_8$ inches high. (Photo by L.G. Eggleston.)

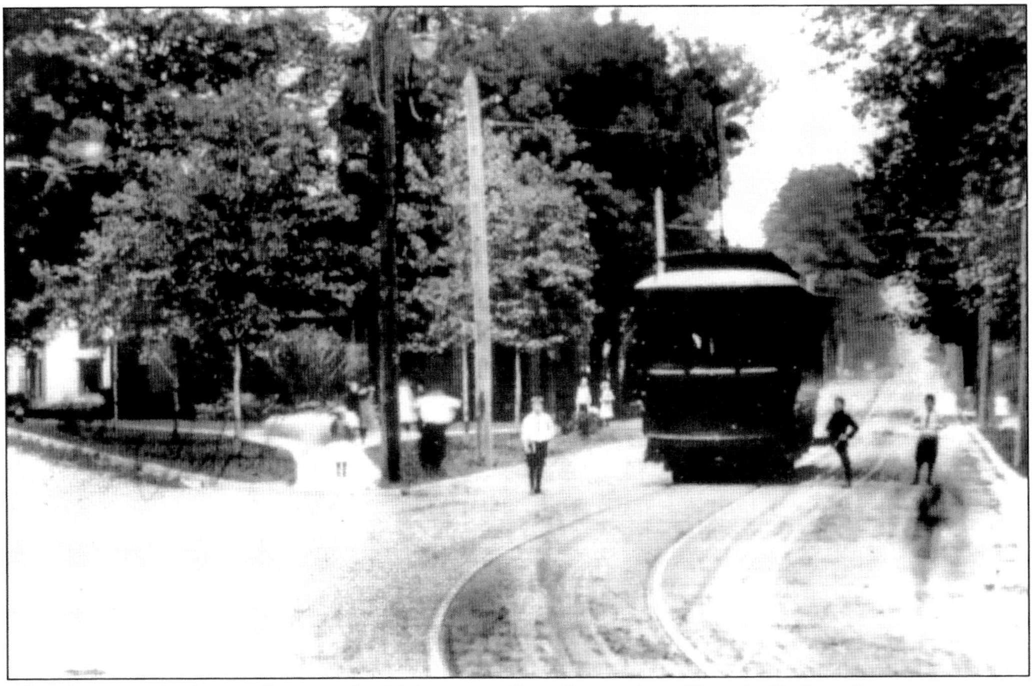

The photograph shown above is the Valparaiso-Gary Interurban Electric Railroad passenger car at the intersection of Franklin Street and Calumet in Valparaiso. (Photo courtesy of L.G. Eggleston.)

Six

Loomis Lake and Spectacle Lake

Loomis Lake/Spectacle Lake Spectacle Lake is located south of Grandview Street between Hillcrest Beach and Anderson Road. (600 N) The lake is a small but deep lake with a surface area of only 12 acres. The lake is on the west side of the watershed and is in the St. Lawrence Basin. Spectacle Lake was referred to by the early settlers as a "Kettle Lake" because of its depth.

In 1924, the Valparaiso Water Department, under the direction of Mr. Elbert Leslie Loomis, decided to increase the area's water supply. The water department determined that if a pipeline could be placed through the divide between Flint Lake and Spectacle Lake they could create a new man-made lake with the overflow from Spectacle. The pipeline was installed and a dam was constructed at the west end of Spectacle Lake. As the water filled Spectacle Lake it overflowed into the large lowland area which lies south of the east end of the lake. The overflow created a 55-acre man-made lake. This successful endeavor was a very interesting undertaking since it brought fresh water from Flint Lake, which lies in the Mississippi Basin, to Spectacle Lake, which lies in the St Lawrence Basin. The newly formed lake was named Loomis Lake in honor of Elbert Leslie Loomis. Three fishing and boating camps were set up on this new lake area by Mr. Hughart, Mr. Erickson, and Mr. Knapp. These camps offered rental boats for fishing or pleasure, and picnic areas for visitors.

The City of Valparaiso purchased 85 acres of land around Loomis Lake from Attorney and Mrs. James Chester on February 27, 1961. The city developed the area and on June 19, 1961 the park was opened to the public, even though it was not completely finished. The park was named Lakewood Park. As the development of the park continued, the city purchased another 37 acres, which increased the size of the park to 122 acres as it, is today.

The park offers hiking, exercise trails, boating, paddlewheel rentals, fishing, a disc golf course, skateboarding, picnicking, swimming, and discover day camps. The Valparaiso Park Board conducts year round activities at Lakewood Park.

The park was later dedicated to Harold L. Rogers and became Harold L. Rogers-Lakewood Park. Harold L. Rogers was the first director of the Valparaiso Parks and Recreation Department. He had also been the band director at Valparaiso High School for a number of years.

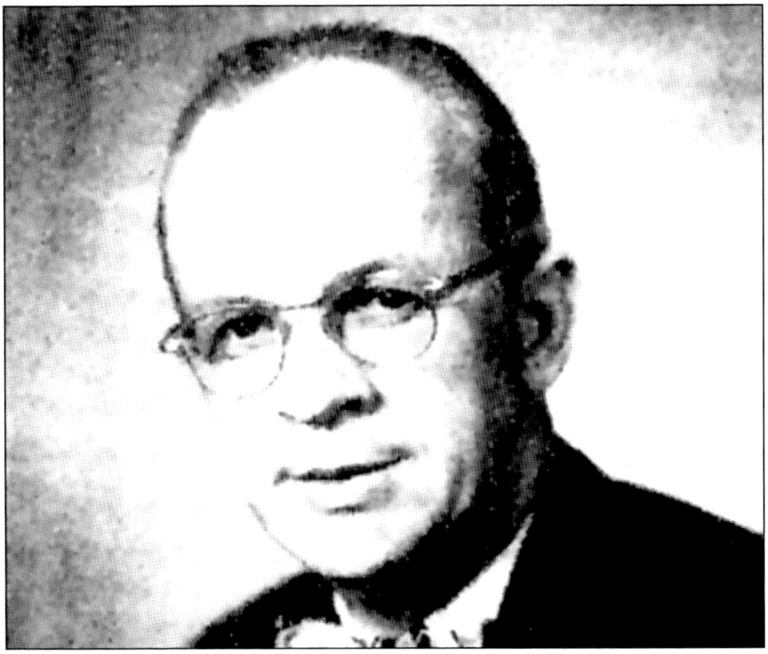

The photograph to the left is of Harold L. Rogers who was the first director of the Valparaiso Parks and Recreation Department. The Harold L. Rogers-Lakewood Park on Loomis Lake was named in his honor. (Photo scanned from the Valparaiso High School 1953 Valenian.)

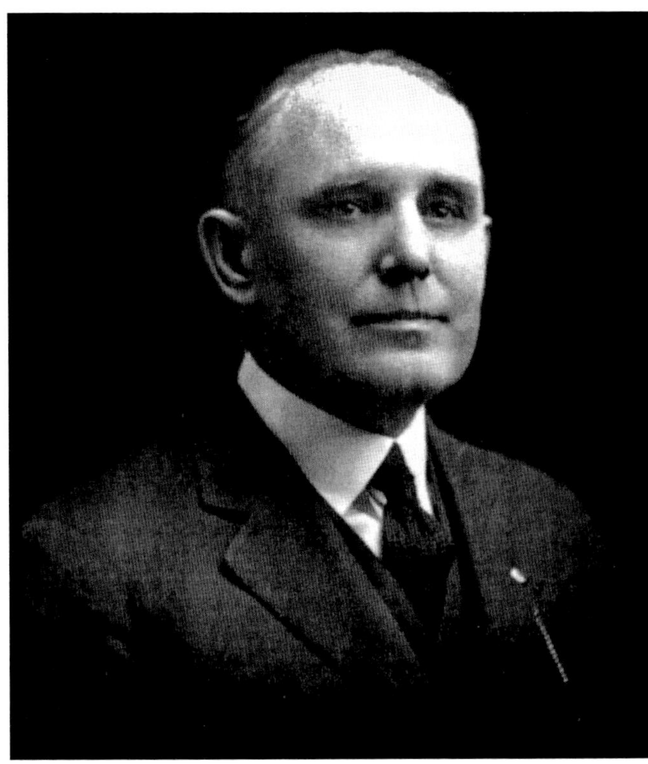

The photograph to the right is of Elbert Leslie Loomis who was head of the Valparaiso Water Department in 1924 when Loomis Lake was created. The new lake was named in his honor. (Photo courtesy of the Valparaiso Water Department.)

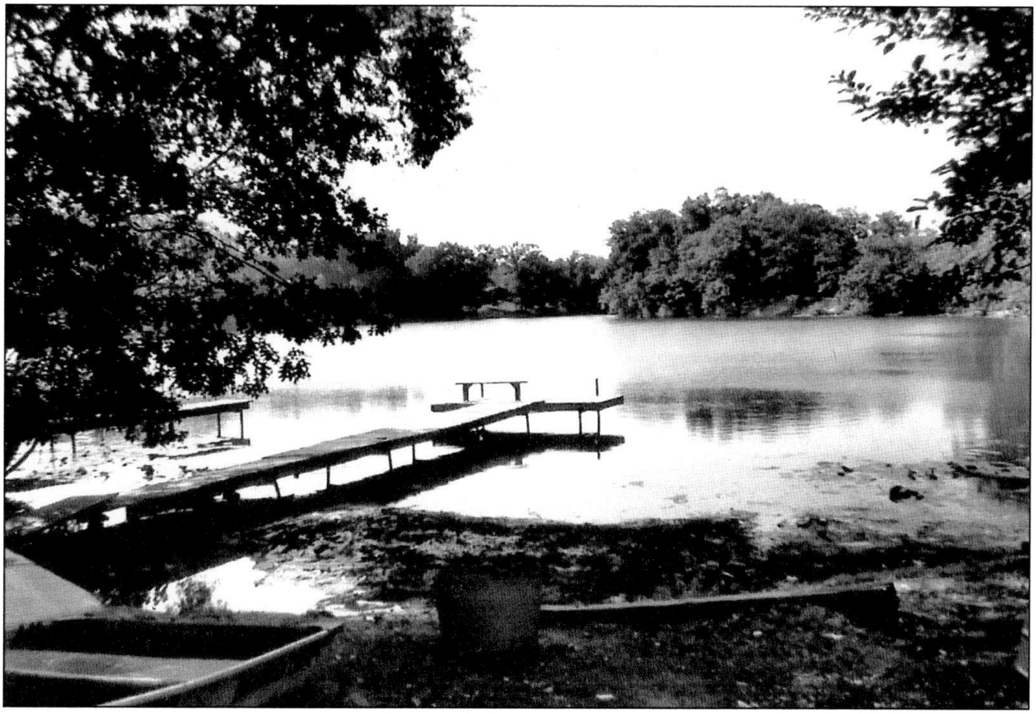

The above photograph is a view of Spectacle Lake from the dam on the west side of the lake. There is currently a boat rental business on this site. (Photo by L.G. Eggleston).

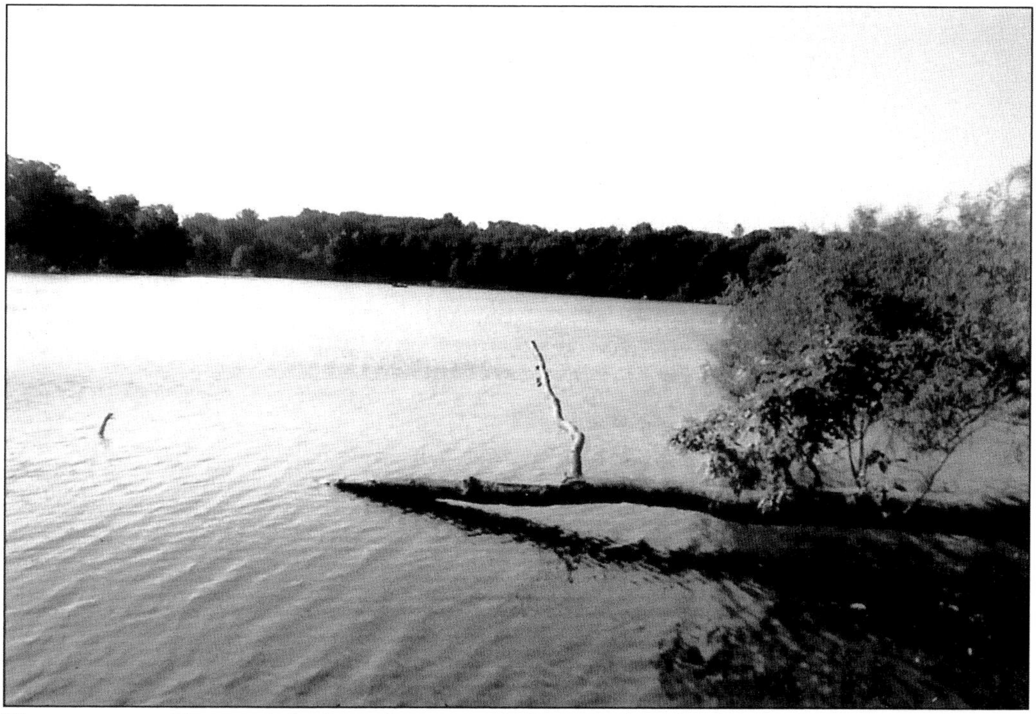

This is a view of Loomis Lake from the east end of Spectacle Lake. (Photo by of L.G. Eggleston.)

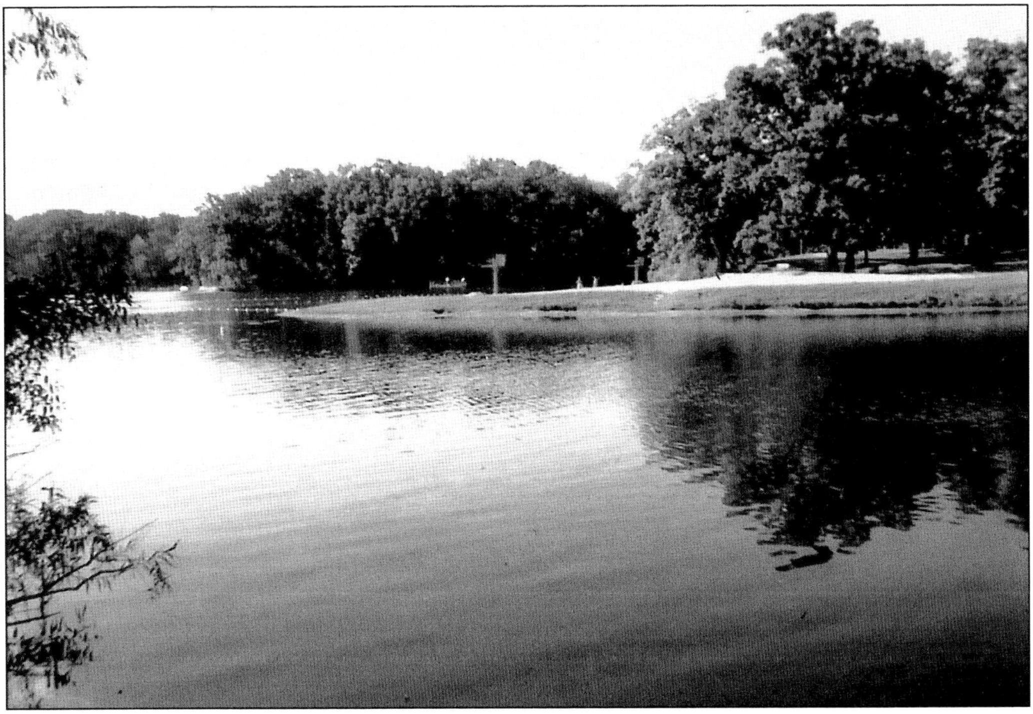

Shown here is a view of the swimming area at Lakewood Park looking across Loomis Lake. During the summer months the water in the lake is checked several times each week to ensure that the lake is safe for swimming. (Photo by L.G. Eggleston.)

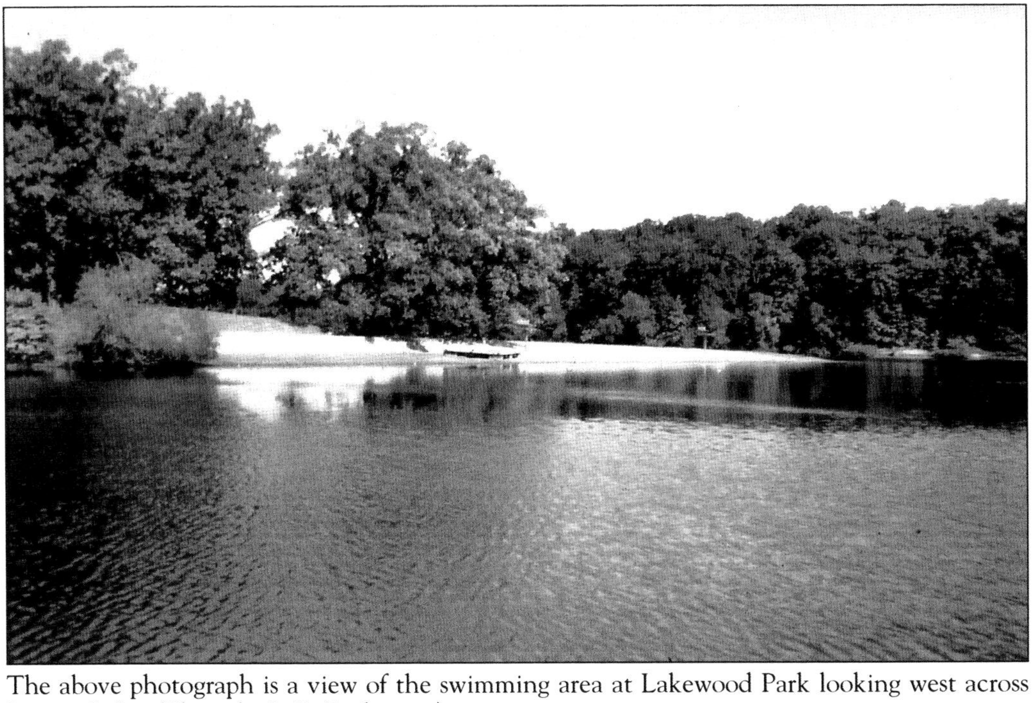

The above photograph is a view of the swimming area at Lakewood Park looking west across Loomis Lake. (Photo by L.G. Eggleston.)

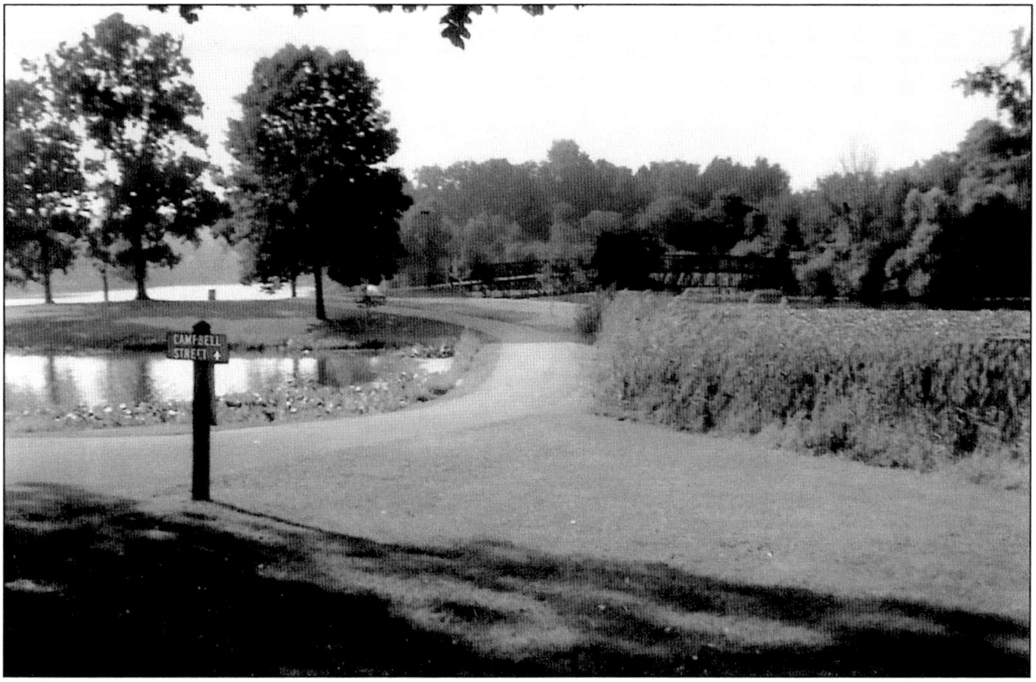

A small island is located at the west side of Loomis Lake. As shown above, it is accessible by the hiking trail seen here and a metal bridge on the other side. (Photo by L.G. Eggleston.)

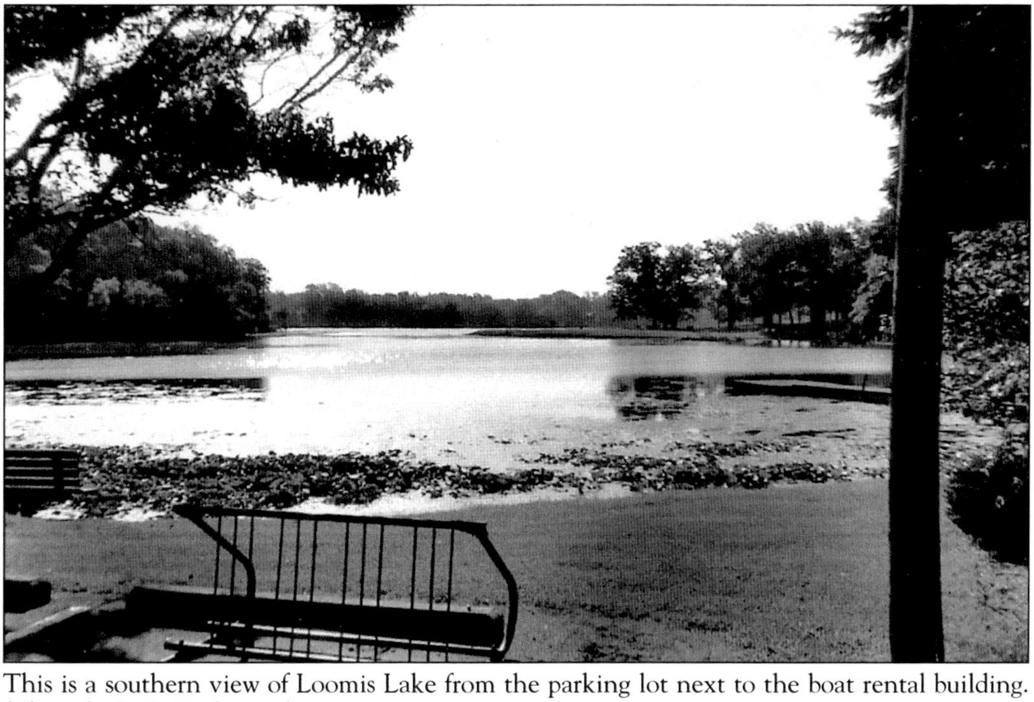

This is a southern view of Loomis Lake from the parking lot next to the boat rental building. (Photo by L.G. Eggleston.)

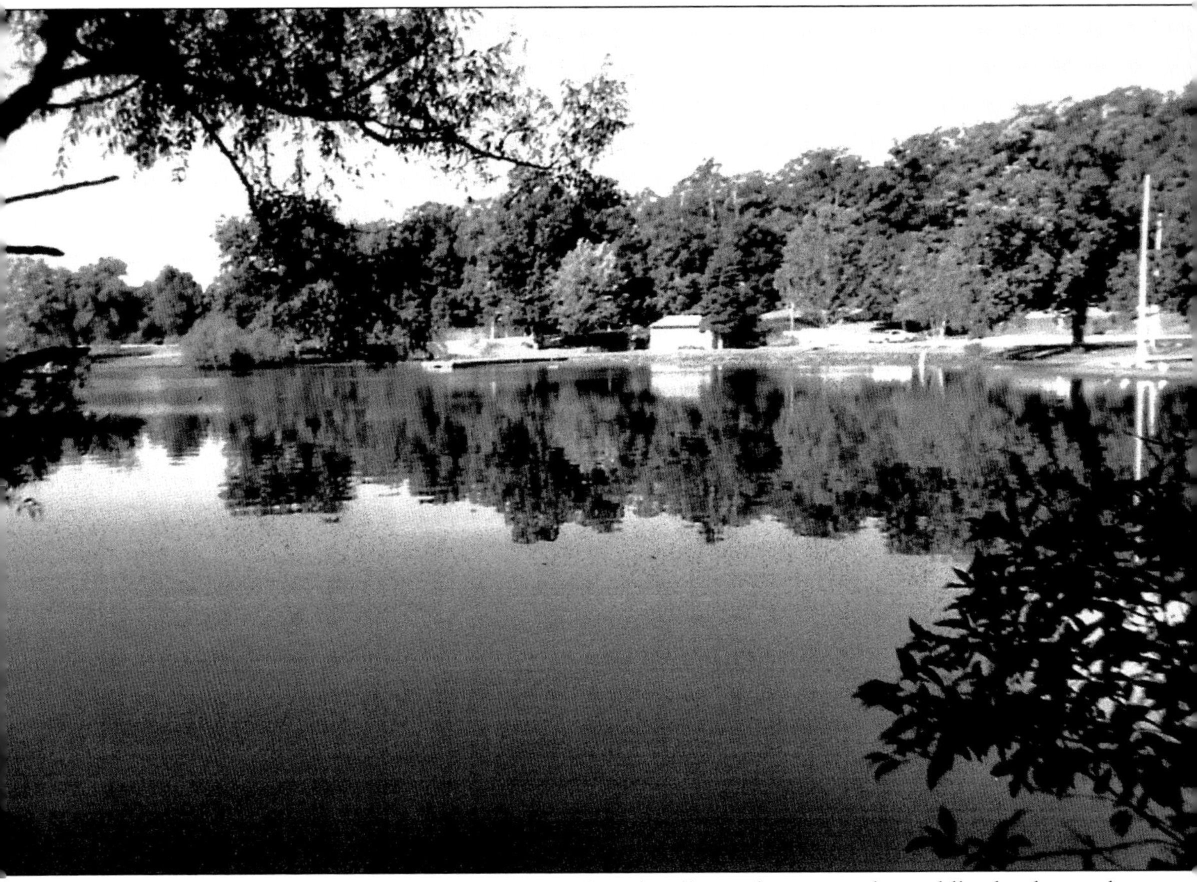

The above view is of the area at Lakewood Park offering boat rentals, paddlewheel rentals, fishing, and a store for supplies. (Photo by L.G. Eggleston.)

When the park originally opened in 1961 the area north of the park entrance was opened for camping. The park was a very popular destination for weekend campers and summer vacationers.

Camping was halted at the park because of the damage to the natural beauty of the park caused by its use as a primitive campground, and the growing need for recreation space for the many organizations, private clubs, and summer activities.

Seven

Lake Michigan Beaches and Resorts

The idea of creating a sand dunes national park was first introduced in 1916 by Senator Thomas Taggart of Indiana who sponsored a resolution in the U.S. Senate. The idea had support from many influential people. This park, if approved, would have been the first national park created from private lands.

Although it was a popular idea it was overshadowed by World War I, which changed national priorities. The idea was revived in 1923 when the Indiana Legislature passed a bill allowing revenue from taxes to be used to purchase the land for a state park.

The collection of tax revenue and funds from private donors allowed the state to purchase 2,182 acres of land on Lake Michigan and the Indiana Dunes State Park was created. The Indiana Dunes State Park opened in 1926 and was an immediate success.

The natural beauty of the Indiana shoreline of Lake Michigan was thus preserved for future generations to enjoy.

Over the next few years the new park was equipped with a huge bathhouse and pavilion, a two-story hotel on the beach, camping areas, picnic areas, hiking trails, a summer home for the Indiana Governor, and a beautiful swimming beach.

Although the hotel and restroom complex has since been torn down, the park has added parking areas, doubled the size of the beach area by the pavilion, added a nature center, added a large campground for RVs as well as tents, and constructed several picnic shelters. The popularity of the Indiana Dunes State Park has continued to grow over the years.

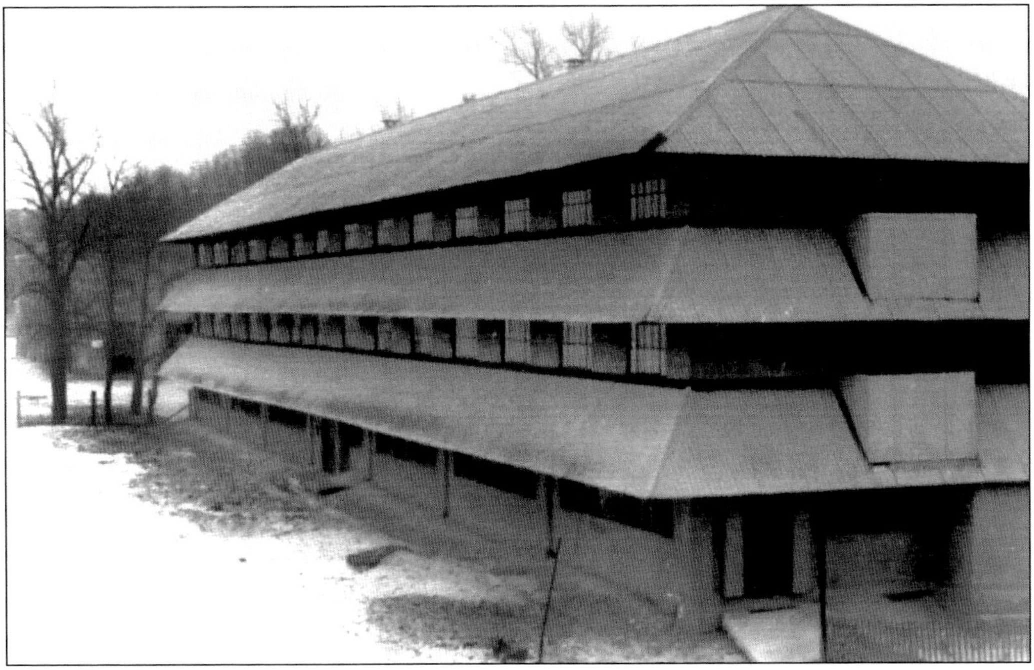

The above resort hotel was constructed in 1930 out of concrete. The hotel was built on the beach west of the pavilion. The cost of staying in the hotel was $5.85 per day, which included three meals. The hotel was torn down in 1972. (Photo courtesy of Edwin Kuehl.)

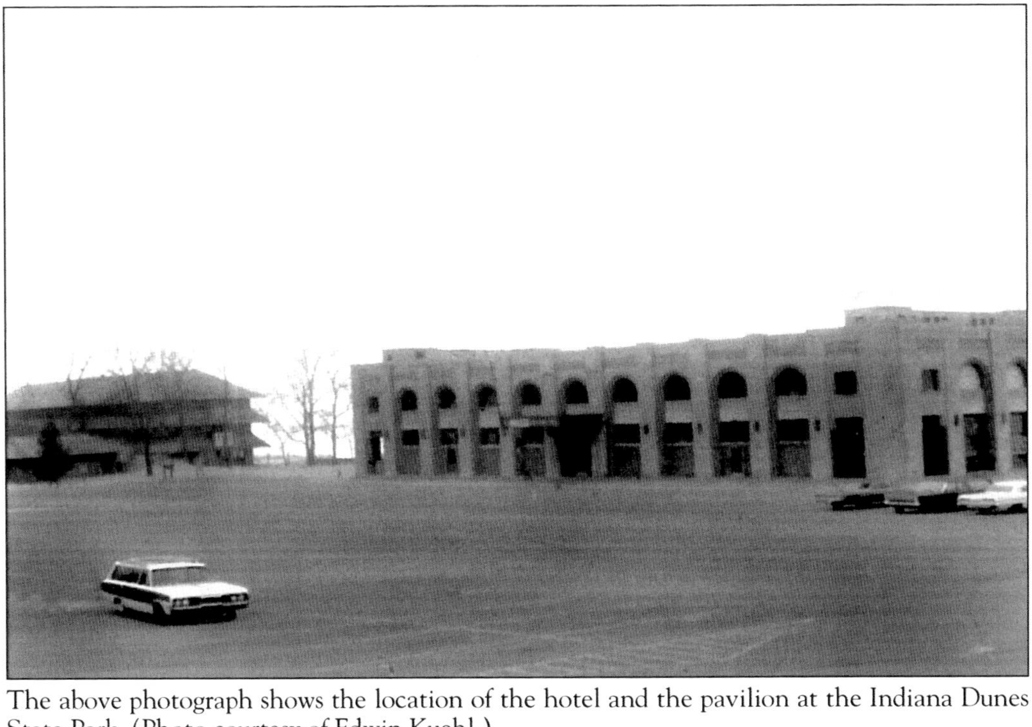

The above photograph shows the location of the hotel and the pavilion at the Indiana Dunes State Park. (Photo courtesy of Edwin Kuehl.)

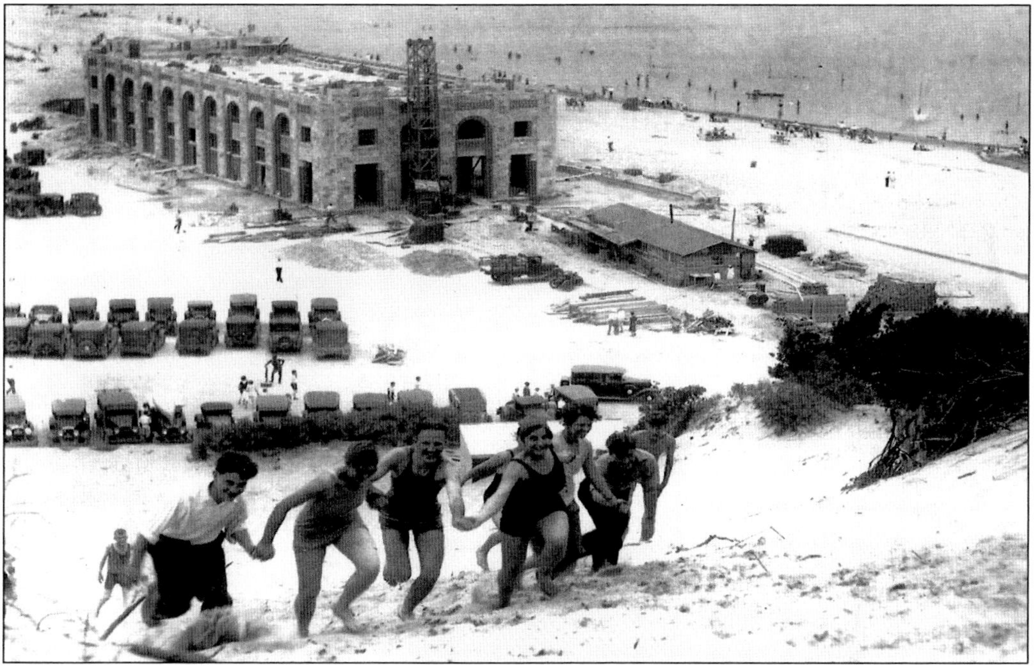

The above photograph shows the pavilion at the Indiana Dunes State Park under construction in 1930. The house to the right of the pavilion was a summerhouse, which was being constructed for use by Indiana Governors. (Photo courtesy of the Indiana State Library.)

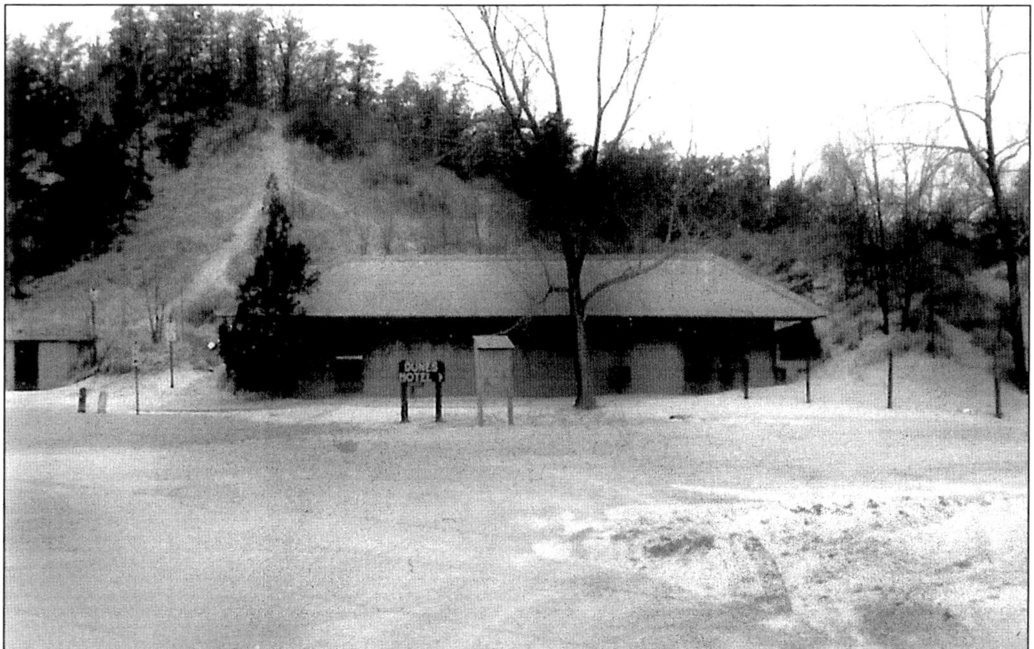

The above photograph is of the public restrooms, which were built in 1930 on the west side of the pavilion parking lot. (Photo courtesy of L.G. Eggleston.)

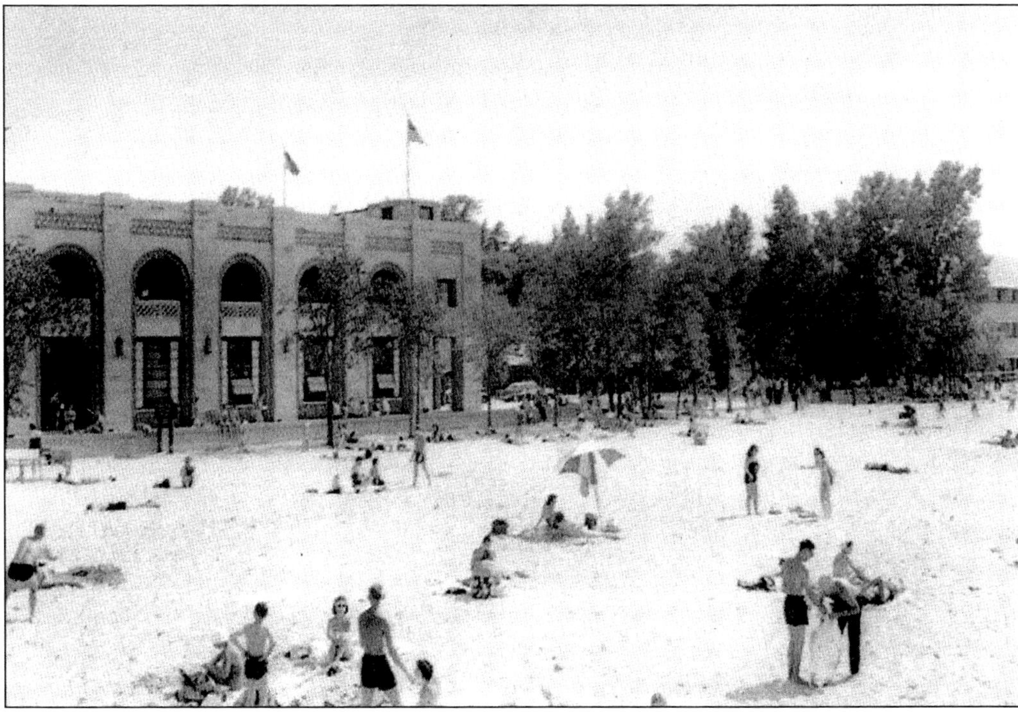

The above area is the beach in front of the pavilion and the hotel. (Photo courtesy of L.G. Eggleston.)

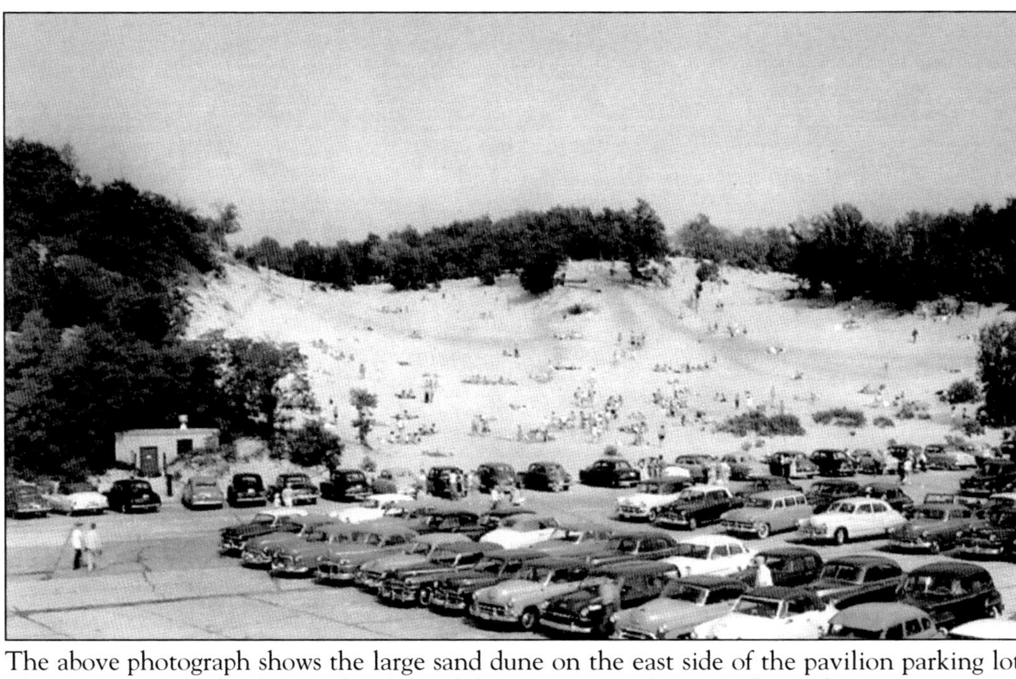

The above photograph shows the large sand dune on the east side of the pavilion parking lot. The dune was called "The Devil's Slide." (Photo courtesy of L.G. Eggleston.)

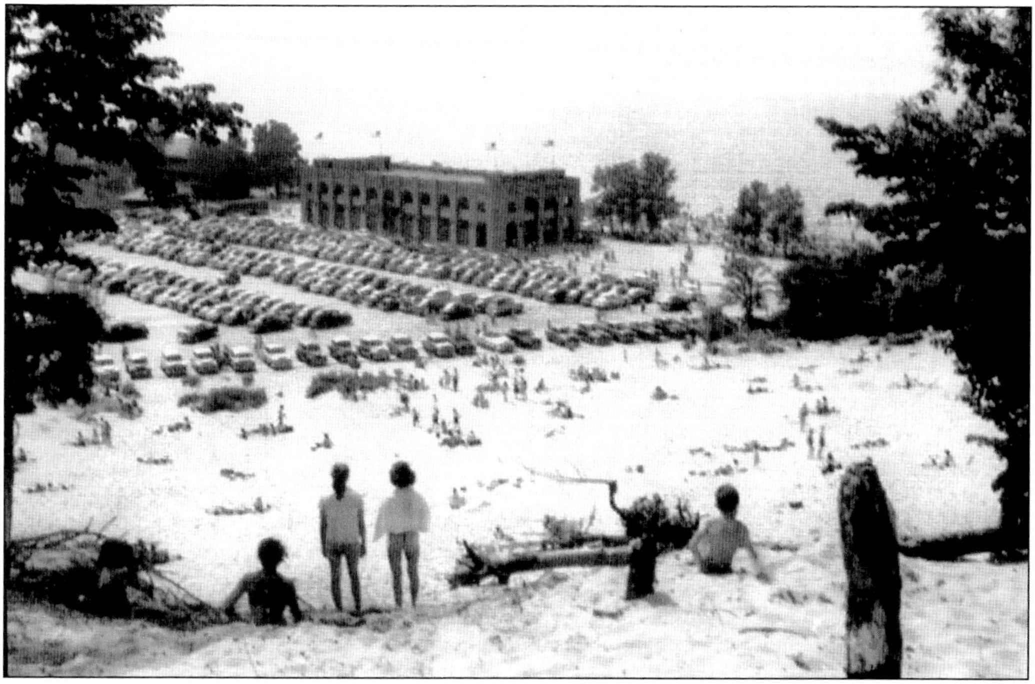

This photograph shows a view of the pavilion parking lot from the top of "Devil's Slide." (Photo courtesy of L.G. Eggleston.)

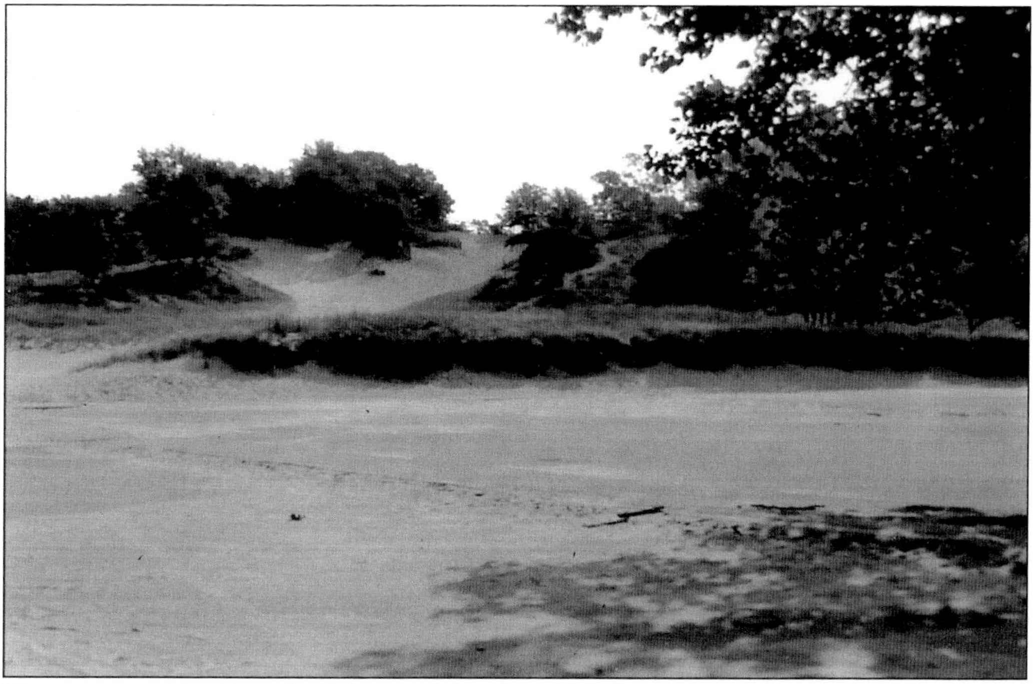

The remains of the "Devil's Slide" sand dune, as it appears today are shown above. (Photo by L.G. Eggleston.)

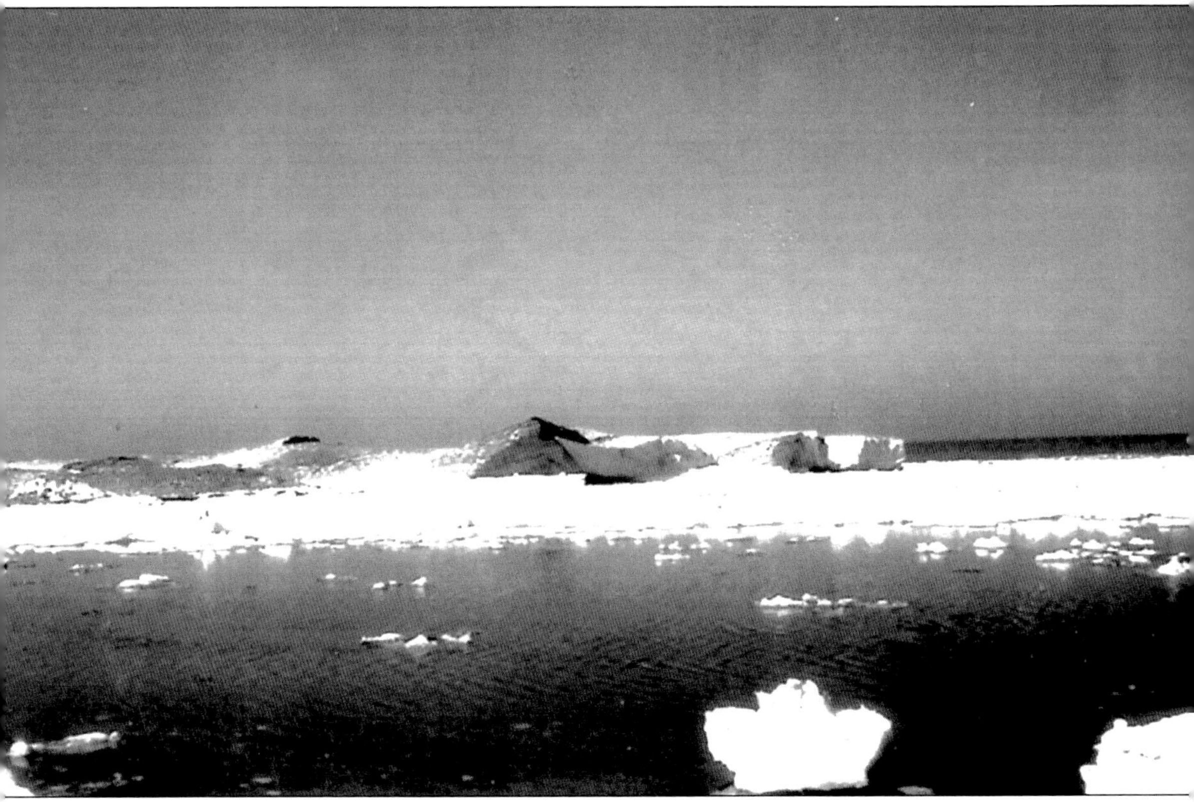

Small icebergs, which form along the shoreline of the Dunes State Park, are pictured here. They measure 10-30 feet high during severe weather. (Photo by L.G. Eggleston.)

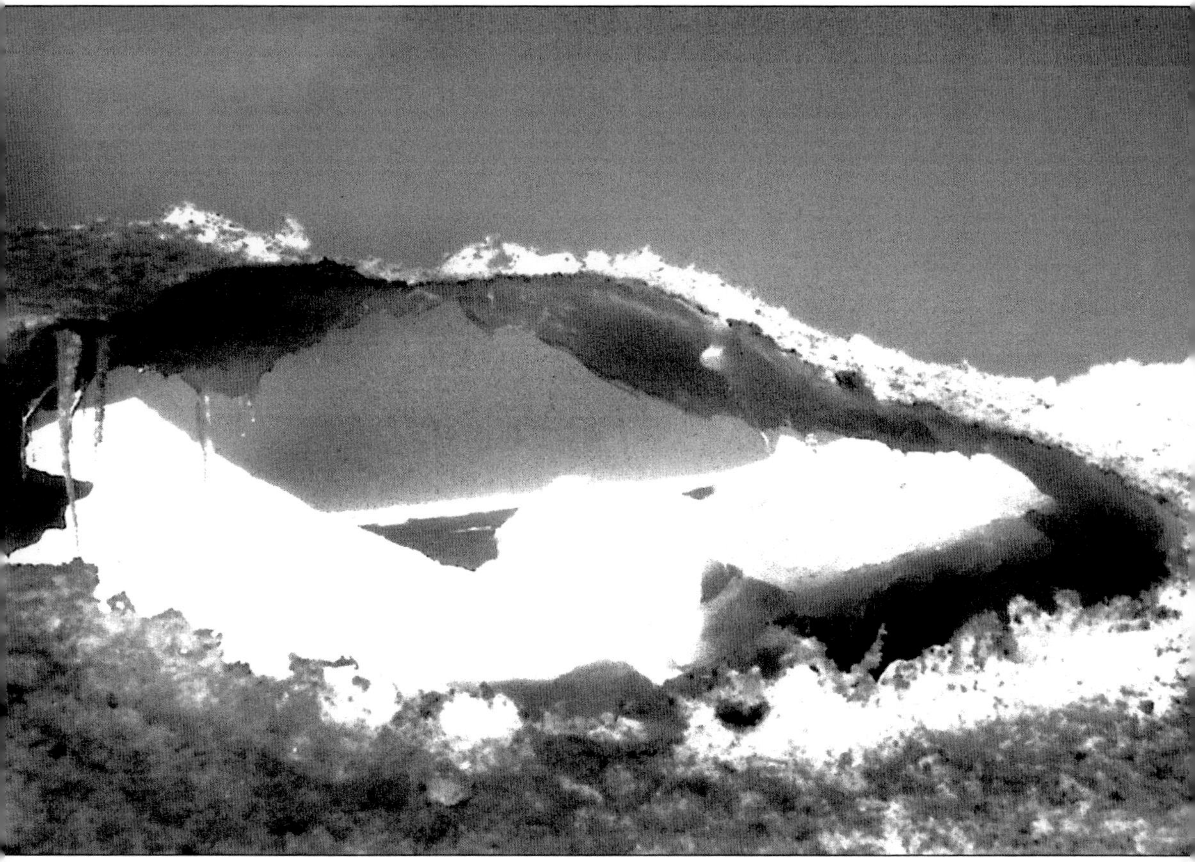

The icebergs shown above, which form on Lake Michigan, melt from the inside in the spring. The coating of blown sand helps the shell of the berg last longer. (Photo by L.G. Eggleston.)

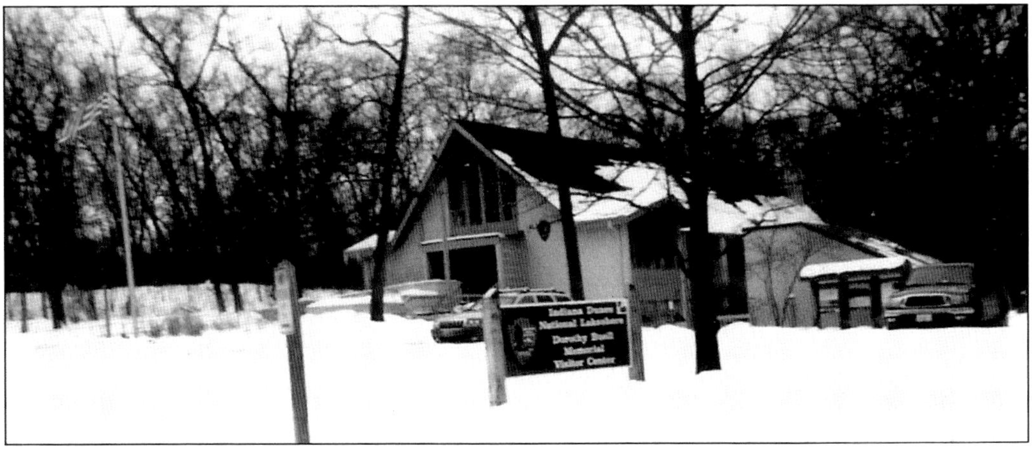

The Dorothy Buell Memorial Visitor's Center of the Indiana Dunes National Lakeshore is shown above. The center is located on the south west corner of Kemil Road and U.S. Highway 12. (Photo by L.G. Eggleston.)

THE INDIANA DUNES NATIONAL LAKESHORE Even though the State of Indiana bought the land on Lake Michigan which was originally wanted for a National Lakeshore, the idea of a National Park did not die. The "Save the Dunes Council" was formed in 1952. The council approached Senator Paul H. Douglas of Illinois for help. Senator Douglas agreed to sponsor legislation for the National Lakeshore Park. In 1966, after many bills had been introduced by Senator Douglas and defeated, the park bill was finally approved and the Indiana Dunes National Lakeshore was created. The size of the park is 15,000 acres, which includes the 2,182 acres of the Indiana Dunes State Park.

Most of the Lake Michigan shoreline in Porter County is part of the National Lakeshore Park. There are six swimming beaches in the park other than the State Park beach. These beaches are West Beach near Ogden Dunes, Porter Beach which is also called Johnson's Beach, Kemil Beach east of the Dunes State Park, Dunbar Beach east of Kemil Beach, Lakeview Beach at Beverly Shores, and Central Beach east of Beverly Shores.

The Bailly Homestead and the Chellburg Farm are also part of the National Lakeshore Park. The Indiana Dunes Environmental Center is located near the Bailly Homestead and offers environmental education programs to allow students to become aware of ecology and the environmental sciences. The center is dedicated to Senator Paul H. Douglas.

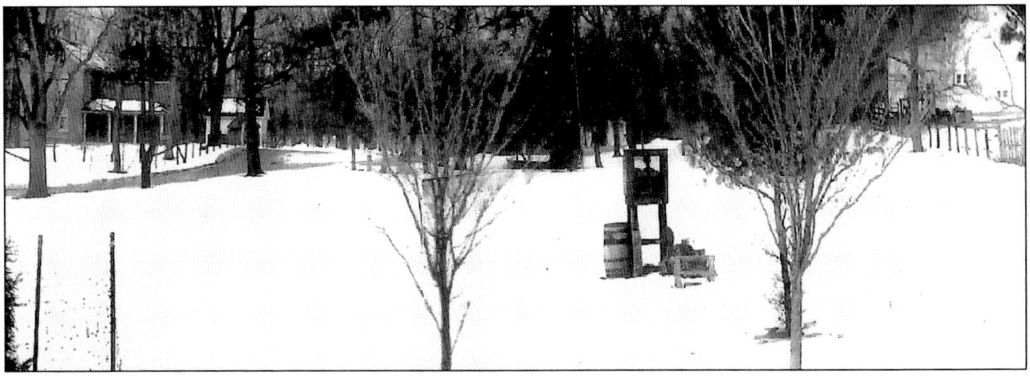

The Chellburg Farm shown here is adjacent to the Bailly Homestead and hosts year round activities such as the Maple Sugartime Festival in March and the Duneland Harvest Festival in September. (Photo by L.G. Eggleston.)

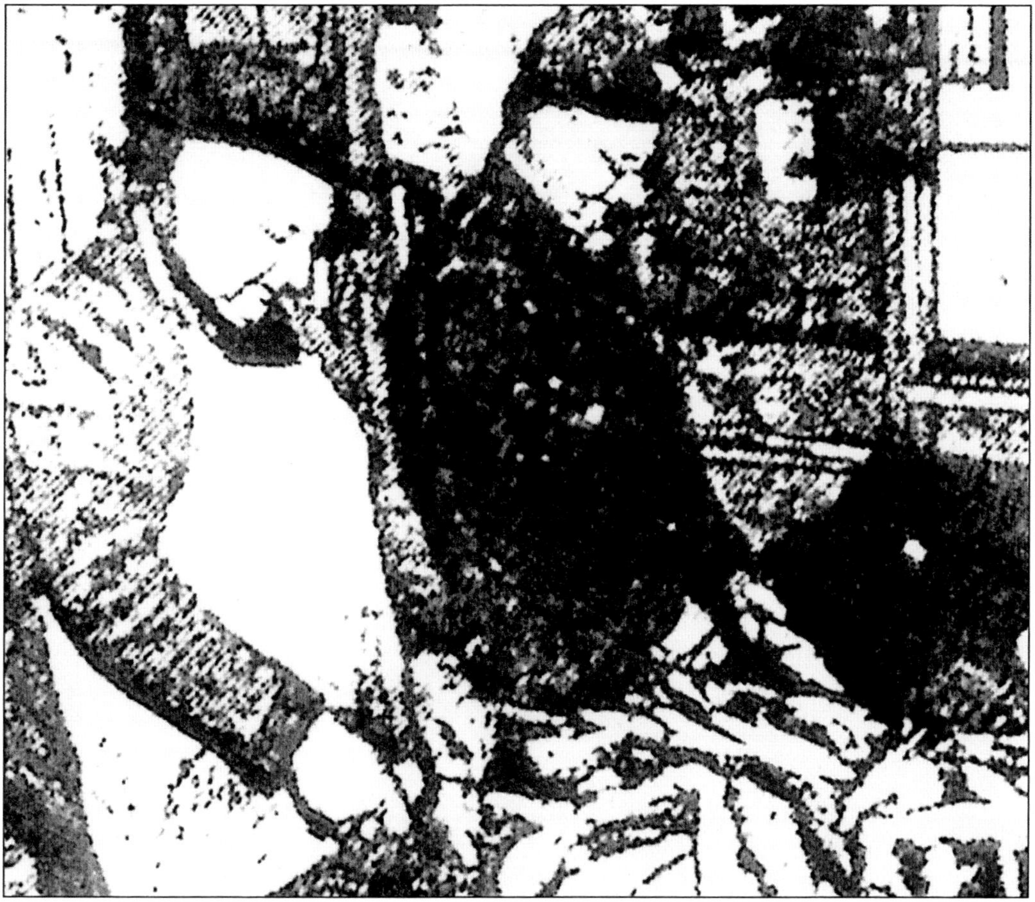

The image above shows Bill and Elmer Johnson hard at work cleaning the morning catch of fish for shipment to Chicago. (Photo courtesy of Eva Hopkins.)

Johnson's Beach On the west side of the Indiana Dunes State Park is an area commonly referred to as Johnson's Beach. The area was originally named Waverly Beach. When the Johnson's Beach lakeshore became part of the Indiana Dunes National Park, the name of the beach was changed to Porter Beach.

Development of this beautiful beach area began in the early 1900s by a fisherman named John Johnson who, with his two sons Bill and Elmer, fished the water's of Lake Michigan. Lake Michigan at that time was teeming with sturgeon, whitefish, peach, and herring.

The abundance of fish allowed them to process and ship many barrels of fish to Chicago each day. The processing of the daily catch was done in a building they referred to as the fish shack. The remains of this building are still standing today. John Johnson was called "Fish Johnson" by the people of the area.

The business interests of the Johnson family changed in 1906 when the South Shore Electric Railroad completed its line to Tremont. With a stop at Waverly Road, visitors could now walk the distance from the South Shore stop to the beach. Because of this new access to Johnson's Beach and the increase in visitors, the Johnson Family decided to build an inn on the beach. Violet and Ida, the wives of Elmer and Bill, applied their cooking skills and the new inn soon became noted for its delicious fish and chicken dinners.

In 1926, when the Indiana Dunes State Park came into being, the Johnson brothers bought the lakeshore land where the inn stands today.

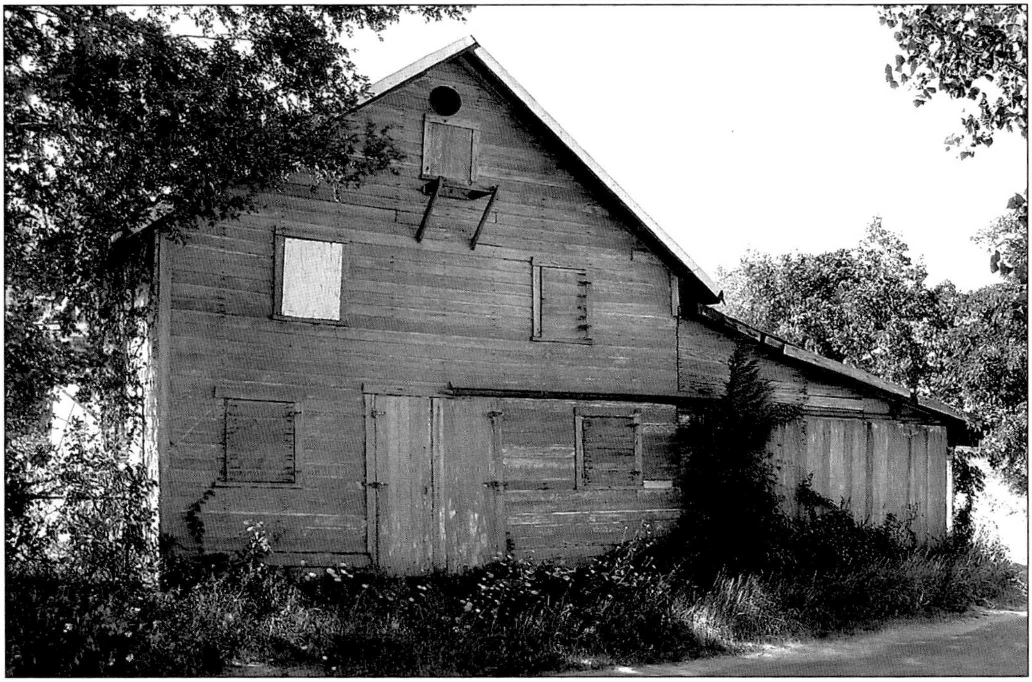

The above photograph is of the original fish shack used by John "Fish" Johnson and his sons to process their catch. (Photo courtesy of Dan Bruhn.)

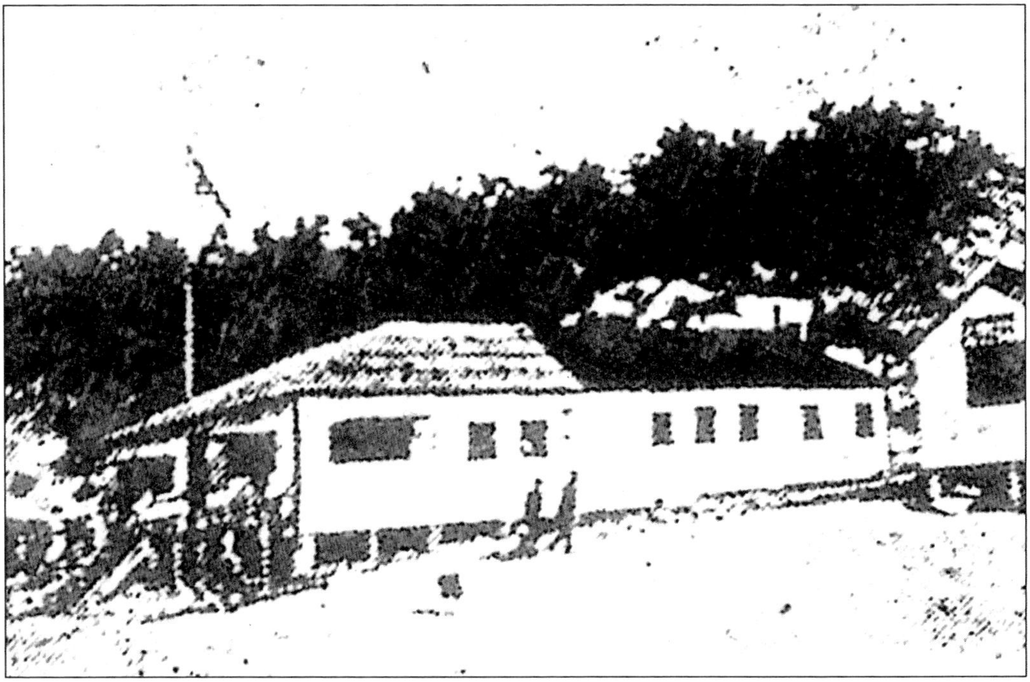

The above photograph is of the original Johnson's Restaurant which specialized in fish and chicken. The restaurant was constructed in 1906. (Photo courtesy of Eva Hopkins.)

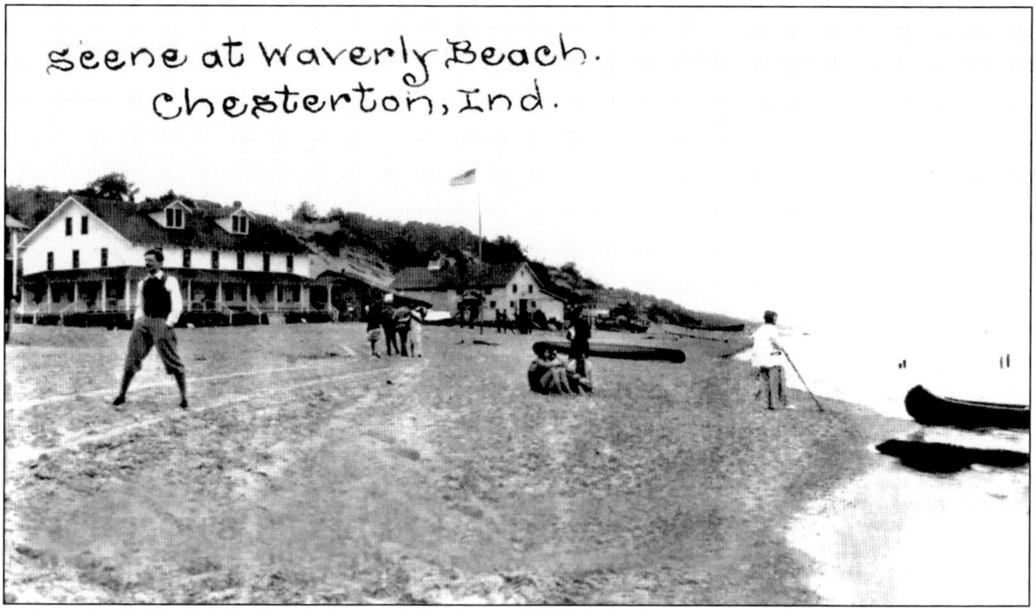

The above photograph shows Johnson's Inn and the fish house from the beach. (Photo courtesy of Dan Bruhn.)

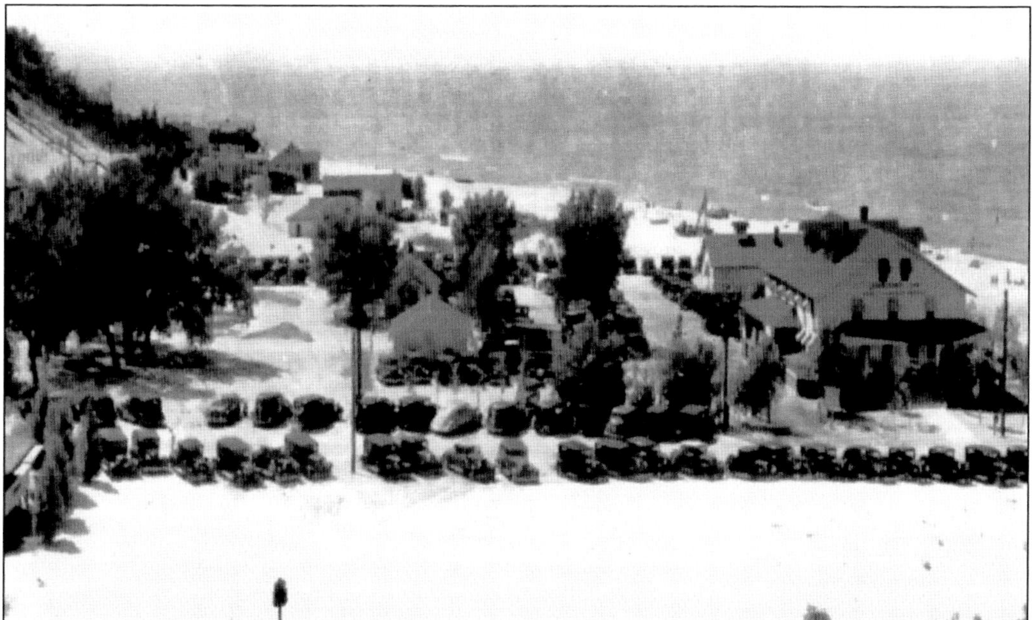
The above view shows the new Johnson's Inn which was constructed in 1930. (Photo courtesy of Eva Hopkins.)

The Johnson brothers contracted with Algot Pearson in 1930 to build a new inn on the newly acquired land. The Inn is still standing today. The new resort area became very popular and attracted people from the entire Calumet Region. The *Vidette Messenger* ran an article on July 7, 1949 titled "Over 1,000 cars at Johnson's Beach."

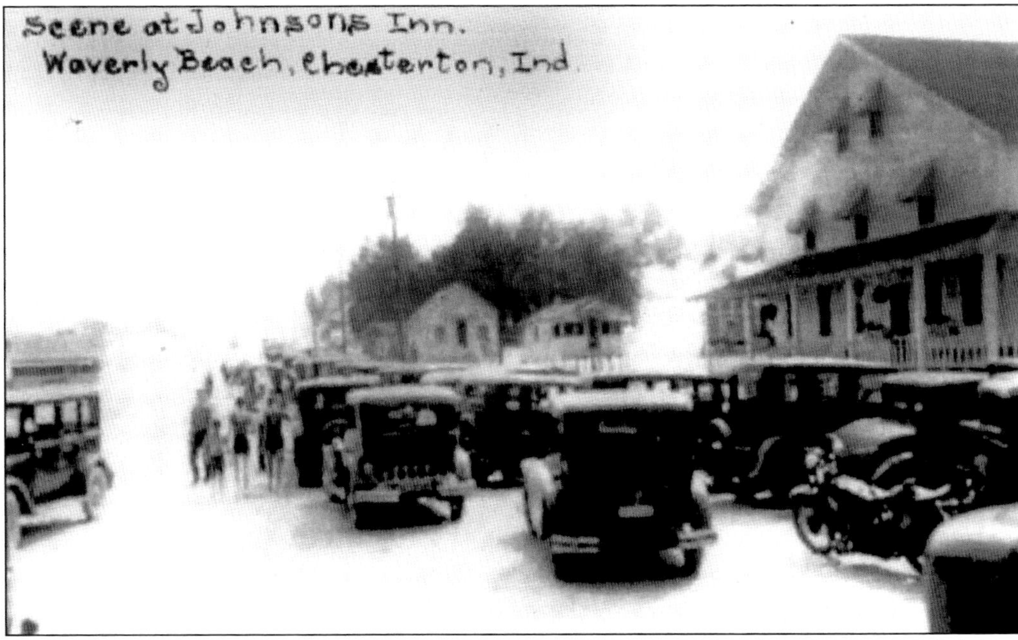

The above scene shows the new Johnson's Hotel and Restaurant shortly after it opened. (Photo courtesy of Eva Hopkins.)

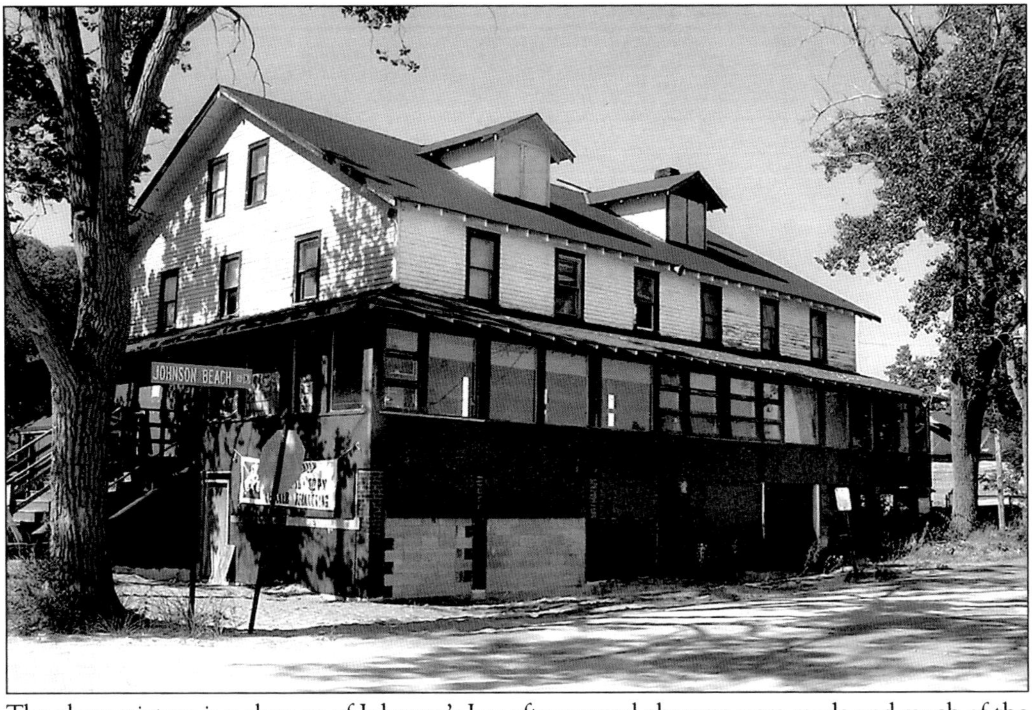

The above picture is a close up of Johnson's Inn after several changes were made and much of the sand that was in front of the inn seems to have been moved. (Photo courtesy of Dan Bruhn.)

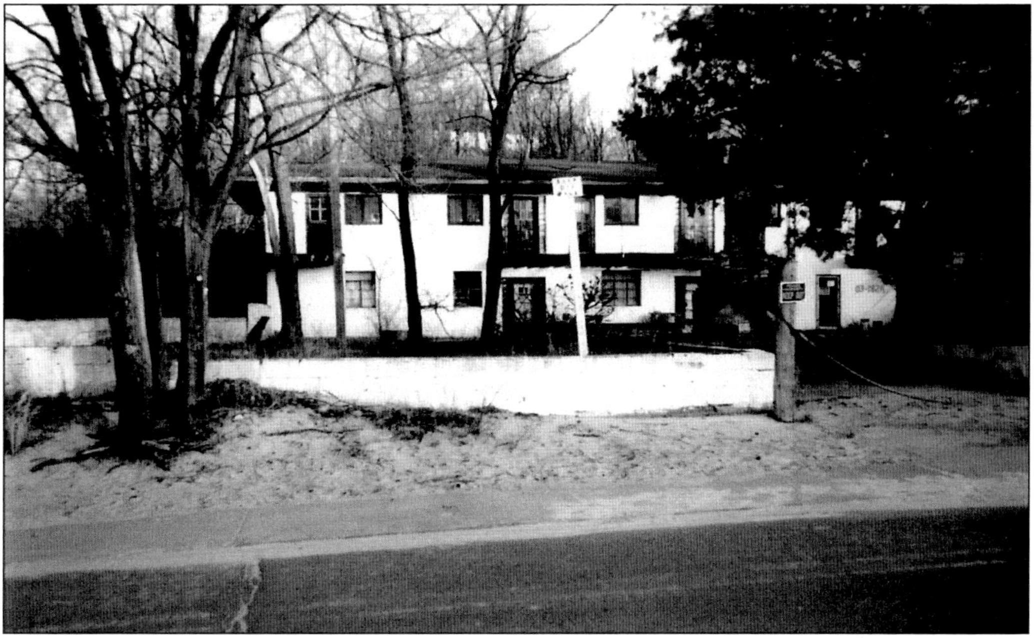

The Wilson's Inn was located on the east side of Waverly Road across from Johnson's Inn. This photograph shows the remains of the once popular Wilson's Inn. (Photo by L.G. Eggleston.)

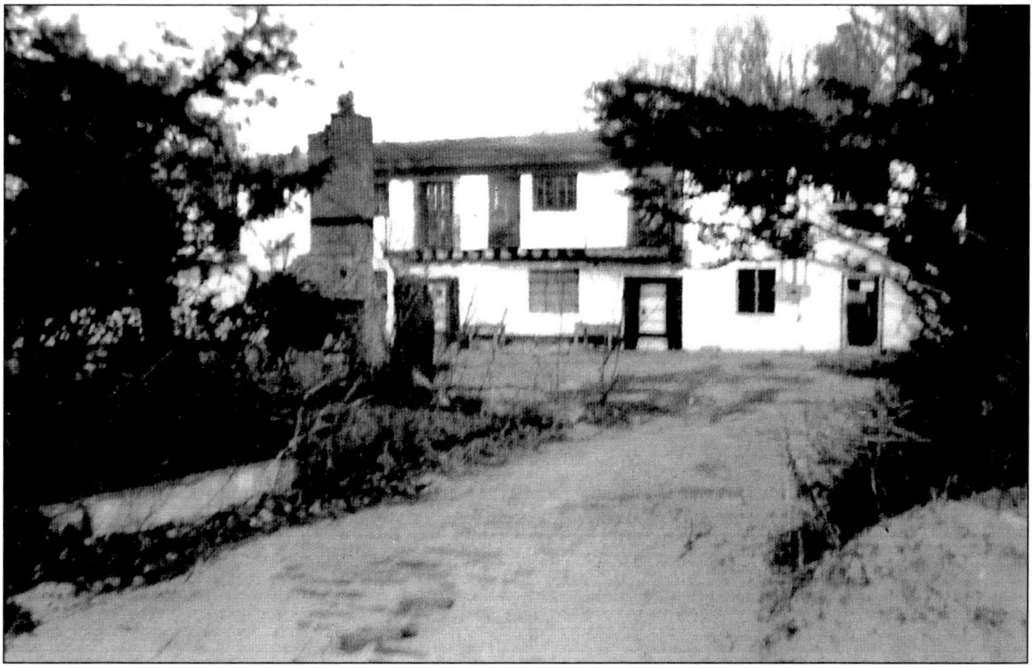

This is another view of the ruins of the Wilson's Inn at Johnson's Beach. The lobby fireplace is seen to the left. (Photo by L.G. Eggleston.)

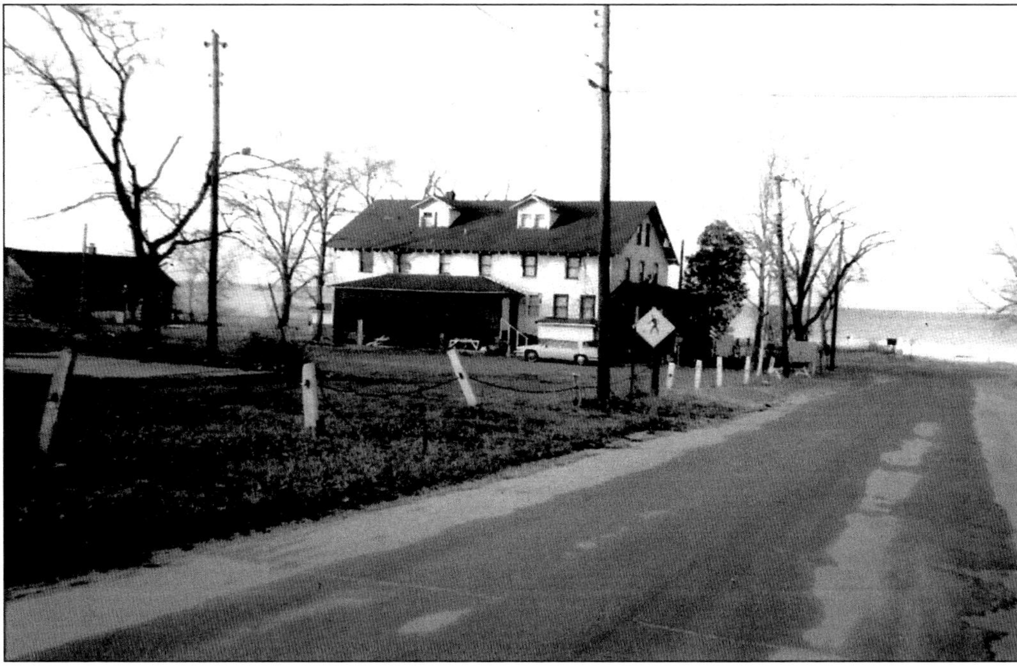

This image is looking down Waverly Road to Lake Michigan. The Johnson's Beach Inn is to the left. (Photo by L.G. Eggleston.)

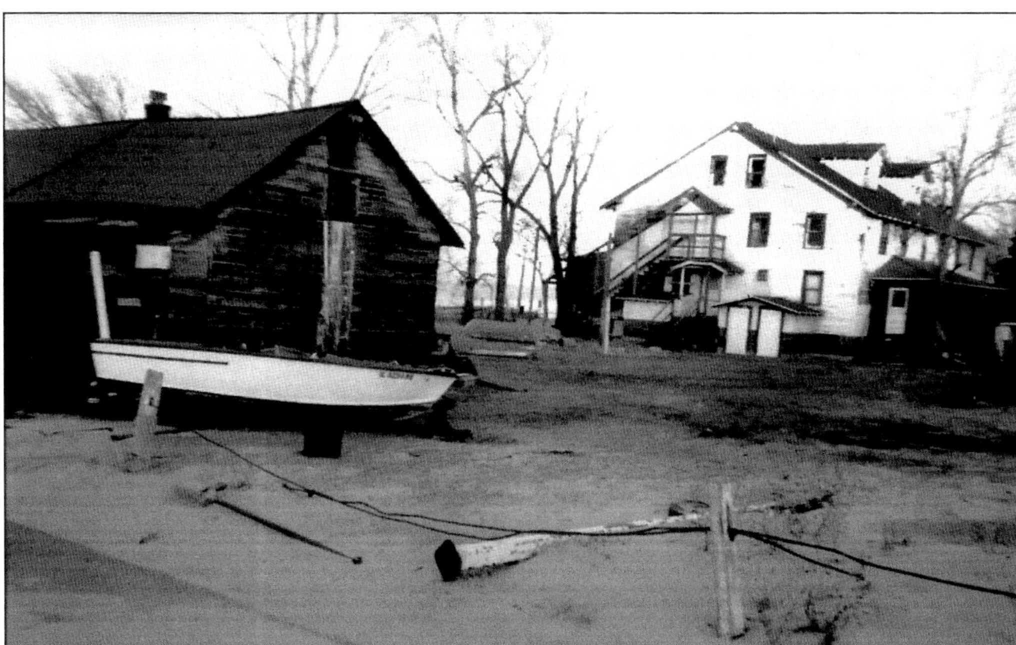

This is a rear view of Johnson's Inn and the original fish shack which is still standing. (Photo by L.G. Eggleston.)

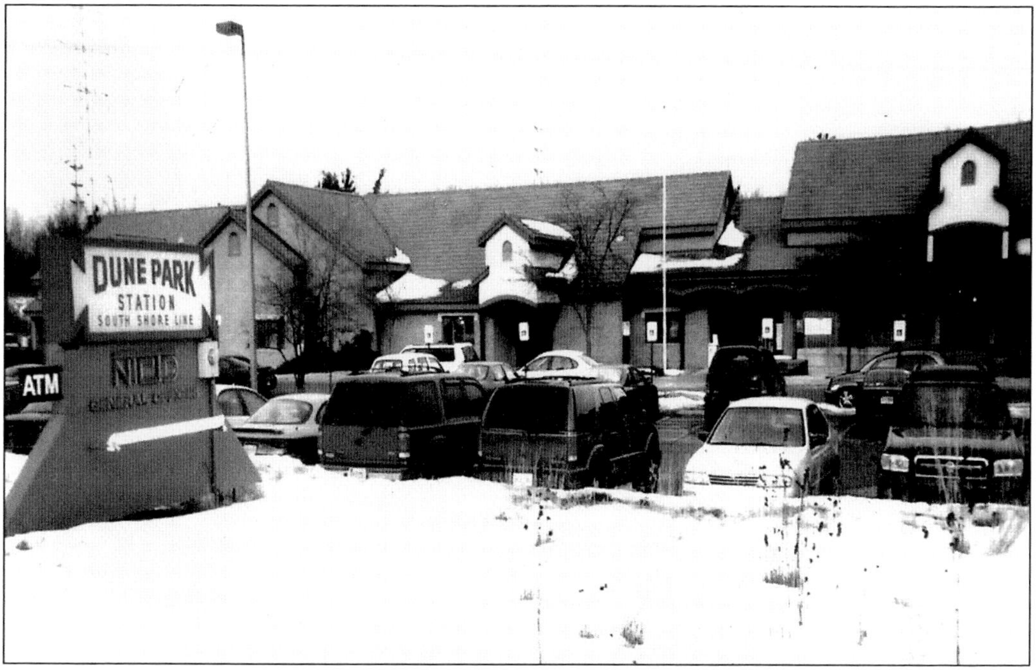

This is the front of the new Dune Park South Shore Electric Railroad Station. The view is from U.S. Highway 12. (Photo by L.G. Eggleston.)

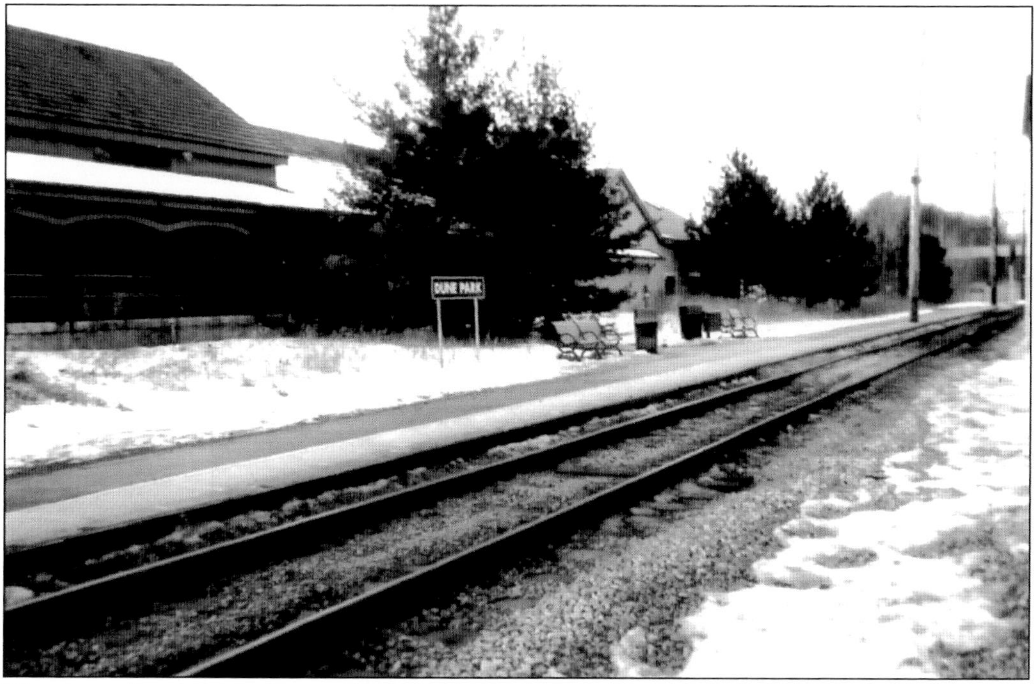

This is another view of the new Dune Park South Shore Station. (Photo by L.G. Eggleston.)

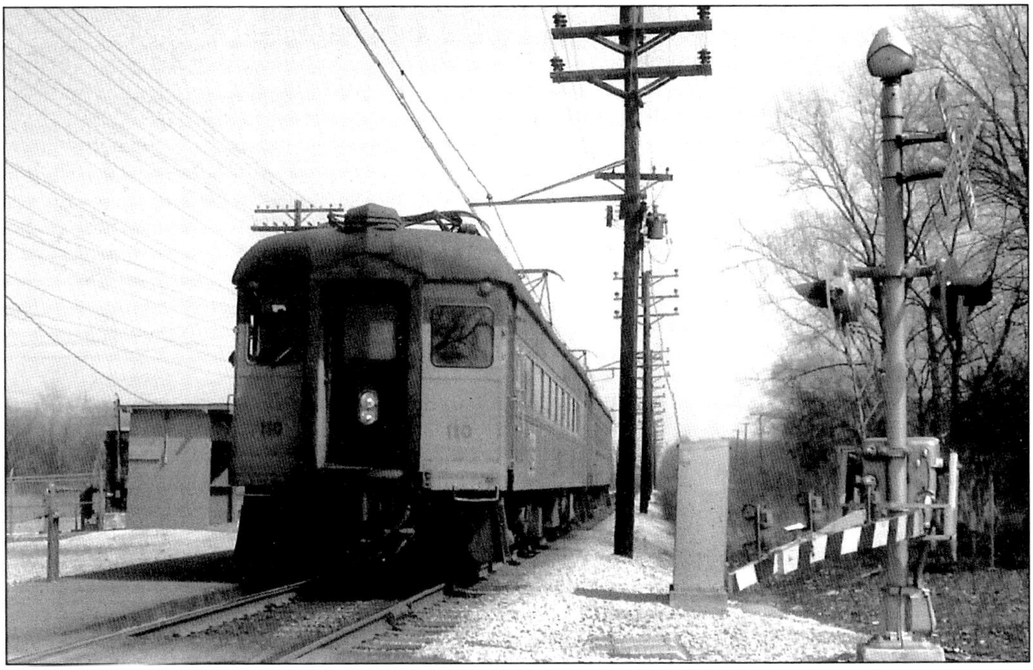

The Waverly Road stop for the South Shore Electric Railroad is shown here. From this stop visitors had a short walk to Johnson's Beach. The stop no longer exists since the new Dune Park Station was built. (Photo courtesy of Edwin Kuehl.)

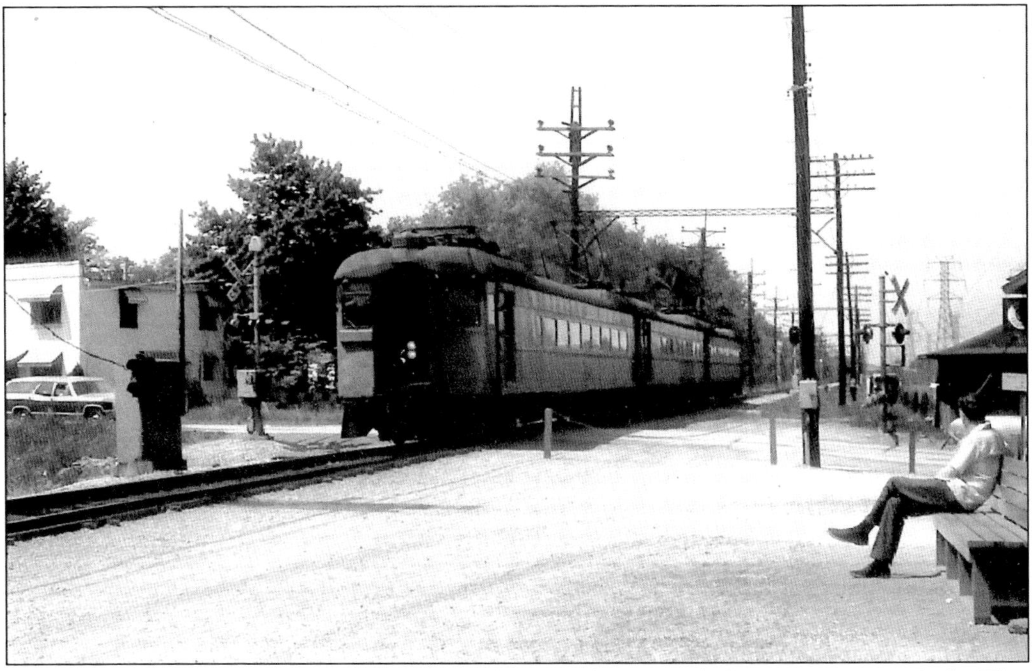

The Tremont train station shown in this photograph serviced the Dunes State Park. This station no longer exists since the new Dune Park Station was built. The new station is closer to the main entrance of the Indiana Dunes State Park. (Photo courtesy of Edwin Kuehl.)

Eight

Moss Lake and Deep Lake

Moss Lake is a small lake, located east of Campbell Street on Wauhob Lake Road (700 N) in Porter County. The lake was originally part of the Moss Lake Farm. Over the years the lake and surrounding land has served as a farm lake, a U.S. Army recreation camp and a camp for the Catholic Diocese of Gary.

Purchase and development of the lake began in 1950 when the Catholic Church began searching for a suitable site to erect a summer camp for the Catholic Youth Organization (CYO). Since the diocese headquarters were located in Fort Wayne, Indiana the children in the CYO program would use the camp at Lake Wawasee north-east of Warsaw in Kosciusko County. The leaders of the church felt that the trip to Camp Wawasee was too long a journey for the children of Lake and Porter Counties.

Through the efforts of Msgr. Lawrence Grothouse the 80-acre track around Moss Lake was selected and purchased in 1950. With the assistance of Dr. Thomas Senese and a dedicated committee of laymen from the Gary CYO program, the land was developed into a summer camp.

Several buildings were constructed beginning with a chapel in honor of Msgr. Grothouse. Barracks for sleeping, dining facilities, and rest rooms were also constructed.

On February 25, 1957, the Diocese of Fort Wayne was split up and the Diocese of Gary was formed which included Lake, Porter, La Porte, and Stark Counties.

From 1957 through 1959 the U.S. Army used the camp as a recreation center for its local troops. The U.S. Army 45th Anti Aircraft Artillery Brigade of NIKE Installation used the base for the soldiers who were manning the local NIKE sites.

Upon the establishment of the new Gary Diocese, Bishop Grutka took an interest in the camp and its value to the people of the area. On August 10, 1958, while the U.S. Army was still using the camp, the Gary Diocese dedicated the camp and named it Camp Lawrence in honor of Msgr. Lawrence Grothouse.

In 1959, after the U.S. Army left, Father William Martin, who was a former Director of the CYO program in Fort Wayne, was appointed as Program and Personnel Director of Camp Lawrence. That first year 752 boys and girls attended the camp. The camp now hosts almost 10,000 boys and girls annually.

In 1964 the Gary Diocese constructed a building called the "Nun's Cabin" which became a popular destination for weekend visits by the religious sisters of the diocese.

On October 11, 1974 the Diocese of Gary purchased Deep Lake which is directly south of Moss Lake. The purchase of Deep Lake not only increased the size of Camp Lawrence but enhanced its natural beauty.

The camp now has 20 buildings which consist of five cabins, a chapel, an administration building, modern restrooms, a dining hall, a gymnasium, a canteen, a craft hall, a tool shop, seminarian's dormitory, seminarian's lounge, nurse's quarters, and four warehouses. It also has two lakes, three ball fields, an archery range, and 30 acres of woods.

Camp Lawrence is not just a summer camp for children. It now hosts many organizations such as CYO, sisters of the diocese, Sierra Clubs, server picnics, GAA groups, search programs, Knights of Columbus activities, Valparaiso University groups, parish retreats, conventions, and numerous other group activities.

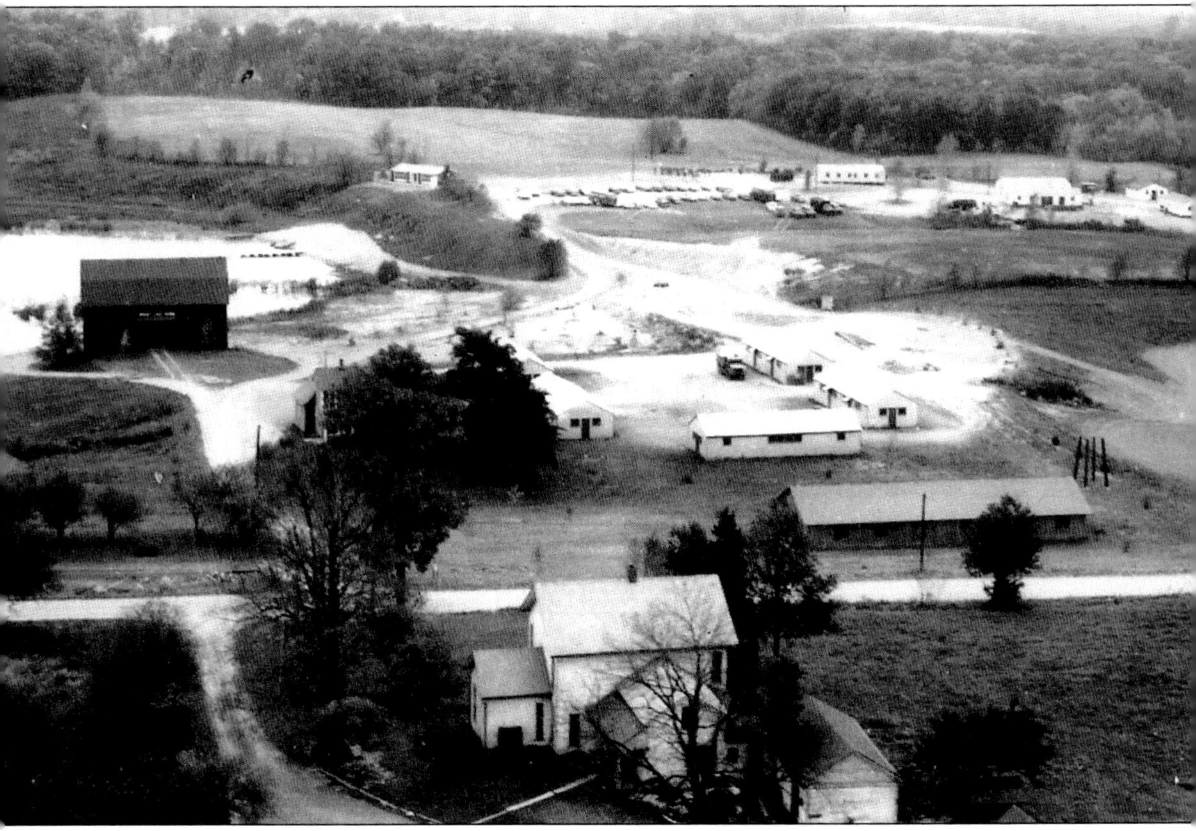

The above picture was taken from an army helicopter during the first stages of development of Camp Lawrence. The top of the picture shows those buildings erected by the U.S. Army. The long building at the right of the picture is the log chapel providing seating for several hundred people. To the left of the picture near the lake stands a well built barn which it was hoped would someday become a recreation center. To the center are seen five corrugated aluminum structures which were used as sleeping quarters for the children. (Photo courtesy of the Catholic Diocese of Gary.)

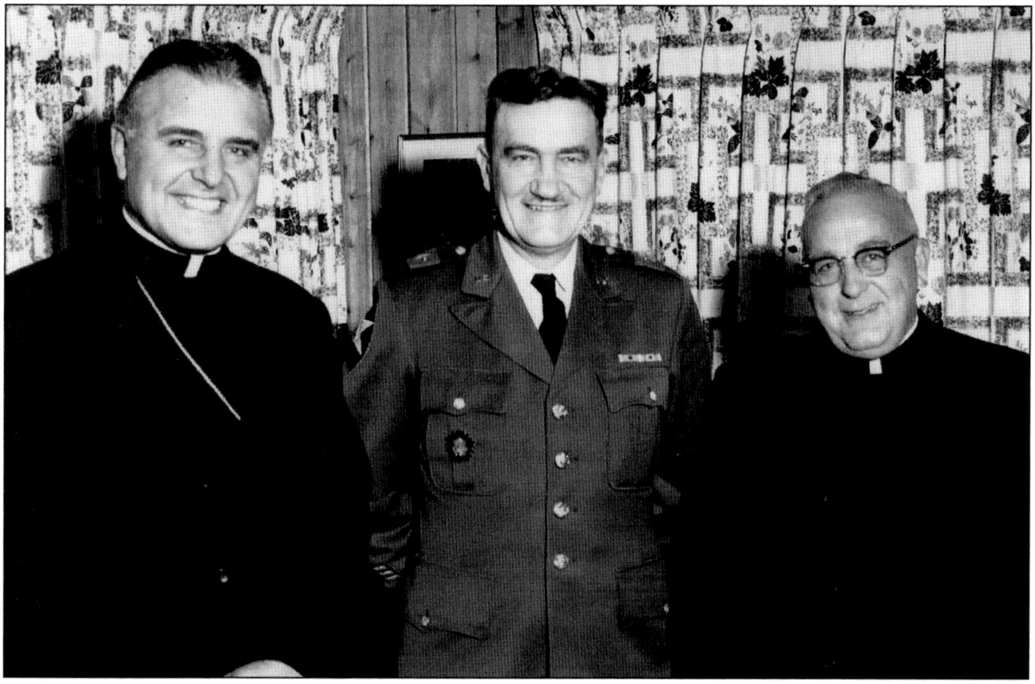

The three men shown in the above photograph are, from left to right, Bishop Grutka, Gen. Peter Schmick, and Msgr. Lawrence Grothouse. This photo was taken at the dedication ceremony for Camp Lawrence. (Photo courtesy of the Catholic Diocese of Gary.)

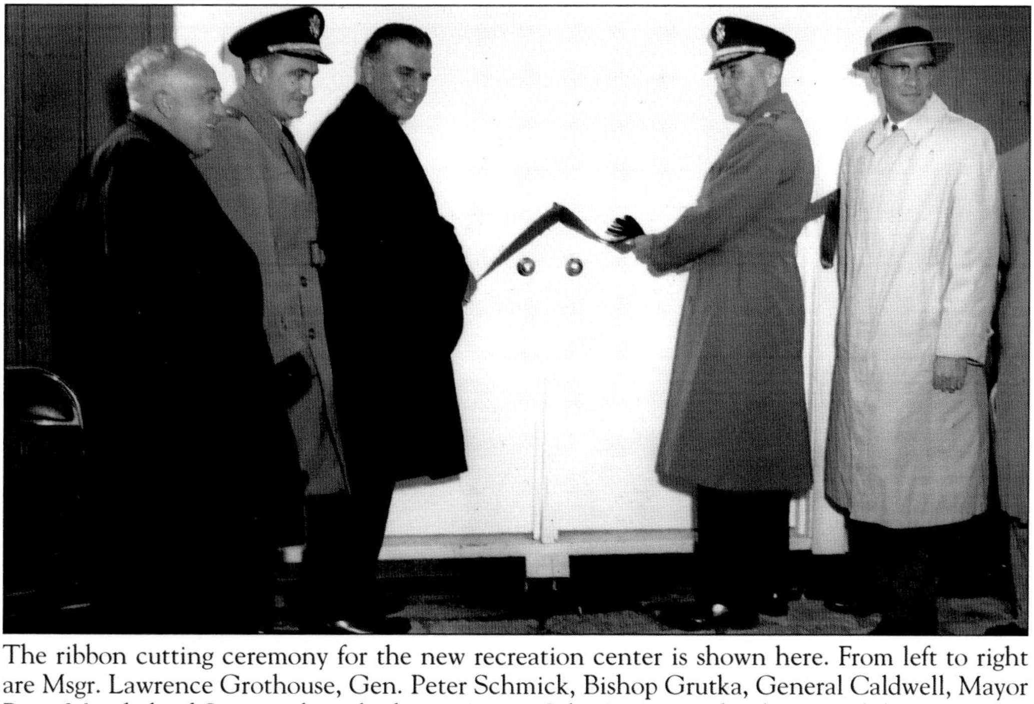

The ribbon cutting ceremony for the new recreation center is shown here. From left to right are Msgr. Lawrence Grothouse, Gen. Peter Schmick, Bishop Grutka, General Caldwell, Mayor Peter Mandich of Gary, and partly shown, Mayor John Wiggins of Valparaiso. (Photo courtesy of the Catholic Diocese of Gary.)

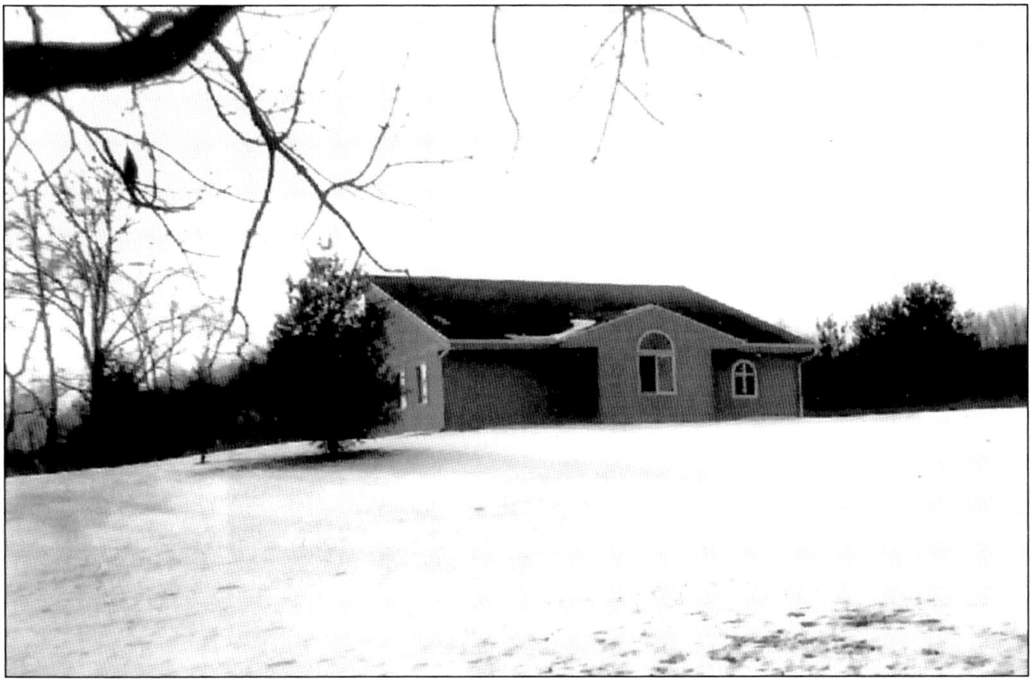

The new chapel at Camp Lawrence is named "Our Lady of the Woods." This chapel sits on a hill overlooking both Moss Lake and Deep Lake. (Photo by L.G. Eggleston.)

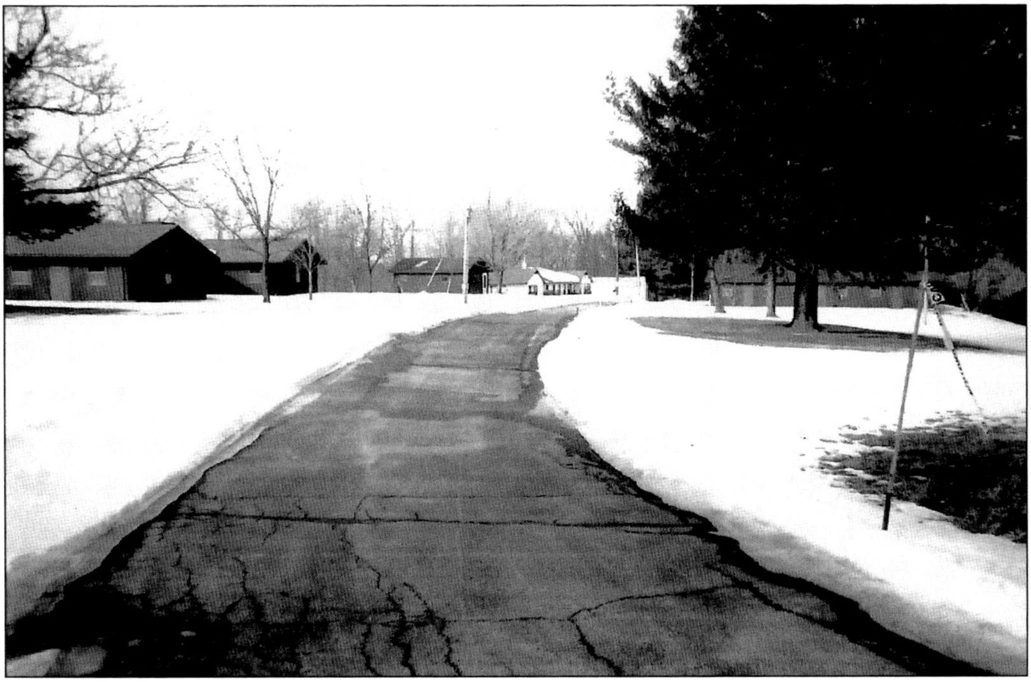

The above buildings are the sleeping quarters for the many guests who come to Camp Lawrence each year. (Photo by L.G. Eggleston.)

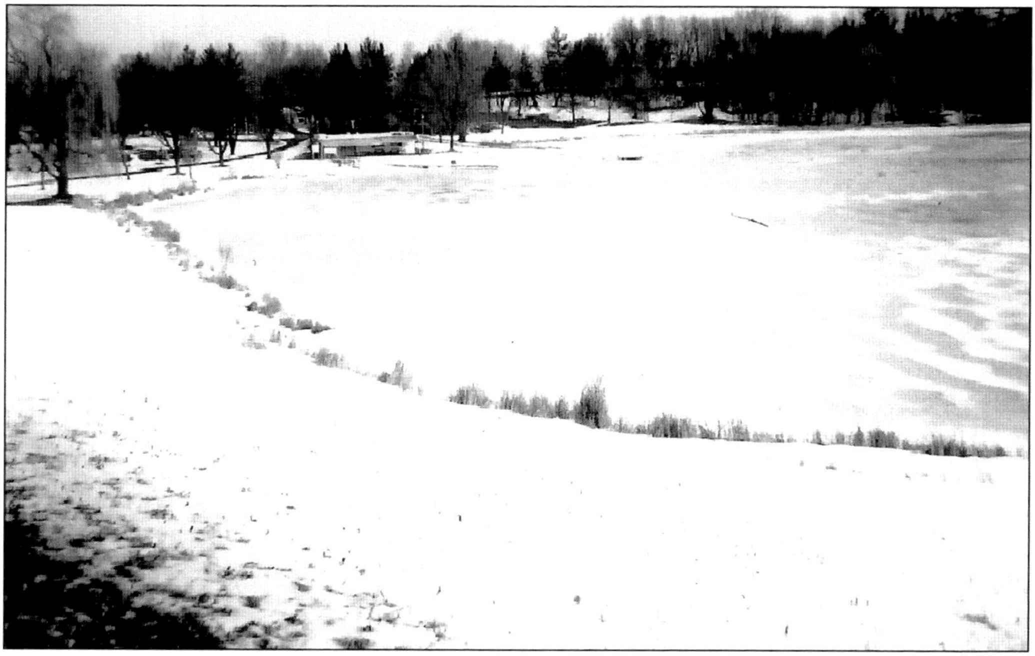

The above view is of Moss Lake with the boat house and swimming beach on the other side of the lake. (Photo by L.G. Eggleston.)

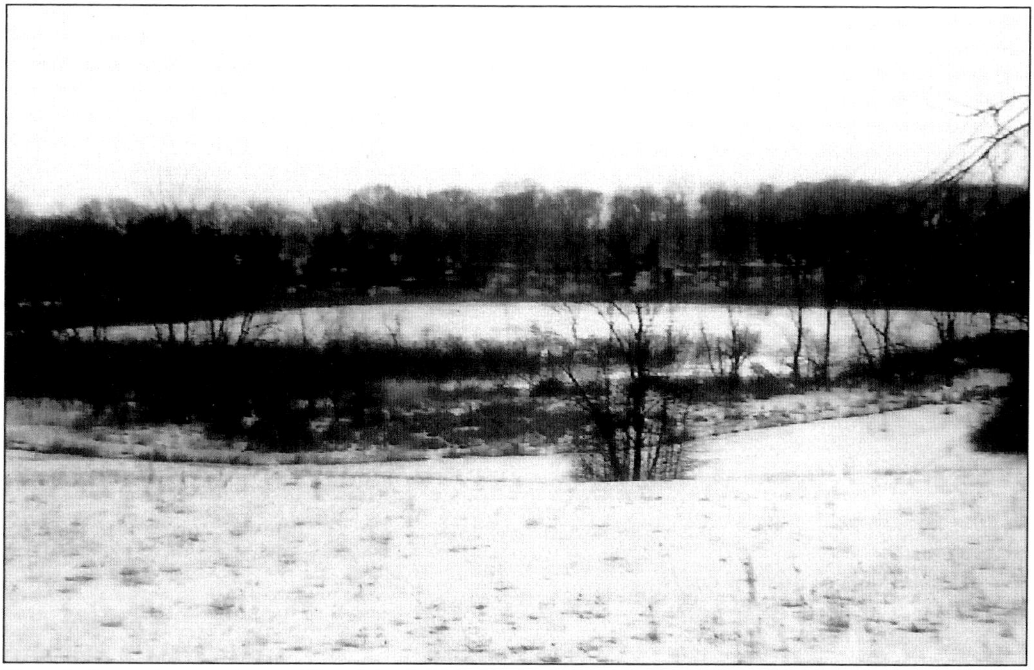

Deep Lake is shown above. This lake is a short distance south of Moss Lake and is part of Camp Lawrence. (Photo by L.G. Eggleston.)

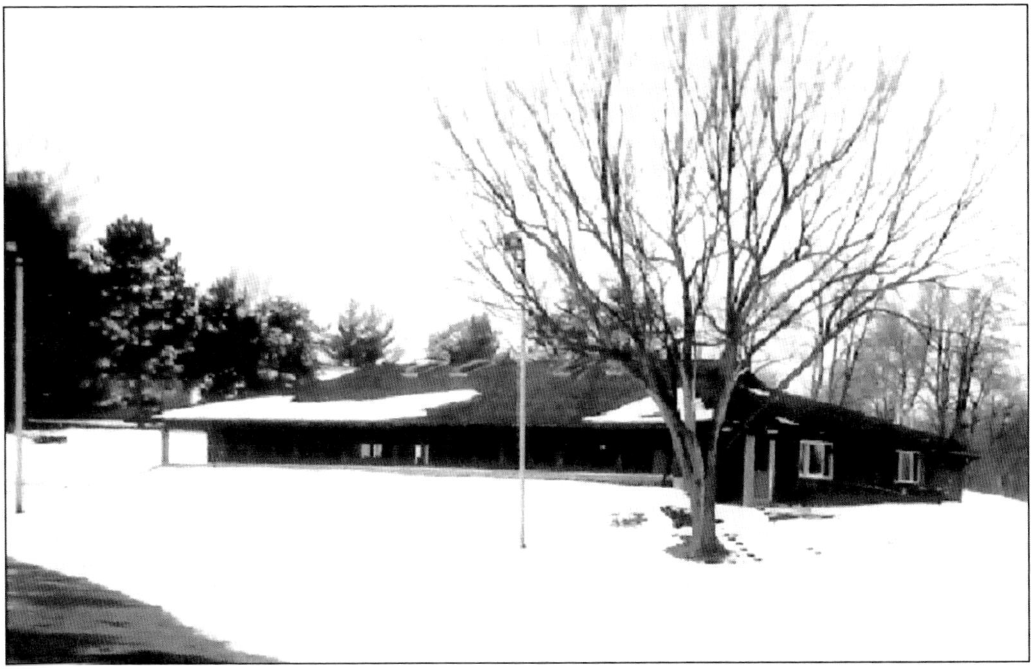

This picture shows the kitchen and dining hall at Camp Lawrence. (Photo by L.G. Eggleston.)

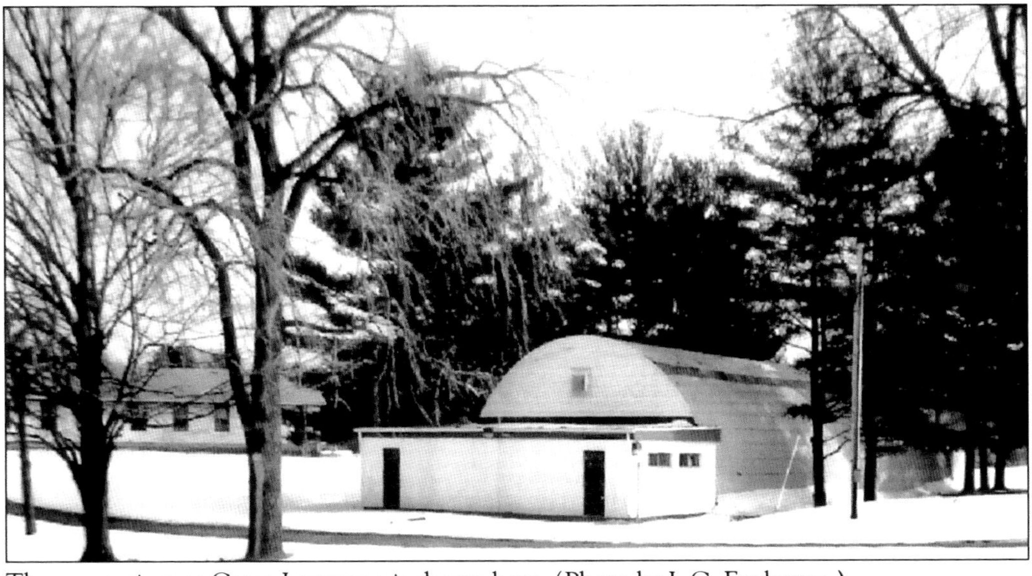

The gymnasium at Camp Lawrence is shown here. (Photo by L.G. Eggleston.)

Nine

The Kankakee River Gun Clubs and Resorts

The first family to settle on the Kankakee River in Porter County was the Eaton family. George Eaton built a cabin for his family at the Potawatomi Ford in 1836. The Potawatomi crossing was the narrowest point in the river and was used by trappers and hunters as well as the Indians. That crossing is now known as Baum's Bridge.

Mr. Eaton operated a ferry boat at the crossing. This was the only crossing on the river in Porter County. In 1894, Mr. Eaton built a wooden toll bridge. The toll was not very popular and shortly after the bridge opened it was burned down.

Mr. Eaton continued to operate the ferry until 1857 when he sold out to a man named Sawyer who in addition to operating the ferry built a saw mill on the river. In 1863, Enos Baum bought the ferry and the lumber mill. He built a wooden bridge across the river. In 1865, the county commissioners of Porter and Jasper Counties took over the bridge. The winding road from the bridge went to Valparaiso and was called the Valparaiso Road.

In 1876, a group of wealthy hunters from Pittsburg, Pennsylvania built a hunting club at Baum's Bridge, and named it the Pittsburg Gun Club. Shortly thereafter another club house was built by a group of wealthy hunters from Louisville, Kentucky. In 1879, hunters from Rockville, Terre Haute, and Indianapolis built a hunting club at Baum's Bridge. The Rockville, Terre Haute and Indianapolis Hunt Club was frequented by Benjamin Harrison who later became president of the United States.

In 1879, another gun club called the White House Hunting Club was built directly west of the Rockville, Terre Haute and Indianapolis Hunting Club at Baum's Bridge.

The Colliers Club House was constructed on the site where the original homes of George Eaton and Enos Baum stood. The site is east of the bridge on the river. The Colliers is the only club house still standing today.

As the popularity of the area grew it began to attract many famous people such as Lew Wallace who acquired a small strip of land west of Baum's Bridge to moor his houseboat. The local inhabitants called his houseboat "The White Elephant." It is commonly thought that his most famous book *Ben-Hur* was partially written on his house boat at Baum's Bridge and partially written at his home in Crawfordsville, Indiana.

Other famous people who frequented these hunt clubs were John "Bronco John" Sullivan, Benjamin Harrison, and Theodore Roosevelt.

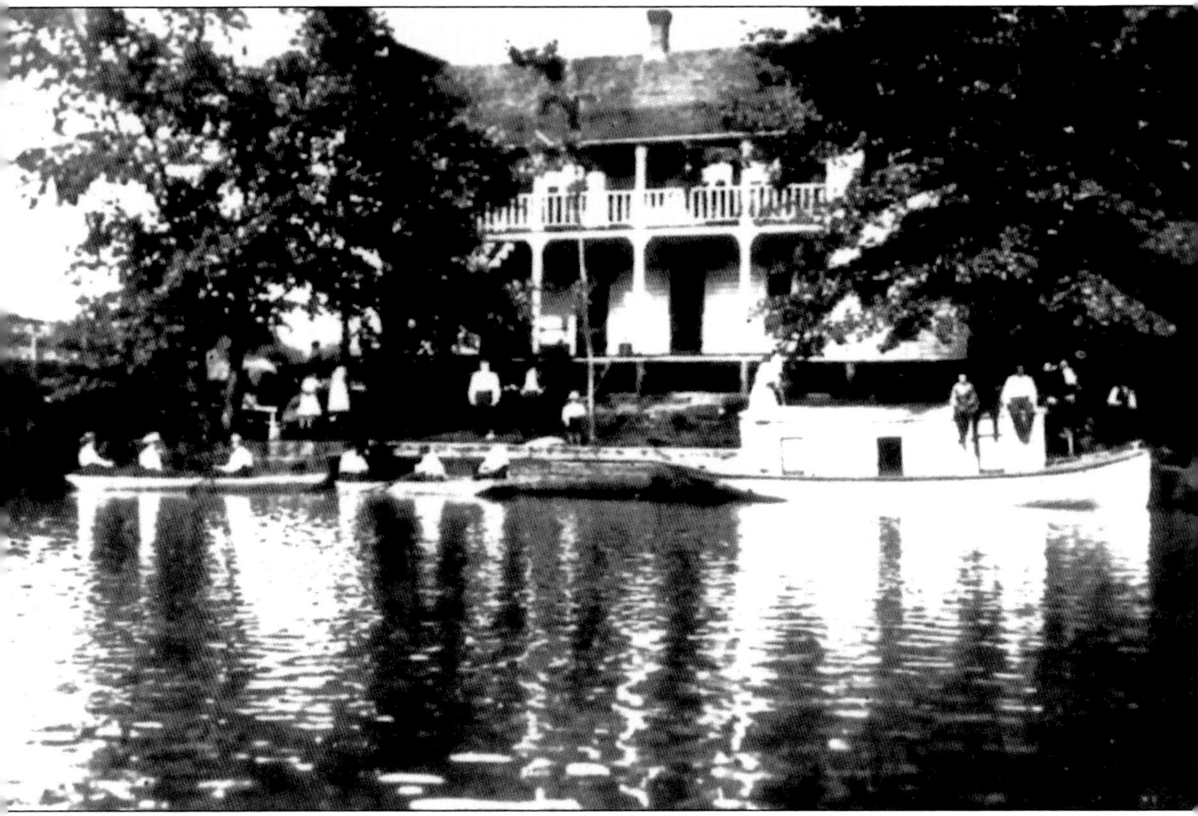

The photograph seen here is the Colliers Club House which is on the left side of Baum's Bridge. The Kankakee River has since been straightened and no longer flows past the lodge. However the channel is still full of water. (Photo courtesy of the Kankakee Valley Historical Society.)

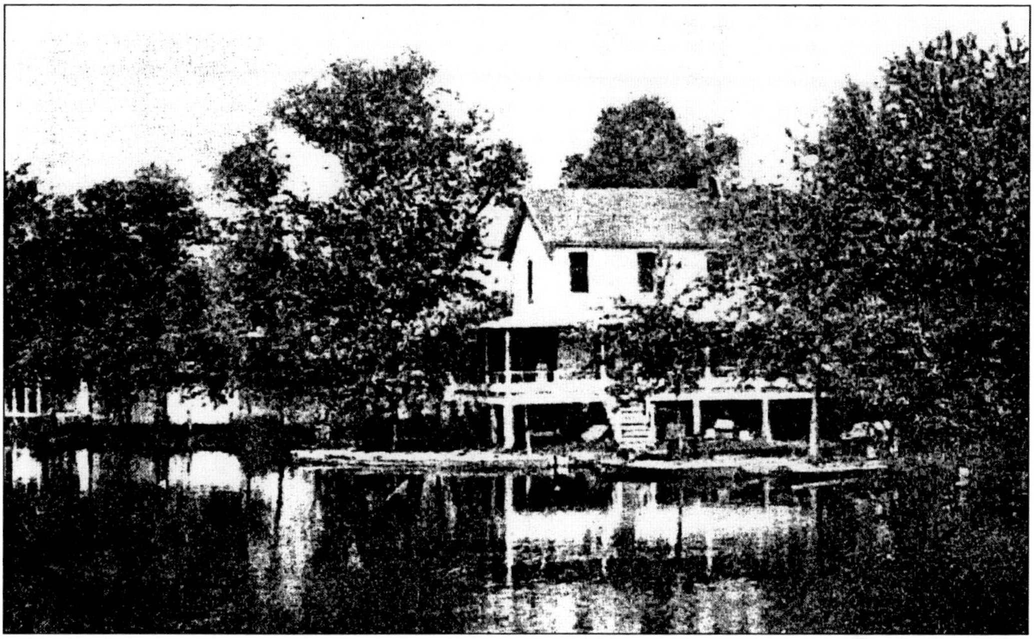

The Rockville, Terre Haute, and Indianapolis Club, shown above, sits on the right side of Baum's Bridge. Next to this club house is the White House Gun Club. This site is currently the site of the Baum's Bridge Inn and Restaurant. (Photo courtesy of the Kankakee Valley Historical Society.)

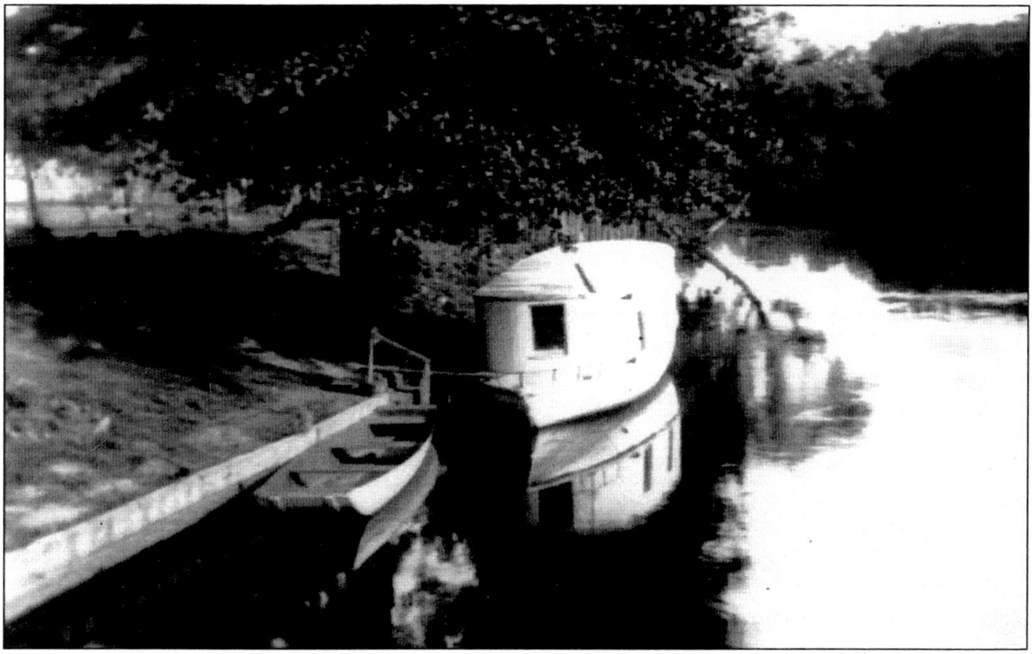

Steam launches such as the one shown above were used to give visitors scenic rides on the Kankakee River. (Photo courtesy of the Kankakee Valley Historical Society.)

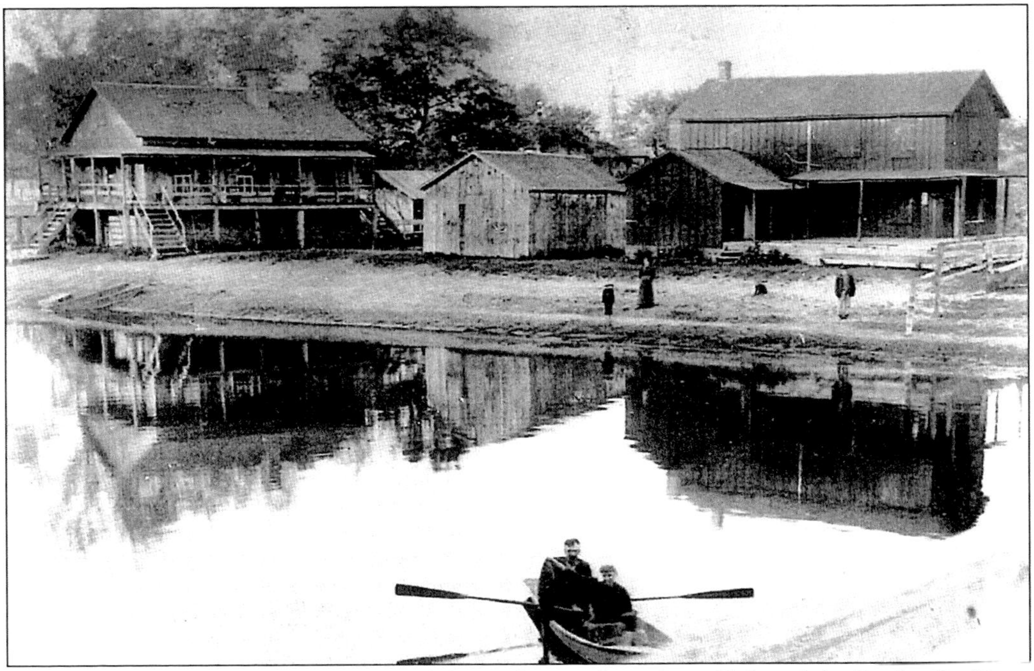

This view was taken from the bridge and shows the Pittsburg Gun Club and the Rockville, Terre Haute, and Indianapolis Club with its wrap-around porch. (Photo courtesy of the Kankakee Valley Historical Society.)

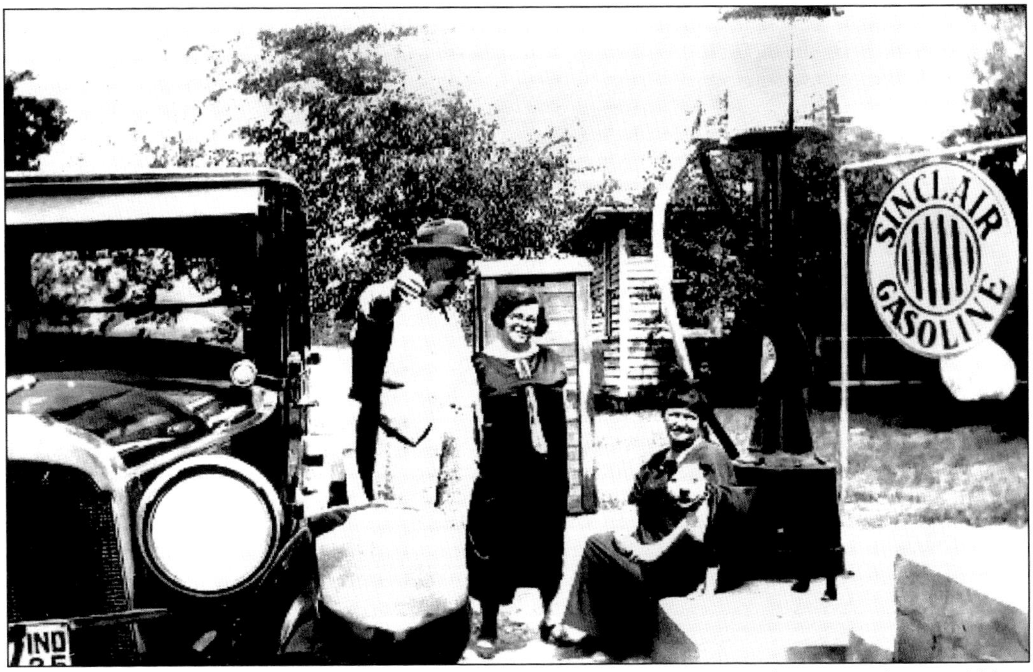

This photograph was taken in 1925 and is at the Colliers Club House where travelers could buy gasoline and supplies before crossing Baum's Bridge. (Photo courtesy of the Kankakee Valley Historical Society.)

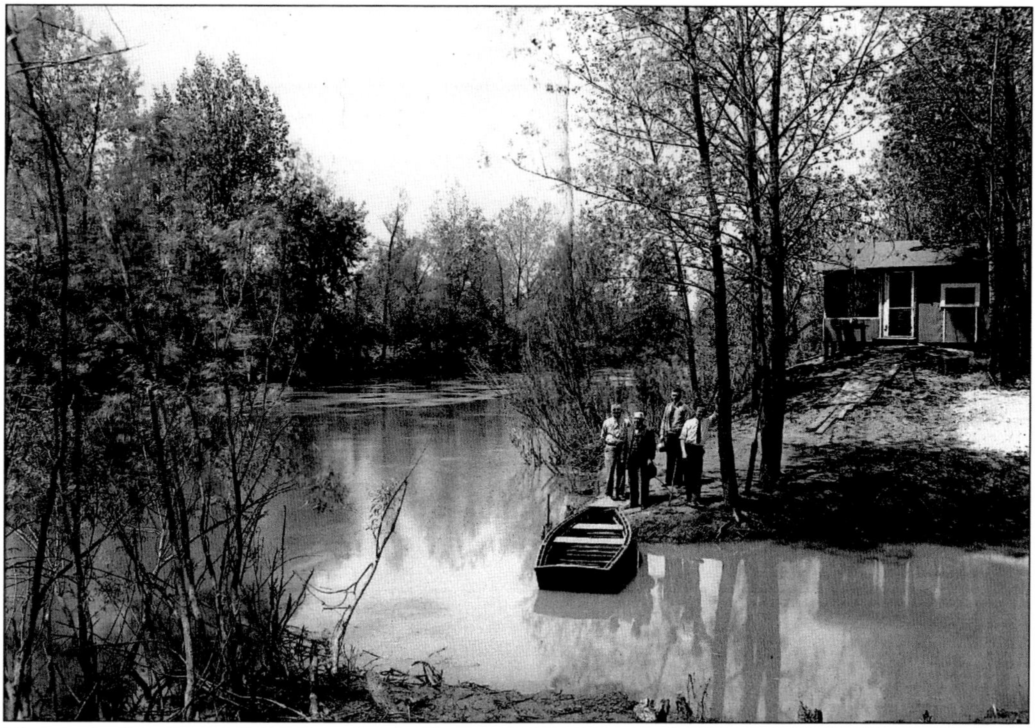

This is the Benke residence on the Kankakee River. This landing site is approximately one half mile east of Baum's Bridge. (Photo courtesy of the Kankakee Valley Historical Society.)

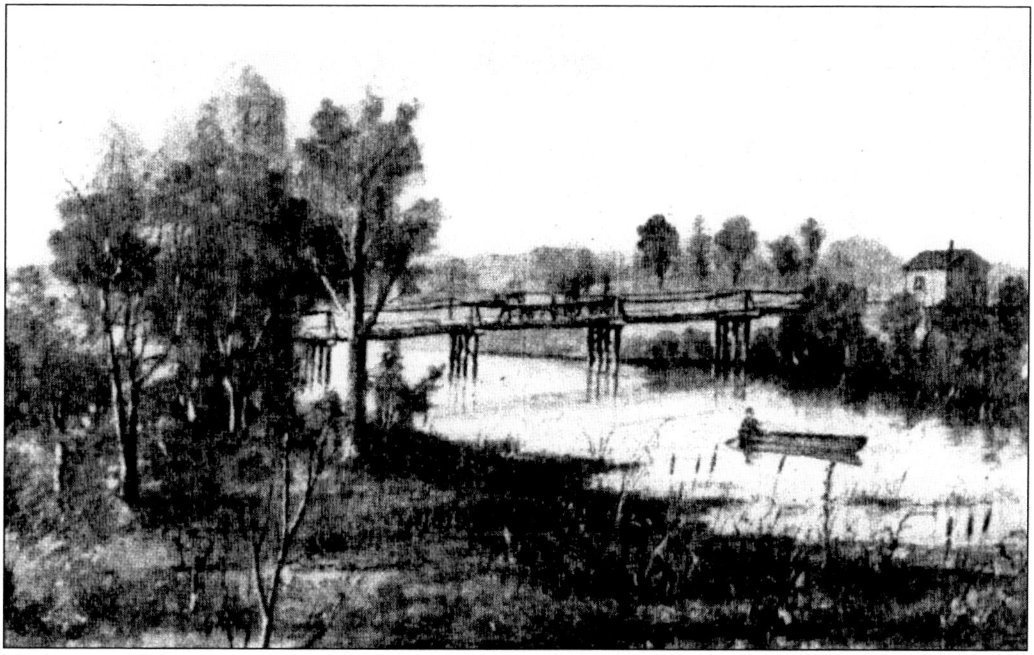

This image shows Enos Baum's house and his wooden bridge over the Kankakee River. The colliers Club House was later built on this site. (Photo courtesy of the Kankakee Valley Historical Society.)

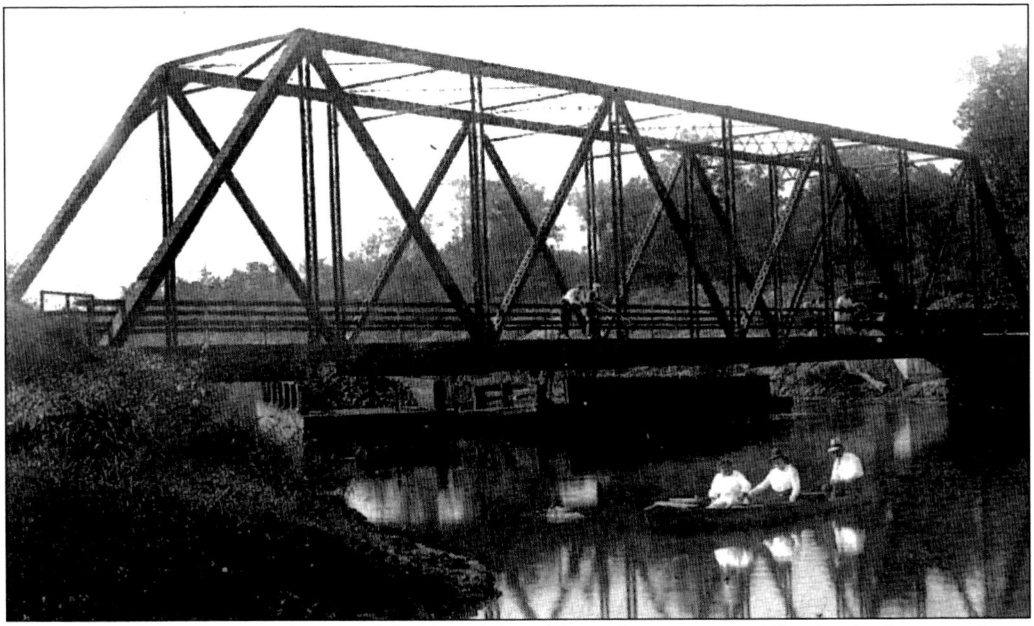

This is the new Baum's Bridge which replaced the old wooden structure. This bridge has now been replaced with a concrete bridge. (Photo courtesy of the Kankakee Valley Historical Society.)

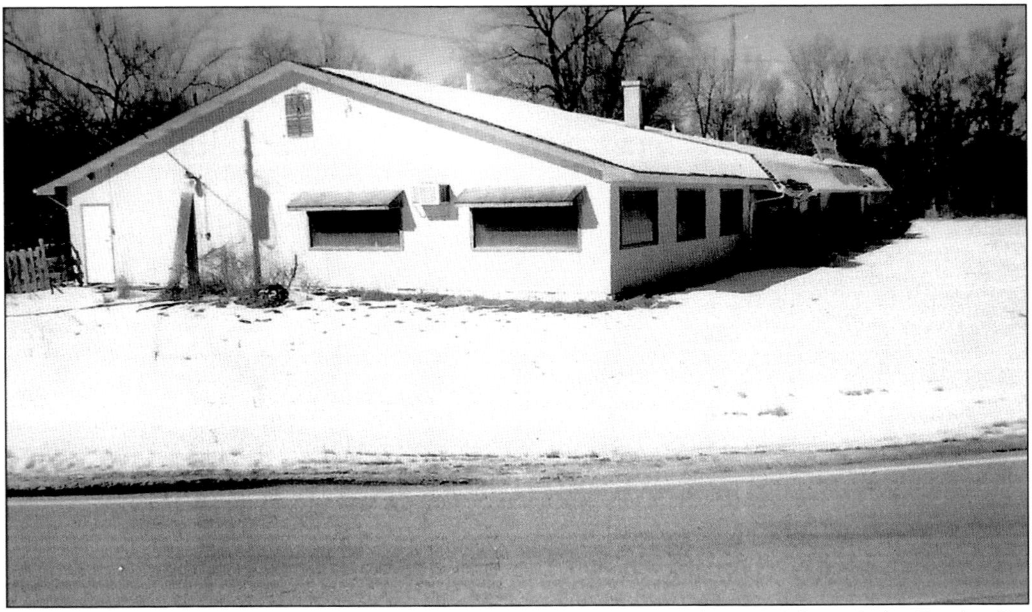

In 1934, this site at Baum's Bridge, which once held the Pittsburg Club and the Rockville, Terre Haute, and Indianapolis Club, was the site of a dance hall and roller rink called the Smith Pavilion. The Baum's Bridge Inn and Restaurant shown above now occupy the site. (Photo by L.G. Eggleston.)

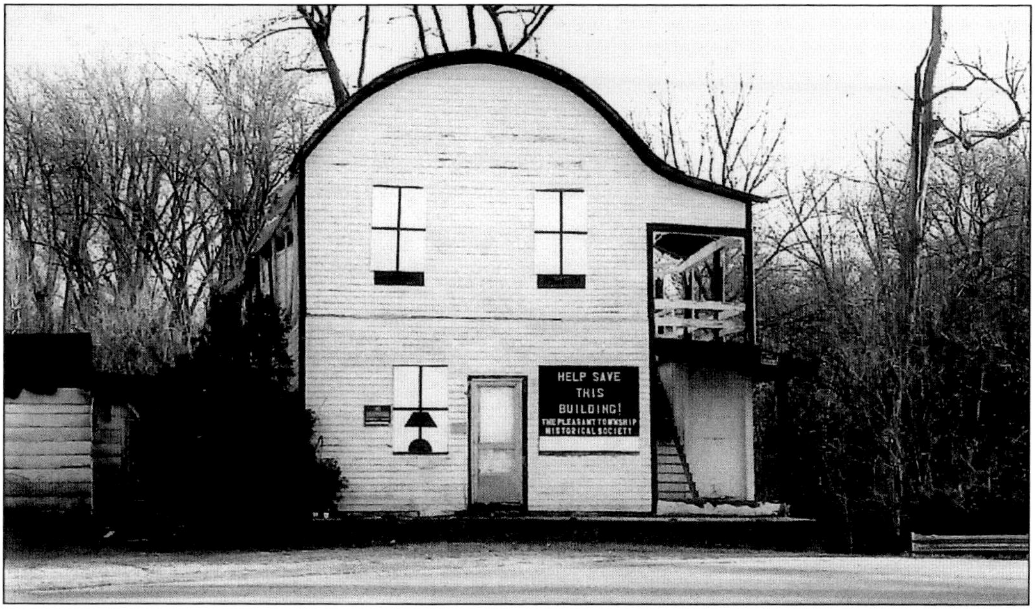

This photograph is of the Colliers Club House as it looks today. The Kankakee Valley Historical Society owns the property and is in the process of getting it placed on the National Register of Historic Places. The historical society plans to restore the building to its original condition. (Photo courtesy of the Kankakee Historical Society.)

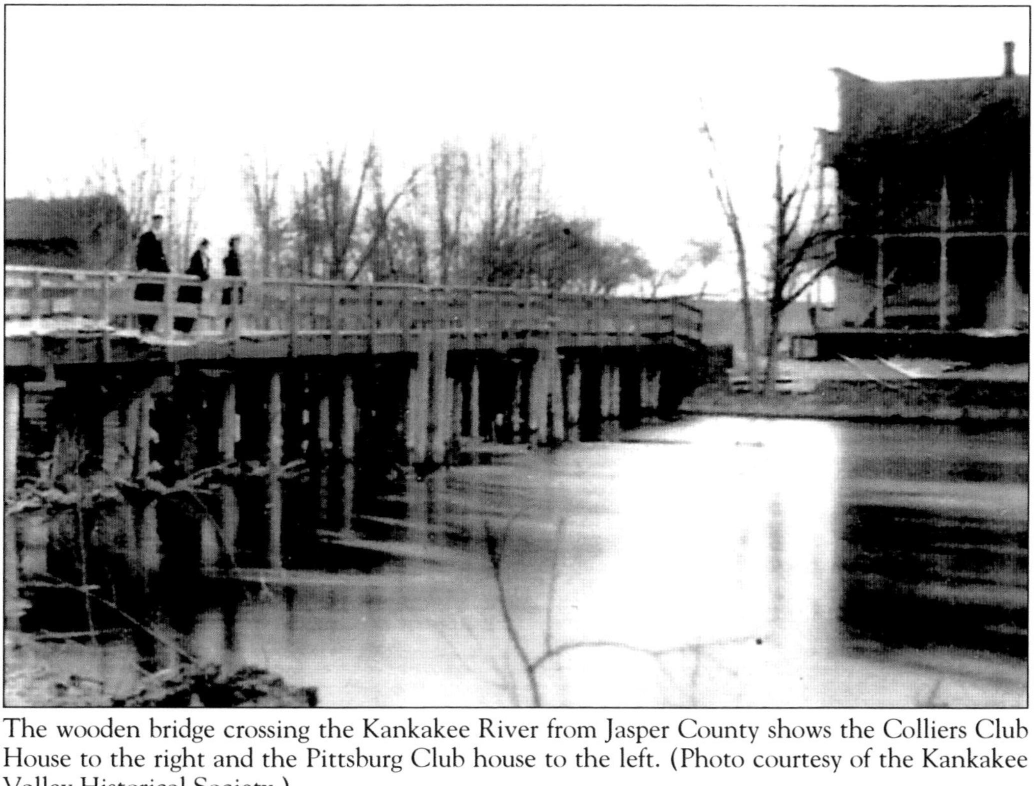

The wooden bridge crossing the Kankakee River from Jasper County shows the Colliers Club House to the right and the Pittsburg Club house to the left. (Photo courtesy of the Kankakee Valley Historical Society.)

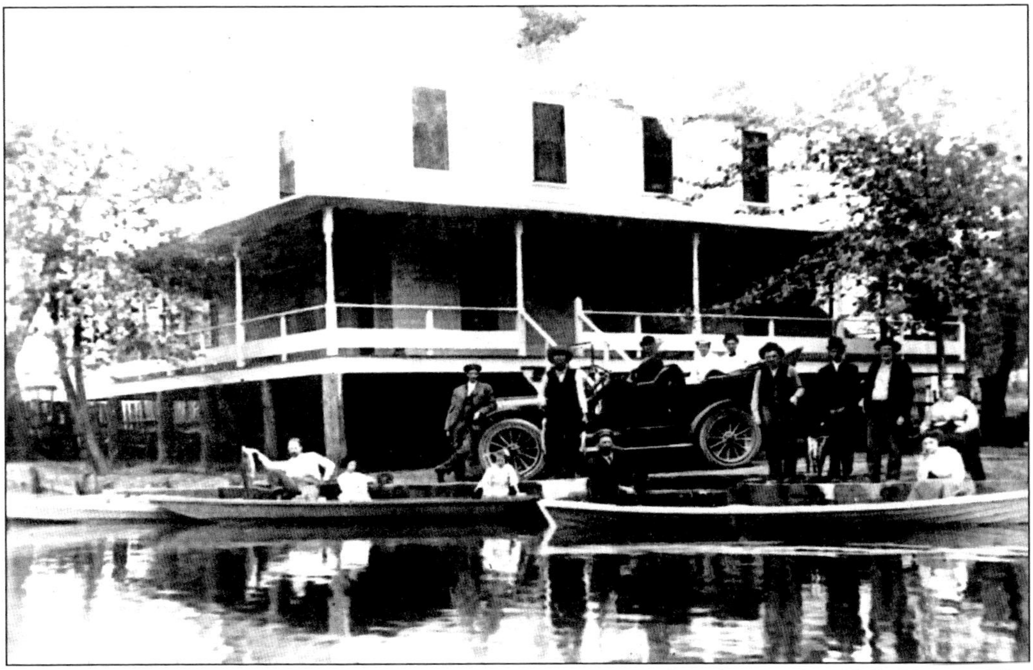

Here is a view of the popular Rockville, Terre Haute, and Indianapolis Club House. The automobile is on the dock in front of the club house. (Photo courtesy of the Kankakee Valley Historical Society.)

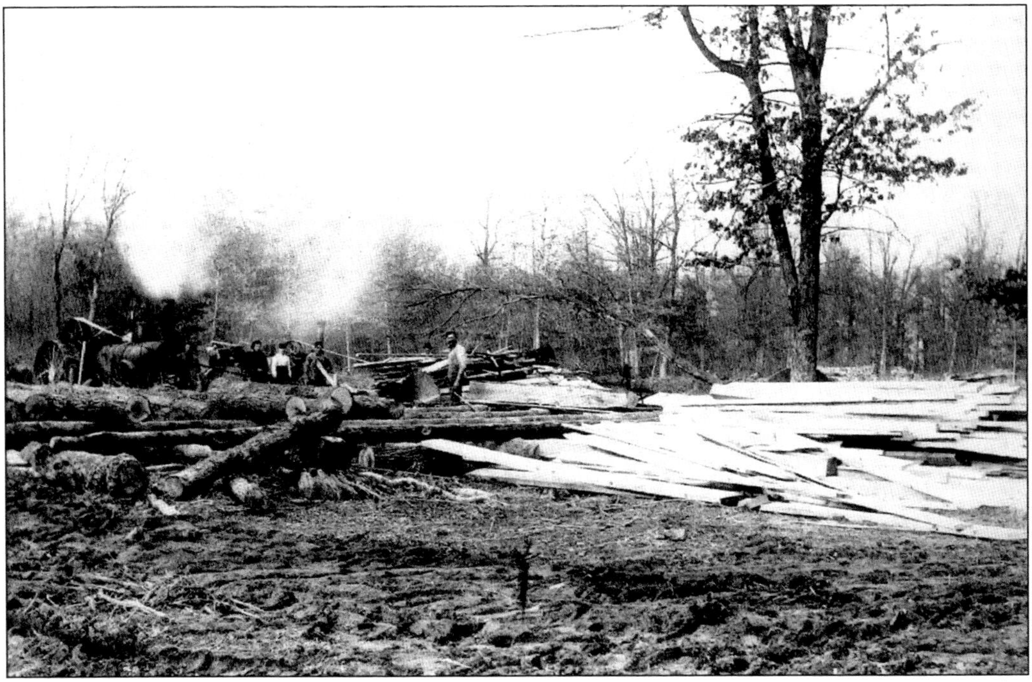

Logging was big business on the Kankakee River. The demand for lumber was increasing as the area grew. Enos Baum had a saw mill on the river in 1863 which he bought from a man named Sawyer. (Photo courtesy of the Kankakee Valley Historical Society.)

Bibliography

Beckwith, Hiram Williams. *Illinois and Indiana Indians, Mid-America.* New York: Arno Press, 1975.

Bennett, Mrs. L.F. "Centennial Notes: The Legend of Flint Lake," *The Vidette Messenger*, 16 October 1916.

Fry, Ira M. *The Kankakee River*. St. John, Indiana: R & B Fine Printing, 2001.

———. *The Kankakee River Vol. II*. St. John, Indiana: R & B Fine Printing, July 2002.

Isaacs, Marion. *The Kankakee River of History*. Self-Published, 1964.

Kubiak, J. *Great Lakes Indians: A Pictorial Guide*. Grand Rapids, Michigan: Baker Book House Company, 1970.

Marlette, Jerry. *Electric Railroads of Indiana.* Indianapolis, Council for Local History. 1959.

Neeley, George. *City of Valparaiso, A Pictorial History, 125th Anniversary Publication*. St. Louis, Missouri: G. Bradley Publishing, Inc., 1990.

Our Sunday Visitor Staff. "Camp Lawrence-Fun Spot for Youth," *Our Sunday Visitor*, vol. LV, no. 44, p. 17a, 16 February 1967.

Rafert, Stewart. *The Miami Indians of Indiana, A Persistent People, 1654–1994*. Indianapolis, Indiana: Indiana Historical Society, 1996.

Rand McNally Staff. *Map of Indians of Indiana.* Recorder number 314-191143, Detroit, Michigan: Hearne Bros.

Simons, Richard S. *Rivers of Indiana.* Bloomington, Indiana: Indiana University Press, 1985.

The Valparaiso Bicentennial Committee. *The Vale of Paradise Valparaiso, Indiana.* Valparaiso, Indiana: Boy-Con Printers, Inc., 1976.

Vidette Messenger Staff. "Baum's Bridge," *The Vidette Messenger*, 2 September 1965.

———. "Centennial Issue-Special Edition," *The Vidette Messenger*, 16–21, August 1936.

———. "Electric Trains have Vanished with Nary a Trace," *The Vidette Messenger*, 3 April 1970.

———. "Over 1,000 Cars at Johnson's Beach," *The Vidette Messenger*, 7 July 1949.

Waldron, Larry. *The Indiana Dunes*, Conshohocken, Pennsylvania: Eastern National Park and Monument Association, 1998.

Wallace, William Orman. "The Stories of Porter County By the Stroller," *The Vidette Messenger*, Vol. 1., pp. 76–79, 118-120.

Wilcox, George. *The Diary of a Kankakee River Guide*. St, John, Indiana: R & B Fine Printing, July 2003.

Willis, Wanda Lou. *Haunted Hoosier Trails*. Zionsville, Indiana: Guild Press Emmis Publishing, LP, 2002.

Winger, Otho. *The Pottawatomi Indians*. Elgin, Illinois: The Elgin Press, 1939.